100 Activprimary™ WHITEBOARD LESSONS

TERMS AND CONDITIONS

IMPORTANT - PERMITTED USE AND WARNINGS - READ CAREFULLY BEFORE USING

Minimum specification:
- PC with a CD-ROM drive and at least 128 MB RAM
- Pentium III 800 MHz processor
- Microsoft Windows 2000 or higher
- Microsoft Office 2000 or higher
- Interactive whiteboard
- Activprimary software
- Facilities for printing and sound (optional)

YEAR 4
Scottish Primary 5

CREDITS

Authors
Jon Audain (foundation subjects and science), Rhona Dick (history), Eileen Jones (English), Ann Montague-Smith (mathematics), Alan Rodgers and Angella Streluk (geography)

Project Editor
Wendy Tse

Editor
Frances Ridley

Assistant Editor
Niamh O'Carroll

Illustrators
Jim Peacock (book and flipchart illustrations), William Gray, Theresa Tibbetts (additional flipchart illustrations)

Series Designer
Joy Monkhouse

Designers
Rebecca Male, Allison Parry, Helen Taylor, Andrea Lewis and Melissa Leeke

CD-ROM developed in association with
Q & D Multimedia

Flipcharts created in association with
Promethean Technologies Group Ltd

Published by Scholastic Ltd
Villiers House
Clarendon Avenue
Leamington Spa
Warwickshire CV32 5PR
www.scholastic.co.uk

Printed by Bell and Bain Ltd, Glasgow

1 2 3 4 5 6 7 8 9   6 7 8 9 0 1 2 3 4

Text © 2006 Jon Audain (foundation subjects and science), Rhona Dick (history), Eileen Jones (English), Ann Montague-Smith (mathematics), Alan Rodgers and Angella Streluk (geography)

© 2006 Scholastic Ltd

British Library Cataloguing-in-Publication Data
A catalogue record for this book is available from the British Library.

ISBN 0-439-96575-6
ISBN 978-0439-96575-0

The rights the authors of this work have been asserted by them in accordance with the Copyright, Designs and Patents Act 1988.

Extracts from The National Literacy Strategy and The National Numeracy Strategy © Crown copyright. Material from the National Curriculum © The Queen's Printer and Controller of HMSO. Reproduced under the terms of HMSO Guidance Note 8.

Extracts from the QCA Schemes of Work © Qualifications and Curriculum Authority.

ACKNOWLEDGEMENTS

Activprimary™ is a trademark of Promethean Technologies Group Ltd.

Microsoft Office, Word and Excel are either registered trademarks or trademarks of Microsoft Corporation in the United States and/or other countries.

With grateful thanks for advice, help and expertise to Margaret Allen (Business Development Manager), Peter Lambert (Business Development Manager) and Sarah Aspden (Digital Producer) at Promethean Technologies Group Ltd.

All Flash activities designed and developed by Q & D Multimedia.

Interactive Teaching Programs (developed by the Primary National Strategy) © Crown copyright.

With thanks to Mike Longden for the use of various photographs.

The publishers gratefully acknowledge:
The Chicken House for the use of the publicity blurb for *The Conch-Bearer* by Chitra Banerjee Divakaruni from the website www.doublecluck.com © 2005, The Chicken House.
Scholastic Children's Books for the use of publicity blurbs for *Buster Baylis: Night of the Living Veg* by Philip Reeve (2005, Scholastic) and *The Stunning Science of Everything* by Nick Arnold (2005, Scholastic).

Every effort has been made to trace copyright holders for the works reproduced in this book, and the publishers apologise for any inadvertent omissions.

Designed using Adobe InDesign.

Adobe, the Adobe logo, and Reader are either registered trademarks or trademarks of Adobe Systems Incorporated in the United States and/or other countries.

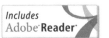

Made with Macromedia is a trademark of Macromedia, Inc. Director ® Copyright © 1984-2000 Macromedia, Inc.

CONTENTS

100 ACTIVPRIMARY™ WHITEBOARD LESSONS

'There is a whiteboard revolution in UK schools.'

(Primary National Strategy)

Interactive whiteboards are fast becoming the must-have resource in today's classroom as they allow teachers to facilitate children's learning in ways that were inconceivable a few years ago. The appropriate use of interactive whiteboards, whether used daily in the classroom or once a week in the ICT suite, will encourage active participation in lessons and should increase learners' determination to succeed. Interactive whiteboards make it easier for teachers to bring subjects across the curriculum to life in new and exciting ways.

What can an interactive whiteboard offer?

For the **teacher**, an interactive whiteboard offers the same facilities as an ordinary whiteboard, such as drawing, writing and erasing. However, the interactive whiteboard also offers many other possibilities to:
- save any work created during a lesson
- prepare as many pages as necessary
- display any page within the flipchart to review teaching and learning
- add scanned examples of the children's work to a flipchart
- change colours of objects and backgrounds instantly
- use simple templates and grids
- link flipcharts to spreadsheets, websites and presentations.

Using an interactive whiteboard in the simple ways outlined above can enrich teaching and learning in a classroom, but that is only the beginning of the whiteboard's potential to educate and inspire.

For the **learner**, the interactive whiteboard provides the opportunity to share learning experiences as lessons can be delivered with sound, still and moving images, and websites. Interactive whiteboards can be used to cater for the needs of all learning styles:
- kinaesthetic learners benefit from being able to physically manipulate images
- visual learners benefit from being able to watch videos, look at photographs and see images being manipulated
- auditory learners benefit from being able to access audio resources such as voice recordings and sound effects.

With a little preparation all of these resource types could be integrated in one lesson, a feat that would have been almost impossible before the advent of the interactive whiteboard!

Access to an interactive whiteboard

In schools where learners have limited access to an interactive whiteboard the teacher must carefully plan lessons in which the children will derive most benefit from using it. As teachers become familiar with the whiteboard they will learn when to use it and, importantly, when not to use it!

Where permanent access to an interactive whiteboard is available, it is important that the teacher plans the use of the board effectively. It should be used only in ways that will enhance or extend teaching and learning. Children still need to gain practical first-hand experience of many things. Some experiences cannot be recreated on an interactive whiteboard but others cannot be had without it.

100 Activprimary™ Whiteboard Lessons offers both teachers and learners the most accessible and creative uses of this most valuable resource.

Safety note: Avoid looking directly at the projector beam as it is potentially damaging to eyes, and never leave the children unsupervised when using the interactive whiteboard.

Introduction

About the series

100 Activprimary™ Whiteboard Lessons is designed to reflect best practice in using interactive whiteboards. It is also designed to support all teachers in using this valuable tool by providing lessons and other resources that can be used on a whiteboard with little or no preparation. These inspirational lessons cover all National Curriculum subjects. They are perfect for all levels of experience and are an essential for any users of Promethean's Activprimary™ software.

About the book

This book is divided into four chapters. Each chapter contains lessons and photocopiable activity sheets covering:
- English
- Mathematics
- Science
- Foundation subjects.

At the beginning of each chapter a **planning grid** identifies the title, the objectives covered and any relevant cross-curricular links in each lesson. Objectives are taken from relevant National Strategies, National Curriculum Programmes of Study (PoS), or the QCA Schemes of Work. All of the lessons should therefore fit into your existing medium-term plans. The planning grids have been provided in Microsoft Word format on the CD-ROM for this purpose.

Lesson plans

The lessons have a consistent structure with a starter activity, activities for shared and independent work and a plenary to round up the teaching and learning and identify any assessment opportunities. Crucially, each lesson plan identifies resources required (including photocopiable activity sheets 🄿 and flipcharts that are provided on the CD-ROM 💿). Also highlighted are the Activprimary™ tools that could be used in the lesson.

Photocopiable activity sheets at the end of each chapter support the lessons. These sheets provide opportunities for group or individual work to be completed away from the board, but link to the context of the whiteboard lesson. They also provide opportunities for whole-class plenary sessions in which children discuss and present their work.

Two general record sheets are provided on pages 170 and 171. These are intended to support the teacher in recording ways in which the interactive whiteboard is used, and where and how interactive resources can be integrated into a lesson.

What's on the CD-ROM?

The accompanying CD-ROM provides an extensive bank of Activprimary™ flipcharts. The flipcharts support, and are supported by, the lessons in this book. As well as texts and images, a selection of flipcharts include the following types of files:

- Embedded Microsoft Office files: These include Microsoft Word and Excel documents. The embedded files are launched from the flipchart and will open in their native Microsoft application.

- Embedded interactive files: These include specially commissioned interactive files as well as Interactive Teaching Programs (ITPs) from the Primary National Strategy.

Printable PDF versions of the photocopiable activity and record sheets, as well as the answers to the mathematics, are also provided on the CD-ROM.

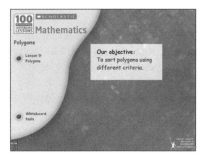

The flipcharts

All of the flipcharts have a consistent structure as follows:

Title and objectives page

Use this page to highlight the focus of the lesson. You might also wish to refer to this page at certain times throughout the lesson or at the end of the lesson to assess whether the learning objective was achieved.

Starter activity

This sets the context to the lesson and usually provides some key questions or learning points that will be addressed through the main activities.

Main activities

These activities offer independent, collaborative group, or whole-class work. The activities use the full range of Activprimary™ tools and include

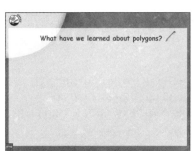

some opportunities for voting. Although Activote devices are useful, these pages can be used without them. Alternative methods of voting include:

- taking a tally of answers on individual whiteboards
- hand counts
- using coloured cards for true/false or yes/no questions, for example, blue for *yes* and red for *no*.

What to do boxes are also included in many of the prepared flipcharts. These appear as tabs in the top right-hand corner of the screen. To access these notes, simply pull out the tabs to reveal planning information, additional support and key learning points.

Plenary

A whole-class activity or summary page is designed to review work done both at the board and away from the board. In many lessons, children are encouraged to present their work.

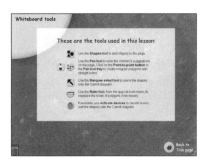

Whiteboard tools page

The whiteboard tools page gives a reminder of the tools used in the lesson and provides instructions on how they are used.

HOW TO USE THE CD-ROM

Setting up your screen for optimal use

It is best to view the Activprimary™ flipcharts provided on the CD-ROM at a screen display of 1024 × 768 pixels. To alter the screen display, select Settings, then Control Panel from the Start menu. Next, double-click the Display icon and click on the Settings tab. Adjust the Screen area scroll bar to 1024 × 768 pixels. Click OK.

If you prefer to use a screen display setting of 800 × 600 pixels, ensure that your Activprimary™ Page Scale is set to Best Fit. To alter the Page Scale, launch Activprimary™ and click on the Teacher tools menu button. Next, click on the Menu button and then Page Scale. Finally, select the Best Fit button. If you use this screen display setting, text in the prepared flipchart files may appear larger when you edit on screen.

Introduction

Viewing the printable resources

Adobe® Reader® is required to view the printable resources. If you do not have it installed already, a version is provided on the CD-ROM. To install this, right-click on the Start menu on your desktop and choose Explore. Click on the + sign to the left of the CD drive entitled *100WBLY4* and open the folder called Adobe Reader. Run the program contained in this folder to install Adobe® Reader®.

If you experience any difficulties viewing the PDF files, try changing your Adobe® Reader® preferences. Select Edit, then Preferences, within Adobe® Reader®. You will then be able to change your viewing options. For further information about Adobe® Reader® visit the Adobe® website at **www.adobe.com**

Getting started

It is advisable to launch Activprimary and to switch to Desktop mode before running the *100 Activprimary™ Whiteboard Lessons* CD-ROM. The program should run automatically when you insert the CD-ROM into your CD drive. If it does not, use My Computer to browse to the contents of the CD-ROM and click on the *100 Activprimary™ Whiteboard Lessons* icon.

When the program starts, you are invited to register the product either online or using a PDF registration form. You also have the option to register later. If you click this option, you will be taken, via the Credits screen, to the Main menu.

Main menu

The Main menu divides the flipcharts by subject: English, mathematics, science and foundation subjects. Clicking on the appropriate blue button for any of these options will take you to a separate Subject menu (see below for further information). The activity sheets are provided in separate menus. To access these resources, click Printable resources.

Individual flipcharts or pages can be located using the search facility by keying in words (or part words) from the resource titles in the Search box. Press Go to begin the search. This will bring up a list of the titles that match your search.

The Web Links button takes you to a list of useful web addresses. A help button is included on all menu screens. The Help notes on the CD-ROM provide a range of general background information and technical support for all users.

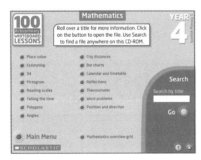

Subject menu

Each Subject menu provides all of the prepared flipcharts for each chapter of the book. Roll over each flipchart title to reveal a brief description of the contents in a text box at the top of the menu screen; clicking on the blue button will open the flipchart. Click on Main menu to return to the Main menu screen.

Printable resources

The printable PDF activity sheets are also divided by chapter. Click on the subject to find all the activity sheets related to that subject/chapter. The answers to Chapter 2, mathematics, are also provided.

To alternate between the menus on the CD-ROM and other open applications, hold down the Alt key and press the Tab key to switch to the desired application.

English

The lessons in the English chapter are arranged chronologically to match the medium-term planning in the National Literacy Strategy. There is a balance of word-, sentence- and text-level activities, which also interact with each other. For example, in the sentence-level work, that term's fiction and non-fiction writing are frequently used as a vehicle for putting the grammar into practice.

The interactive whiteboard offers pace and visual excitement. Words can be made to appear or disappear; text can be manipulated; the children can see sentences being constructed and watch paragraphs and stories emerging.

Be generous with the wonderful powers of the whiteboard and involve the children as much as possible in operating the board's tools. This will bring special benefits to children with dominant visual and kinaesthetic styles of learning. The interactive whiteboard is a stimulating resource for the teaching of English. Its role should always be to support the interaction between you, the children and literacy.

Lesson title	Objectives	What children should know	Cross-curricular links
Term 1			
Lesson 1: Verbs and tense	**S2** To investigate verb tenses (past, present and future). **W7** To spell regular verb endings.	• Verbs can be in the present or past.	**History** QCA Unit 18 'What was it like to live here in the past?'
Lesson 2: Irregular tense changes	**W8** To spell irregular tense changes.	• Verbs change spelling.	**ICT** QCA Unit 4A 'Writing for different audiences'
Lesson 3: Character sketches	**T11** Write character sketches, focusing on small details to evoke sympathy or dislike. **S3** Identify the use of powerful verbs.	• Experience of thinking about fictional characters.	**History** QCA Unit 6 'Why have people invaded and settled in Britain in the past?'
Lesson 4: Adverbs	**S4** To identify adverbs and understand their functions in sentences.	• The function of verbs.	**Citizenship** QCA Unit 01 'Taking part – developing skills of communication and participation'
Lesson 5: Story planning	**T4** To explore narrative order: identify and map out the main stages of the story. **T15** To use paragraphs in story writing to organise and sequence the narrative.	• Text is divided into paragraphs.	**History** QCA Unit 9 'What was it like for children in the Second World War?'
Lesson 6: Collecting and classifying words	**W9** To recognise and spell suffixes.	• Word beginnings may be grouped.	**History** QCA Unit 6A 'Why have people invaded and settled in Britain in the past?'
Lesson 7: Written instructions	**T22** To identify features of instructional texts. **T26** To improve the cohesion of written instructions and directions through the use of link phrases and organisational devices.	• The term *instruction*.	**Design and technology** QCA Unit 4B 'Storybooks – To design and make a book that has moving parts for a particular purpose' **ICT** QCA Unit 4A 'Writing for different audiences'

English Chapter 1

Lesson title	Objectives	What children should know	Cross-curricular links
Lesson 8: Alphabetical order	**W12** To use 3rd and 4th place letters to locate and sequence words in alphabetical order.	• Lists are often in alphabetical order.	**Speaking and listening** Objective 39: Group discussion and interaction: To take different roles in groups.
Lesson 9: Newspaper stories	**T21** To predict newspaper stories from the evidence of headlines, making notes and then checking against the original. **T24** To write newspaper style reports.	• Familiarity with some IT texts.	**Citizenship** QCA Unit 11 'In the media – what's the news?'
Lesson 10: Commas	**S5** To practise using commas within sentences; link to work on editing and revising own writing. **T24** To write newspaper style reports, using IT to draft and lay out reports.	• Common use of a comma.	**Citizenship** QCA Unit 11 'In the media – what's the news?'
Lesson 11: Homophones	**W6** To distinguish between the spelling and meanings of common homophones.	• Different words may sound the same.	**History** QCA Unit 6A 'Why have people invaded and settled in Britain in the past?'
Lesson 12: Adjectives	**S1** To revise and extend work on adjectives from Y3. **T10** To develop use of settings in own writing, making use of work on adjectives and figurative language to describe settings effectively.	• Adjectives describe nouns.	**Speaking and listening** Objective 41: To respond appropriately to the contributions of others in the light of alternative viewpoints.
Term 2			
Lesson 13: Spelling patterns	**W5** To investigate what happens to words ending in -*f* when suffixes are added.	• The term *suffix*.	**Speaking and listening** Objective 41: To respond appropriately to the contribution of others in the light of alternative viewpoints.
Lesson 14: Expressive writing	**T13** To write own examples of descriptive, expressive language based on those read. Link to work on adjectives and similes.	• Knowledge of adjectives.	**Speaking and listening** Objective 44: To tell stories using voice effectively.
Lesson 15: Apostrophes	**S2** To use the apostrophe accurately to mark possession. **T11** To write poetry based on the structure and/or style of poems read.	• Apostrophes can mark possession.	**Science** QCA Unit 4C 'Keeping warm'
Lesson 16: Word order	**S3** To understand the significance of word order. **S4** To recognise how commas, connectives and full stops are used to join and separate clauses.	• Punctuation aids comprehension.	**History** QCA Unit 7 'Why did Henry VIII marry six times?'
Lesson 17: Explanations	**T19** To identify how and why paragraphs are used to organise and sequence information. **T20** To identify from the examples the key features of explanatory texts. **T25** To write explanations of a process, using conventions identified through reading.	• Experience of non-fiction texts.	**Science** QCA Unit 4D 'Solids, liquids and how they can be separated'
Lesson 18: Spelling patterns	**W6** To spell words with the common endings: -*ight*, and so on.	• Spelling does not follow one set of rules.	**Citizenship** QCA Unit 9 'Respect for property'

Lesson title	Objectives	What children should know	Cross-curricular links
Lesson 19: Collecting and presenting information	**T21** To make short notes, for example, by abbreviating ideas, selecting key words, listing or in diagrammatic form.	• Information can be abbreviated.	**Science** QCA Unit 4D 'Solids, liquids and how they can be separated'
Lesson 20: Prefixes	**W7** To recognise and spell the prefixes: *-al*, and so on.	• The order of the alphabet.	**History** QCA Unit 7 'Why did Henry VIII marry six times?'; Unit 8 'What were the lives of rich and poor people in Tudor times'
Term 3			
Lesson 21: Writing poetry	**T15** To produce polished poetry through revision. **S1** To understand that some words can be changed in particular ways and others cannot.	• Editing and rewriting are important. • Words belong to different classes.	**Speaking and listening** Objective 44: Identifying the ways presentational features contribute to message and impact.
Lesson 22: Word roots	**W7** Collect/classify words with common roots.	• Knowledge of root words.	**History** QCA Unit 6A 'Why have people invaded and settled in Britain in the past?'
Lesson 23: Punctuation	**S2** To identify the common punctuation marks.	• Awareness of punctuation marks in text.	**History** QCA Unit 6A 'Why have people invaded and settled in Britain in the past?'
Lesson 24: Summaries	**T20** To summarise a sentence or paragraph by identifying the most important elements and rewording them in a limited number of words.	• Not every word is of equal importance.	**History** QCA Unit 6A 'Why have people invaded and settled in Britain in the past?'
Lesson 25: Its and it's	**W10** To distinguish the two forms: *its* and *it's*.	• Words may sound the same but be spelled and used differently.	**Science** QCA Unit 4B 'Habitats'
Lesson 26: Word endings and classes	**S1** To understand that some words can be changed in particular ways and others cannot.	• Words are divided into classes.	**Speaking and listening** Objective 44: To tell stories using voice effectively.
Lesson 27: Spelling compound words	**W11** To investigate compound words and recognise that they can aid spelling even when pronunciation obscures it.	• Pronunciation does not always help spelling.	**History** QCA Unit 6A 'Why have people invaded and settled in Britain in the past?'
Lesson 28: Sentence types	**S3** To understand how the grammar of a sentence alters when the sentence type is altered.	• Not all sentences are the same type.	**History** QCA Unit 18 'What was it like to live here in the past?'
Lesson 29: Advertisements	**T19** To evaluate advertisements for their impact, appeal and honesty, focusing in particular on how information about the product is presented. **T25** To design an advertisement.	• Experience of seeing advertisements.	**Science** QCA Unit 4C 'Keeping warm'
Lesson 30: Connectives	**S4** The use of connectives to structure an argument.	• The term *connective*.	**Citizenship** QCA Unit 11 'In the media – what's the news?'

Verbs and tense

Starter
Revise the term *verb*. Define a verb as a *doing* or *being* word. It can express an action, a happening, a process or a state. Remind the children that:
● every sentence needs a verb
● a verb can be a chain of words.
Open the flipchart 'Max's party' and look at the text on page 2. Together, read the passage, identify the verbs and highlight them.

Whole-class shared work
● Go to page 3. The three hyperlinked football buttons lead to the invitation to Max's party, the voiceover Max wrote to go with a video of the day and the entry Max wrote in his diary at the end of the day.
● Click on the football button next to *The invitation*. Read it and together identify the verbs. Ask volunteers to highlight them. Reveal the correct answers by moving the spyglass over the text.
● Move to *Max's voiceover* and repeat the process, highlighting the verbs first, and then checking the answers with the spyglass.
● For *Max's diary*, ask the children to drag the verbs into the text before using the spyglass to check that they are correct.
● Challenge the children to explain the difference between the verbs in each passage. (They are in different tenses.)
● Revise the word *tense:* the tense of a verb gives information about when the action took place. Identify the tenses of these three pages of information: present, past and future.
● Investigate how the tenses are formed. Focus on the verb endings in each text. Point out the frequent use of *-s, -ing* and *-ed*. Explain that these are some of the regular verb endings. If required, use page 7 to write notes about verb tenses and the different verb endings.
● Look again at the paragraph on page 2. Encourage the children to say what tense has been used here? (Present.)

Independent work
● Ask the children to write two more paragraphs in their exercise books to continue the text on page 2. One paragraph should be about education in the past, the other about education in the future.
● The children should use the verbs that they highlighted on page 2, but change their tense.
● Supply opening words for both paragraphs:
  ● *When our great grandparents were children...*
  ● *In the future...*
● Provide a framework for the sentences for less confident children, with a box of verbs for each paragraph.
● As an extra challenge, ask the children to convert other paragraphs in the past tense into the present tense.

Plenary
● Invite the children to share their work. Write examples of their sentences on page 8. Discuss the verb forms used.
● Look for examples of the usual spelling patterns: *-s, -ed* and *-ing*. Identify instances of verbs doubling a consonant (for example, *chats* becomes *chatted*).

Irregular tense changes

Learning objective
NLS Term 1
● W8: To spell irregular tense changes.

Resources P
Photocopiable page 41 'Now and Then' for each child; individual whiteboards and pens.
Prepared flipchart file with the following sentences written in separate text boxes:
Tom blinked fast.
Harry shuts his eyes.
Dad went white.
Mum wrote an email.
The neighbours fled.
The baby wept.
The postman runs.
Shaun reads a story.
Stacey raced to the rescue.

Links to other subjects
ICT
QCA Unit 4A 'Writing for different audiences'
● Provide opportunities for the children to use computers to make their poems into appealing texts for a class poetry anthology.

Starter
Open your prepared flipchart. Ask the children to identify the verbs and challenge them to sort the sentences into two groups. Give thinking time before you ask a volunteer to demonstrate this on the whiteboard, creating:
● a group in the present tense
● a group in the past tense.
Focus on the second group. Ask: *How can this group be divided again into two groups?* Encourage the children to look carefully at the spelling and construction of the past tense verbs. Highlight the different endings in different colours. Finally, create two groups:
● sentences with verbs ending in -*ed*
● sentences with different verbs.

Whole-class shared work
● Explain that the regular ending for past tense verbs is -*ed*. Irregular past forms show other changes, usually to the medial vowel (*blow* becomes *blew; rise* becomes *rose*).
● Point out that the children probably make many of these tense changes without thinking. Play an oral game of *Boasting* to prove this. Make a boastful statement about yourself in the present: *I begin karate this week.*
● Ask the children to better this, making the same boast about themselves in the past: *I began karate last week.*
● Record the tense changes on the whiteboard. Look for verbs that can be grouped together, and group them under headings. For example: -*ing* becomes -*ang* (*sing* – sang, *ring* – rang); -*ind* becomes -*ound* (*find* – found, *wind* – wound); -*ow* becomes -*ew* (*blow* –blew); -*ell* becomes -*old* (*sell* – sold).
● Allow the children time to play a further a short session of *Boasting* with a partner. Ask them to keep a record of their verb changes on individual whiteboards.
● Share results by letting children add examples to the headings on the whiteboard. Create new headings if verbs can be grouped together.
● Point out that some past tenses follow no set pattern. Demonstrate how to use a dictionary to check past tenses.

Independent work
● Ask the children to complete the poem on the photocopiable sheet, comparing themselves *Now* in Year 4 to *Then* in babyhood.
● The *Now* lines use present tense verbs. The children must use these verbs in the past tense in the *Then* lines.
● Making rough drafts and checking awkward verbs in a dictionary will help the children to produce a polished, final poem.
● Give less able learners a box of past tense verbs to fit into their lines.
● As an extra challenge, ask children to write additional pairs of *Now* and *Then* lines.

Plenary
● Scan in and view some of the results from the Independent work.
● Ask some children to read their poems to the class. Are any unusual tense changes discovered?

Whiteboard tools
Use the Floating keyboard in the Text editor tray to enter text.

 Pen tool

 Text editor tool

Highlighter tool

 Marquee select tool

Floating keyboard

Character sketches

Learning objectives
NLS Term 1
● T11: Write character sketches, focusing on small details to evoke sympathy or dislike.
● S3: Identify the use of powerful verbs.

Resources
'Dragon Invaders' flipchart file; individual whiteboards and pens, or Activote devices (if available).

Links to other subjects
History
QCA Unit 6 'Why have people invaded and settled in Britain in the past?'
● Link the text to information about the Viking raiders.

Starter
Display page 2 of the flipchart. Read the text and discuss it. Find out whether the majority like or dislike Father and Mother by asking the children to vote. They could do this by writing *Like* or *Dislike* by each character's name on individual whiteboards and holding them up, or by having an Activote session. Discuss the results. Highlight parts of the text which could have affected feelings (not wanting to share, not being rich, the word *schemed*).

Whole-class shared work
● Display page 3. Discuss the events of the text (Aled's actions, dragons coming by sea).
● Focus on the character, Aled. Ask: *What sort of person do you think he is? How can you tell? Do you like or dislike him? Why?* Encourage discussion and different viewpoints, emphasising that people respond to writing differently.
● Point out specific details from the passage. Discuss each of the details in turn, asking the children to think about how the words make them feel about Aled. (For example, *He got rid of all signs of his presence* might show that Aled has a careful nature.)
● Ask the children whether the words add information about the character? Does it make them feel more sympathetic towards him? Does one detail make them dislike Aled? Encourage varied viewpoints.
● If required, draw out details from the text by double-clicking on it with the Marquee select tool, then clicking on Edit text in the Object edit toolbox. Highlight the words you want to isolate and drag them outside the text box. This adds the words to the page as a separate object.
● Focus on the verbs the writer has chosen. Are they good choices? (The verbs are often weak and there is repetition.)
● Make the point that more powerful verbs could improve this passage.
● Highlight some weak verbs in the first two lines.
● Print a copy of the text for every child.

Independent work
● Ask the children to read the text by themselves. They should highlight at least 15 verbs to replace.
● They should then write their replacement, powerful verbs.
● Support less able learners by focusing on a smaller number of replacements of the weakest verbs (*put, saw, got*).
● As an extra challenge, ask more able learners to write the next part of the story, using powerful verbs and small details to evoke more sympathy or dislike of Aled.

Whiteboard tools
Double-click on the text with the Marquee select tool to view the Object edit toolbox. Select Edit text to edit existing text and to add words from existing text to the page as a separate object.

 Highlighter tool

 Marquee select tool

 Edit text tool

Activote (optional)

Plenary
● A copy of the text is on page 4 of the flipchart. Let the children use this to demonstrate their replacement verbs.
● Discuss the effect more powerful verbs have on audience reaction. Return to the original version on page 3 so that other children can write alternative verbs.
● There is a text using stronger verbs on page 5 of the flipchart, but other verbs are, of course, possible.

Adverbs

Learning objective
NLS Term 1
● S4: To identify adverbs and understand their functions in sentences.

Resources
'Dragon Invaders' flipchart file; photocopiable page 42 'The meeting' for each child.

Links to other subjects
Citizenship
QCA Unit 01 'Taking part – developing skills of communication and participation'
● During circle time, ask the children to write the adverb that best describes how they feel about a school issue. Share the words, and use them as a starting point for an exchange of views.

Starter
Look at page 6 of the flipchart. Remind the children that words belong to different classes. A word's class depends on its function in a sentence. Revise familiar word classes: verbs and nouns. Ask the children to highlight the nouns (*Margaret, labels*) and verbs *(held, looked)*. Ask: *What class do the words in red belong to?* Identify them as adverbs. Deconstruct the text to draw out and list the adverbs. Remember to switch back to Presentation mode.

Whole-class shared work
● Display page 7. Explain that an adverb's usual function is to add meaning to a verb.
● Investigate the adverbs used in the Starter text. Point out that most answer the question *How?* (For example, *clearly* explains how the names were written; *shyly* explains how Margaret looked.) Question the children about *wearily, tightly,* and *silently*. (They all answer *How?*)
● Focus on *Eventually*. Agree that it answers the question *When?*
● Ask if they have noticed anything special about the spellings of adverbs. Explain that adverbs commonly (but not always) end in *-ly*.
● Investigate the position of the adverbs. Can the children tell which word the adverb adds meaning to? (Verb.) Which word should it stay near? (Verb.) *Eventually* is an exception in this text.
● Look at page 8 of the flipchart. Can the children spot an adverb ending in *-ly*? (*Finally*.) Highlight the word.
● Suggest improving the text with eight to ten adverbs. Share ideas and make additions to the whiteboard. Page 9 demonstrates adverbs that could be used in the text.
● Warn against unnecessary adverbs: the verb may already express the meaning of a suggested adverb.
● Adverbs are useful in dialogue passages because they help the reader to *see* a speaker's face and to *hear* the tone of voice. (For example, *"I don't know," John replied glumly*.)
● Encourage the children to suggest more adverbs that could describe how people speak, and write a few of their ideas on page 7. (For example: loudly, quietly, cheerfully, miserably, happily.)

Independent work
● Ask the children to complete the dialogue on photocopiable page 42 'The meeting'.
● Explain that each of the speaking verbs needs an adverb to bring the text to life. The spoken words must suit the adverbs chosen.
● Provide less able learners with a list of adverbs to use.
● As an extra challenge, ask more able learners to write their own narrative with dialogue, using a different set of adverbs.

Plenary
● Invite the children to share their finished texts. Add examples of their sentences to page 10, highlighting the adverbs used.
● Discuss whether the spoken words suit the adverbs chosen.
● Let the children speak the words in the appropriate voice. This can be recorded using the Sound recorder ◀)) if a microphone is available.

Whiteboard tools
To deconstruct text, enable Design mode, right-/barrel-click on the word you want to use, and select Deconstruct word from the pop-up menu. Convert handwriting to text with the Recognition tool. If a microphone is available, use the Sound Recorder to record speech.

⬉ Marquee select tool

🖉 Pen tool

🖍 Highlighter tool

🔤 Recognition tool

◀)) Sound recorder (optional)

🛠 Design mode

Ⓣ Edit text tool

Story planning

Starter
Display page 2 of the flipchart 'Story planning'. Read the text and ask the children what they notice about it. (The narrative is not in the correct sequence.) Keeping the story in paragraphs, invite children to change the paragraph order. When you have agreed on a correct sequence, use the Fill tool to change the colour for each circle and reveal the correct order.

Whole-class shared work
● Discuss paragraphs, making notes on page 3. Explain that paragraphs mark different stages in the a: they help writers to organise their thoughts and readers to follow the story line.
● Explain that paragraphs can vary in length: the introduction and the ending to a story are often shorter than other paragraphs.
● Go to page 4 and open the *Story Planning* activity. Discuss the picture sequence. Ask: *What do you think is happening? Which events are important? Is there a main character?*
● Ask the children what is wrong with the pictures. (They are in the wrong order.) Challenge them to decide and note on their individual whiteboards what the picture order should be.
● Discuss their answers and agree on an order. Move the frames into the correct sequence. How does it compare with their individual whiteboard suggestions? Were there points the children had not thought about?
● Take a snapshot of the correct story sequence using the Camera tool and add it to the flipchart page.
● Suggest that each picture represents a paragraph. Annotate each picture with a planning sentence.
● Write these stage names next to the pictures, discussing each one as you do so:
  1. introduction
  2. build-up
  3. climax
  4. resolution
  5. ending.
● Go to page 5 of the flipchart. Ask the children to plan another story about the evacuees using the stages that have been discussed. Write a few subject ideas on page 5, for example: *Mum's first visit; an adventure with local children; problems at the village school.* Emphasise that the children's own ideas should be better.

Independent work
● The children should plan their stories on the photocopiable sheet and write the opening paragraph in their exercise books.
● Work in a group with less able learners by, explaining each story stage.
● As an extra challenge, suggest that not every story stage has to be the same length: for example, the build-up could have two paragraphs.

Plenary
● Scan in and view some of the children's plans and opening paragraphs.
● Discuss the progression and the sequence of events in some of the story plans.
● Listen to some of the children read their introductions, and discuss as a class how effective they are.
● Use an extended writing session to finish the story.

Learning objective
NLS Term 1
● W9: To recognise and spell suffixes.

Resources
'Suffixes and prefixes' flipchart file; individual whiteboards and pens, or Activote devices; printed copy of page 5 of the flipchart for each child.

Links to other subjects
History
QCA Unit 6A 'Why have people invaded and settled in Britain in the past?'
● Provide etymological dictionaries for investigation work. Ask the children to identify the Latin root word and find out the meaning of these words: *centurion, century, centenary, cent, porcupine, pork, porcelain, granary, granite, pomegranate, tractor, distract, attract, terrier, interred, territory, puncture, punctuation, punctual, audition, auditorium, audible.*

Whiteboard tools

🖉 Pen tool

🖰 Marquee select tool

🖌 Highlighter tool

🖶 Print button

◉ Activote (optional)

Collecting and classifying words

Starter
Display page 2 of the flipchart. Discuss how to sort the words, eventually moving them so that they are grouped like this:
● Group 1: champion, member, owner, neighbour
● Group 2: partnership, childhood, ownership
Explain that the words in Group 1 are root words and the words in Group 2 are made from root words plus additional letters.
Show the children how *owner* with *ownership* make a pair. Ask volunteers to supply the missing word to pair with the root words on the page (*champion - championship; member - membership; neighbour - neighbourhood; partner - partnership; child - childhood*).

Whole-class shared work
● Explain that a suffix is a group of letters added to the end of a word. Each root word in the Starter uses a suffix to become another word.
● Focus on the suffix -*ship*. Brainstorm words ending this way, such as *fellowship* or *partnership*. Write them on to page 3. Ask the children to highlight the root words.
● Discuss how the suffix affects the meaning of the new word. Encourage the class to think about what -*ship* means in these words. Establish that it is a way of living or a skill.
● Display page 4 of the flipchart. Point to a root word and ask children to choose a suffix for it, writing *a* or *b* on their individual whiteboards or using Activote devices, if available.
● Ask volunteers to drag the words into the correct boxes. Note that *silly* does not work in either, although *silliness* is a valid word. Point out that the addition of a suffix can alter the spelling of the root word: if the root word ends in *y*, the *y* usually changes to *i* when a suffix is added.
● Reverse the activity, looking at the new, extended word and identifying the original, root word.

Independent work
● Print off a copy of page 5 for each child. The children must choose a suffix for each root word, listing the root word and the new word in the correct column.
● Encourage the children to use dictionaries for their investigation.
● Reduce the list of root words and limit the choice of suffixes to two for less confident children.
● As an extra challenge, ask more able learners to make their own additions to the columns.

Plenary
● Display page 5 and invite children to drag the words into the table.
● Note the words that do not work because of spelling changes.
● Encourage the children to suggest other words that could be added to the lists. Use page 6 to work together on lists of words for the suffixes -*dom, -ance, -ence, -ology, -ation.*

Written instructions

Learning objectives
NLS Term 1
● T22: To identify features of instructional texts.
● T26: To improve the cohesion of written instructions and directions through the use of link phrases and organisational devices.

Resources
'Making a storybook' flipchart file; one computer for each pair of children, if available. (Microsoft Word is required to view the embedded text document in the flipchart.)

Links to other subjects
Design and technology
QCA Unit 4B 'Storybooks - To design and make a book that has moving parts for a particular purpose'
ICT
QCA Unit 4A 'Writing for different audiences'
● The work in this lesson links well to both of the objectives above.

Whiteboard tools
Activprimary will automatically switch to Desktop mode when the embedded file on page 3 is opened.

 Pen tool

 Highlighter tool

Marquee select tool

Desktop mode

 Return to main screen

Starter
Display page 2 of the flipchart 'Making a storybook'. Discuss the text. Ask the children to explain the process in their own words to a partner. Point out the emphasis on correct sequential order. Ask questions such as: *What has to be done first? What is the final step?* Ask the children to identify words reinforcing this sequence. Highlight these words: *First, Then, Eventually, Finally.* Explain that they are link words.

Whole-class shared work
● Display page 3 and read the text aloud. Can the children identify the text type as instructions?
● Investigate the special features of instruction texts, using this example.
   1. Highlight its different sections:
      ● Title: the objective of the text is stated.
      ● Requirements: necessary materials are listed.
      ● Method: the reader is told what to do.
   2. Highlight some of the verbs (*discuss, display, demonstrate*). Explain that they are *imperative* (command) verbs. Point out their sentence position (the start of the sentence). Question the children about the verbs' tense (present).
   3. Draw the children's attention to the use of short sentences and the importance of sequential order.
● Encourage the children to recall written instructions that they have used. Are there any in their text books? Investigate examples.
● Ask the class: *Can you think of additional features missing from here?* Agree on important, missing features. Use page 4 of the flipchart to add them to the list, for example:
   ● Dividing the text into sections.
   ● Having a subheading for each section.
   ● Listing the requirements vertically.
   ● Starting a new line for each instruction.
   ● Using organisational devices, such as numbers, letters, or bullet points.
   ● Including informative illustrations or diagrams.
   ● Varying the font to make the information clearer.
   ● Using link phrases.

Independent work
● Print a copy of the story-making instructions on page 3 for each child. Ask the children to work in pairs to plan improvements.
● Suggest that the children have subheadings for these three sections:
   1. What you need
   2. What to do
   3. How to display
● Once planned, let the children produce a new copy of the text, preferably on a computer. (An editable version of the text is available by clicking on the button on page 3.)
● Support less able learners by suggesting where to divide the text.
● As an extra challenge, ask children to write instructions for making a storybook using the computer.

Plenary
● Scan in some of the children's texts, and discuss which organisational features were the most popular. Make a note of the techniques on page 5.
● Look at instructional texts on the classroom walls. Do any need improving? How would the children improve them?

 17

Alphabetical order

Learning objective
NLS Term 1
● W12: To use 3rd and 4th place letters to locate and sequence words in alphabetical order.

Resources
'Making a storybook' flipchart file; copy of photocopiable page 44 'Alphabetical order' for each child; individual whiteboards and pens.

Links to other subjects
Speaking and listening
Objective 39: Group discussion and interaction: To take different roles in groups.
● Allow group discussion when children contribute to the whole-class ordering of words.

Starter
Play some oral games to revise alphabetical order, for example, creating an animal alphabet, reciting the alphabet backwards, or starting from a letter and finding the letter before or after it.

Whole-class shared work
● Display page 6 of the flipchart. Highlight the *p* words.
● Encourage the children to put the words in alphabetical order. Draw the words out from the text by selecting Edit text in the Object edit toolbox, highlighting the relevant word, and dragging it to the white box at the side.
● Compare the children's results. Ask: *How did you decide?* Agree on the need to look past the first letter *p*. Underline the second letter in each of the words. Encourage the children to decide which of these is first in the alphabet. Drag this word to the bottom of the screen.
● Repeat this process with the other words, placing them in order. What problem do the children notice? (Two words have *e* as a second letter.) Agree to look at the third letter. Continue until you have: *paper, pens, pencils, pictures.*
● Repeat the exercise with the *d* words. Point out that for *discuss* and *display* you have to move to the fourth letter.
● Display page 7. Give each pair of children a word to write on their individual whiteboard and ask them to underline the second letter. Explain that you will recite the alphabet slowly and when they hear you say the underlined letter they must raise their hands.
● Start reciting, stopping when children raise their hands and allowing them to come to the board and move their words into the vertical list.
● Now review the list. Ask: *Are there problems? Do any words have the same second letter?* Remove those words from the list, placing them to one side.
● The owners of those words should then underline their third letters. Repeat the process of calling out the alphabet. When their letter is reached, the children move to the front and place their words in the line.
● Again look for problems. Do any words have the same third letter? If so, check the fourth letter. Agree on the final list.

Independent work
● Ask the children to complete photocopiable page 44 'Alphabetical order'.
● Support less able learners by reducing the list.
● As an extra challenge, ask more able learners to make their own *b* section.

Plenary
● Display page 8 of the flipchart and ask for volunteers to order the words correctly. Highlight words where third and fourth place letters have to be taken into account.
● Using page 9 of the flipchart, compile an alphabetically ordered list of first names in the class.

Whiteboard tools
To draw out words from the text before ordering, select Edit text in the Object edit toolbox, highlight the relevant word, and drag it to the white box at the side.

 Highlighter tool

 Marquee select tool

 Text editor tool

 Edit text tool

 Recognition tool

Newspaper stories

Learning objectives
NLS Term 1
● T21: To predict newspaper stories from the evidence of headlines, making notes and then checking against the original.
● T24: To write newspaper style reports.

Resources **P**
Photocopiable page 45 'Story summaries'; example of local newspaper; example of online newspaper such as **www.timesonline.co.uk** individual whiteboards and pens.

Links to other subjects
Citizenship
QCA Unit 11 'In the media – what's the news?'
● Select newspaper stories that are of local or national interest.

Starter
Read one of the summaries on the photocopiable sheet to the class, leaving out the book title. Ask the children to propose a title. Choose the one closest to the author's and write it onto a blank flipchart page. Use a different colour to write the real title. Which version do the children think is better? Why? Repeat this with the other story summaries. Play the game with some of the children's stories. Ask: *What does the title say about the plot? Does it make you want to read it?* Discuss what a title should achieve.

Whole-class shared work
● Open an online newspaper or magazine. Explain that stories in a newspaper do not have titles; they have headlines.
● Use the Spotlight tool 🕙 to focus on one news headline. What do the children think this story will be about? Read some of the story to them. Discuss whether it is what they expected from the headline.
● Return to the front page. Choose another headline. Repeat the process, predicting the content of the story, and then checking to see if the story meets expectations.
● What do the children notice about the headlines? Agree on common features and write them on the whiteboard. For example:
  ● eye-catching
  ● quick to read
  ● arouses interest
  ● uses key words rather than lengthy sentences
  ● encourages the reader to read the story.
● Read some news headlines from a local newspaper. Challenge the children to guess what the story will be about. Read the subheadings and discuss whether these give any more information. Invite the children to make brief notes on their individual whiteboards, predicting a story's content.
● Read parts of the reports to the children. Ask: *Were the headlines helpful? Are subheadings a good device? How well do your notes match the story?*

Independent work
● Type up these headlines onto a blank flipchart page:
  ● Protest over lunch
  ● Swarm stings school!
  ● Why did they win?
  ● School sees sense
● Suggest that the headlines all relate to (imaginary) school news.
● Ask the children to choose a headline and write a newspaper report for the school newspaper. Tell them to write it in their exercise books, as they will be editing it in another lesson.
● Less confident children could work with a partner.
● As an extra challenge, ask the children to write two reports with different events but the same headline.

Whiteboard tools
Use the Spotlight tool to focus on newspaper headlines. Use the Floating keyboard to enter text.

🖊 Pen tool

🕙 Spotlight tool

Ⓣ Text editor tool

⌨ Floating keyboard

Plenary
● Ask some children to read part of their reports, involving as many of them as possible.
● Discuss how much variety there is between different reports. Scan a few reports and display them on the whiteboard.
● Discuss whether headlines predict the reports accurately, and if subheadings are also needed.

 19

Commas

Learning objectives
NLS Term 1
● S5: To practise using commas within sentences; link to work on editing and revising own writing.
● T24: To write newspaper style reports, using IT to draft and lay out reports.

Resources
Computers for the children to use; individual whiteboards and pens.

Links to other subjects
Citizenship
QCA Unit 11 'In the media – what's the news?'
● Follow up the lesson by asking the children to edit and revise their newspaper reports.
● Provide computers, and help the children to lay out their report in a newspaper column format.

Starter
Put a comma on a blank flipchart page and remind children of its name. Ask them to count the commas on a page of their last story. Compare totals. Ask: *Why did you use a comma? Was it essential? Why was it the best punctuation mark?* Record their answers on the whiteboard.

Whole-class shared work
● Write: *A comma is a punctuation mark used to help the reader by separating parts of a sentence. It sometimes corresponds to a pause in speech.*
● Discuss this, and then type the following paragraph:
  ● The editor was furious. The deadline was four o'clock. It was now five past four. No article had appeared. Where was it? He reached for the phone.
● Invite the children to close their eyes while you read the paragraph aloud to them. Can they *hear* any commas? (No.) Discuss why. (The sentences are mainly short.)
● Explain that longer spoken sentences can be difficult for a listener to make sense of, so the speaker will make pauses. Commas break up written sentences in the same way, dividing the sentence into meaningful portions.
● Demonstrate this by reading the following sentence aloud: *Wayne Yorke, the youngest reporter, ignored the phone.*
● Ask the children to write, on their individual whiteboards, which words need commas after them. Repeat the sentence, advising the children that two commas are needed. Finally, write the punctuated sentence on the whiteboard.
● With different colour highlighting, split the sentence into three sections: *Wayne Yorke,   the youngest reporter,   ignored the phone.*
  Explain that:
  ● Section one names someone.
  ● Section two adds extra information about the person.
  ● Section three takes action.
● Repeat this exercise with other sentences of a similar construction. For example: *Suki, the receptionist, opened the biscuits.* Each time, read the sentence aloud for the children to *hear* and decide where to place commas. Afterwards, write the punctuated sentence on the whiteboard or invite a child to add the commas, then highlight the sections.
● Make sure that your intonation helps the children to become confident about identifying the position of the commas.

Independent work
● Ask the children to edit their newspaper report from Lesson 9 by changing, removing and adding words. Encourage them to add three sentences similar to the examples, with two commas in each.
● Support less able learners by dividing the task into stages:
  1. Create sentences with commas.
  2. Place the sentences in their report.
● As an extra challenge, ask children to do further editing, combining and changing their short sentences so that commas are needed.

Plenary
● Encourage some children to read their sentences aloud. Can others *hear* commas?
● Ask some children to write their sentences on the whiteboard and highlight each part.

Whiteboard tools
 Pen tool

 Text editor tool

 Highlighter tool

 Floating keyboard

Homophones

Learning objective
NLS Term 1
● W6: To distinguish between the spelling and meanings of common homophones.

Resources
'Homophones' flipchart file; individual whiteboards and pens; copy of photocopiable page 46 'Letter from Britain' for each child.

Links to other subjects
History
QCA Unit 6A 'Why have people invaded and settled in Britain in the past?'
● Link the lesson to work on the Roman invasion of Britain.

Whiteboard tools
Remove unwanted objects by clicking on the Delete button in the Object edit toolbox.

 Highlighter tool

 Marquee select tool

 Delete button

 Pen tool

 Eraser tool

Activote (optional)

Starter
Look at page 2 of the flipchart 'Homophones'. Ask the children what the three words under the pictures have in common (they are pronounced the same way). Point out that although they are said the same way, they are spelled differently.

Explain that you want to sort the words on page 3 into small groups by playing *Sound Snap*. Drag one word into one of the circles, and ask a volunteer to identify another that sounds the same. If the answer is wrong, the turn passes to someone else. If correct, say *Snap* and drag the matching word to the circle.

Some of the words are in groups of three. In these cases, highlight a word in a circle for the children to guess the third one of the group. Keep going until all the words are in circles. If the children find the sound matching difficult, play the game more than once.

Whole-class shared work
● Point to the word *Homophone* on page 4. Ask the children what they think it means. Reveal the definition behind the red box.
● Explain that the words they played *Sound Snap* with are homophones.
● Encourage the children to suggest other examples and add them to the page 3 in the remaining three circles.
● Play *Solve my Riddle* by asking the children to tell you which word on page 3 fits the clue. For example:
  ● *I am very wet.* (sea)
  ● *I get fried in batter.* (plaice)
  ● *I am more than one.* (four)
  ● *I say baa.* (ewe)
● Allow partner collaboration and thinking time as children write their answers on individual whiteboards. Highlight words as they are identified. Encourage the children to make up some riddles of their own.
● Discuss whether the children confuse particular homophones. Ask: *How do you remember the correct one?* Share helpful memory tips.
● Display page 5 of the flipchart. Work together to invent mnemonics (devices to aid memory).

Independent work
● Give each child a copy of the photocopiable sheet. Explain that the Roman soldier, writing a letter from Britain, has all the words he needs in the box.
● The children must decide which word goes where.
● Advise less able learners which set of homophones to choose from.
● As an extra challenge, encourage more able learners to compose their own Roman letter containing between 10 and 15 deliberate mistakes. Can someone else spot the mistakes?

Plenary
● Display page 6 of the flipchart. Discuss possible answers before allowing children to drag the correct words from the *Homophones* box into the text. Delete incorrect words. Move the spyglass to reveal the correct answers.
● If time allows, use pages 7 and 8 to assess the children's learning with a quick voting session.

Adjectives

Learning objectives
NLS Term 2
● S1: To revise and extend work on adjectives from Y3.
● T10: To develop use of settings in own writing, making use of work on adjectives and figurative language to describe settings effectively.

Resources
'Another world' flipchart file; exercise books and pens.

Links to other subjects
Speaking and listening
Objective 41: To respond appropriately to the contributions of others in the light of alternative viewpoints.
● Encourage children to express opinions about the adjectives used.

Starter
Open page 2 of the flipchart, firstly enabling the Reveal tool 🖬 to keep the second paragraph hidden. Read the text to the children. Question them about their reactions. Ask: *How does the description make you feel? What mood do the words create?*

Now reveal the second paragraph. Read it to the children and repeat the questions. Compare the texts. Ask: *Does the second version make you feel differently when it is read? How? Why?* Note down some comments on the whiteboard. Express the view that the second text arouses expectations, making you want to see what will happen.

Whole-class shared work
● Highlight the additional words and the changed final word in the second extract on page 2.
● Ask the children what class these words belong to. (Adjectives.)
● Define *adjective*: a word describing somebody or something. Investigate which nouns are described by the adjectives.
● Discuss the benefits of adding adjectives to this text. (Tension is built.)
● Play a game in which the children suggest an adjective to describe a given classroom object. Encourage informative or expressive adjectives, rather than bland ones, for example: a *grazed* knee; a *tanned* face; a *modern* computer; a *useless* box; a *confused* expression.
● Display page 3 of the flipchart, read it to the children and discuss it together. How does it make the children feel?
● Point out the word *afraid*. Does this piece of writing make the children feel afraid? Suggest that well-chosen adjectives could add to the mood.
● Work together, experimenting with adding adjectives. Encourage adjectives of sufficient intensity, avoiding those that are too obvious. (An amended version of the text, showing possible adjectives, appears on page 4.)
● Ask the children to think up an imaginary world. List some of their ideas on page 5 of the flipchart. Some examples are given below, but encourage the children's own ideas:
    ● A world on the other side of an ordinary doorway.
    ● A place reached by travel.
    ● A world reached through a theme park ride.
    ● A house that changes as night falls.

Independent work
● Ask the children to write a description of their world. They should use well-chosen adjectives to create atmosphere and tension.
● Suggest writing a rough draft, before editing and producing a polished version (computers would be useful).
● Direct less able learners to the ideas on the whiteboard.
● As an extra challenge, ask children to describe the same imaginary world but using different adjectives and creating a different atmosphere.

Plenary
● Invite some children to read their descriptions to the class.
● Ask listeners to pick out memorable adjectives and list them on page 5.
● Discuss their reactions to those words.

Whiteboard tools
Use the Reveal tool from the Special tools menu to hide part of the screen. Click on the Edit text button in the Object edit toolbox to amend existing text.

 Pen tool

 Edit text tool

 Highlighter tool

 Reveal tool

🢒 Marquee select tool

Spelling patterns

Learning objective
NLS Term 2
● W5: To investigate what happens to words ending in -*f* when suffixes are added.

Resources
'The shopping list' flipchart file; photocopiable page 47 'A strange shopping list' for each child; writing books and pens.

Links to other subjects
Speaking and listening
Objective 41: To respond appropriately to the contribution of others in the light of alternative viewpoints.
● Encourage the children to use partner discussion to help them identify plurals that sound correct.

Starter
Display page 2 of the flipchart and ask the children to write in the plural forms for the first three words. Use the Eraser tool to reveal the answers on the right and highlight the suffixes that form the plural. Do the same for the next three words. Then extend the work to plurals where -*s* is not added by repeating the activity for the next group of words on page 3.

Whole-class shared work
● Go to page 4 of the flipchart. Group the children in pairs: one partner should read the word in the left-hand column of the table; then the other partner should say its plural form. Ask them to agree on the pronunciation of the plural.
● Discuss the plurals with the class. If there is dispute, let children say answers in sentences. Can they now hear which sounds correct?
● Invite children to write the plural of each word in the central column. Check the answer is right each time, using the Eraser tool.
● When the table is complete, ask the children to study the words and to work out a spelling rule for converting these words from singular to plural.
● Share ideas and write a list on the next page:
  1. Words ending in -f, change to -ves in the plural.
  2. Words ending in -ff, add -s in the plural.
  3. Words ending in -fe, change to -ves in the plural.
● Investigate which rule applies to each word in the table on page 4.
● Write the word *chief* under the rules on page 5. Ask: *Which rule should we apply?* (You would expect to use rule 1.) *What will the plural be?* (Chieves.) *Does it sound correct?* (No.)
● Explain that the correct plural is *chiefs.* Spelling rules cannot always be applied. There are many exceptions.
● Demonstrate how a dictionary can help with problem words.

Independent work
● Ask children to complete photocopiable page 47. (A *plum duff* is a plum pudding.)
● Divide the words into groups for less able learners.
● As an extra challenge, ask children to add further text, using other -*ff*, -*f* and -*fe* words and their plural forms.

Plenary
● Work through the photocopiable sheet together and compare the children's answers with the answers on pages 6 and 7 of the flipchart. Invite children to write the answer you agree upon.
● Show the correct plural forms by reducing the box on the right-hand side of the page.
● Draw attention to *scarf:* the plural can be *scarfs* or *scarves.*
● Share some of the children's spells from their photocopiable sheets.
● Pages 8 and 9 offer the opportunity to assess the children's understanding of the spelling patterns.

Whiteboard tools
Use the Recognition tool or the Pen tool when entering text.

 Pen tool

Highlighter tool

 Recognition tool

Marquee select tool

Eraser tool

Activote (optional)

Expressive writing

Learning objective
NLS Term 2
● T13: To write own examples of descriptive, expressive language based on those read. Link to work on adjectives and similes.

Resources
'Another world' flipchart file; individual whiteboards and pens.

Links to other subjects
Speaking and listening
Objective 44: To tell stories using voice effectively.
● Ask the children to talk about the similes they hear and the images they form from them.

Starter
Use the Reveal tool 🖳 to hide the drawing on page 6 of the flipchart. Display the rest of the page and ask: *What is Dean's shirt compared to?* (Wasp.) *What has colours like a rainbow?* (Sweater.) *What is the third comparison?* (Trousers are compared to a chess board.) *Why do you think his trousers are compared to a chess board?* (Black and white checks.) Reveal the drawing on the right of the page. Highlight the three comparisons in the text. Point out why comparisons improve the text: they bring the writer's descriptions to life, making it easier to form a visual image.

Whole-class shared work
● Use and define the term *simile*: Words that create an image in the reader's mind by comparing a subject to something else.
● Explain that the comparisons in the Starter activity are similes.
● Display page 7 of the flipchart. Point out that similes could add further atmosphere and mood by creating stronger visual images.
● Read the first sentence. Ask the children to think of something that disappears from view very quickly. Agree on something. Ask: *What word should introduce the comparison?* (*Like* or *as.*) Add the simile to the text.
● Continue with a couple more sentences. Ask the children to write ideas on individual whiteboards before you all compare suggestions.
● Encourage imaginative ideas. Stress that there is no *correct* simile: an unusual comparison will make the visual image stronger in a reader's mind.
● Add the similes to the text and discuss what difference they make. Read the sentences to the children and ask them what they *see*. Share visual images.

Independent work
● Ask the children to re-write the last three sentences of the passage on page 7, extending the passage with a new sentence or two of their own.
● They should use at least three similes. Suggest adding similes to compare with:
  ● Twisted trees
  ● Menacing branches
  ● Metal structures
● Less confident children could discuss what to write with a partner before they start work.
● As an extra challenge, ask the children to add similes to their own imaginary world descriptions (Independent writing, Lesson 12).

Plenary
● Hold a Speaking and listening session. Let the children read their sentences aloud.
● As others listen, ask them to describe the pictures put in their minds by the similes.
● Examples of the similes can be added to page 8.

Whiteboard tools
Use the Reveal tool to hide part of the screen. Click on the Edit text button in the Object edit toolbox to amend existing text.

 Reveal tool

 Pen tool

🅣 Edit text tool

⛟ Highlighter tool

Apostrophes

Learning objectives
NLS Term 2
● S2: To use the apostrophe accurately to mark possession.
● T11: To write poetry based on the structure and/or style of poems read.

Resources
'Apostrophes' flipchart file; photocopiable page 48 'Animal possessions' for each child; individual whiteboards and pens.

Links to other subjects
Science
QCA Unit 4C 'Keeping warm'
● Write a pattern possession poem about the materials and products that keep things warm or cold. (For example: *the sun's rays make me hot; the air's wind makes me cold; the sweater's wool warms me up; the T-shirt's cotton keeps me cool; the freezer's ice saves the food, the bear's coat keeps it snug*).

Whiteboard tools
If a microphone is available, use the Sound recorder to record the children reading.

 Pen tool

 Floating keyboard

Ⓣ Text editor tool

 Highlighter tool

Ⓣ Edit text tool

◀)) Sound recorder (optional)

Starter
Tell the children you are going to say something, and you want them to decide how often you push words together (made contractions). Then say:
> *That's very strange. It's the computer: it's never left on! Something's wrong. Someone's definitely been messing around in here. We've got to find out more.*

Repeat the words if necessary, then ask the children to show their answers on individual whiteboards.

Display the text on page 2 of the flipchart 'Apostrophes' and highlight the contractions in the first paragraph. Ask: *What letters have been left out? How should we mark those letters?* (With an apostrophe.) Invite volunteers to add the apostrophes and leave the text on the screen.

Whole-class shared work
● Introduce the term *omission*: letters left out of a shortened form as words are pushed together. This occurs frequently in speech.
● Explain that all the apostrophes used in the Starter are apostrophes of omission. Write an apostrophe in the Key at the bottom of the screen, and highlight it with the same colour that you used before. Beside the apostrophe put *O* for *Omission*.
● Ask the children to read the second paragraph to a partner. Can any of them hear something strange about the words?
● Compare ideas. Agree that *of* phrases are clumsy. Ask the children what the more usual, economical way is of explaining who owns something? (An apostrophe followed by *s*.) Explain that possession is the second use of an apostrophe.
● Invite children to edit the text to make the changes, highlighting the apostrophes in a second colour:
  ● **Jasmine's coat** *was on the floor.* **The boys' instruction books** *were torn in half.* **Jade's bag** *was open. The* **children's diaries** *were open.*
● Add another apostrophe to the key and highlight it in the second colour. Label it *P* for *Possession*.
● Turn to page 3 and read out each phrase. Then ask the children to say the economical, contracted form. Type up the phrases and add a couple more examples of your own.
● Explain the rules:
  1. Singular owners, and other owners not ending in *s*, add '*s*.
  2. Plural owner ending in *s*, just add '.

Independent work
● Ask the children to complete the poem on the photocopiable sheet.
● Divide the task in two to support less able learners: first, write an apostrophe phrase beside each picture; secondly, use the phrases in a poem.
● As an extra challenge, ask more able learners to write a pattern possession poem about their family.

Plenary
● Use the scanner to view a selection of the children's poems on page 4.
● Ask poets to read them aloud to the rest of the class. Use the Sound recorder to record the poetry readings if a microphone is available.

Word order

Learning objectives
NLS Term 2
● S3: To understand the significance of word order.
● S4: To recognise how commas, connectives and full stops are used to join and separate clauses.

Resources
'Word order' flipchart file; photocopiable page 49 'Changing order – changing meaning' for each child.

Links to other subjects
History
QCA Unit 7 'Why did Henry III marry six times?'
● Link the Independent work to the Tudors.

Starter
Go to page 2 of the flipchart. Ask the children to investigate the sentence pairs. Encourage reading aloud to a partner. What do they notice? Conclude that the pairs of sentences use the same words but change the word order. Do the children think this affects meaning? Ask them to try to make up a similar pair of sentences. Invite volunteers to write their sentences on the board.

Whole-class shared work
● Investigate the sentences from the Starter more closely. Discuss sentence types. Explain that:
 1. is a simple sentence (one clause) with an adverb
 2. is a simple sentence with a prepositional phrase
 3. is a compound sentence (two equal clauses)
 4. is a complex sentence (one main clause and a subordinate clause).
● Highlight the words that move in each pair. Identify them:
 1. an adverb is moved
 2. a prepositional phrase is moved
 3. the clauses are reversed.
 4. the clauses are reversed.
● Explain that the type of phrases in these sentences means that the word order can be changed without changing the meaning of the sentence. Point out the punctuation changes that occur: when adverbs and prepositional phrases lead the sentence, a comma follows them in numbers 1 and 2, and a comma separates the main and subordinate clauses in number 4.
● Display page 3 of the flipchart.
● Point out that these sentences also use identical words, but change their order. Ask: *What else has changed?* (Meaning.) Explain that a phrase such as *biggest man* must stay together. If separated, the adjective may describe the wrong noun.
● Go to page 4 of the flipchart. Experiment with ordering the words in different ways, typing up different sentences, for example:
 ● *The dog bit the man nastily.*
 ● *Nastily, the dog bit the man.*
● Point out punctuation changes for each version.

Independent work
● Ask the children to complete the photocopiable sheet.
● Remind them to think about punctuation.
● Ask less confident children to write one sentence from each line of words.
● As an extra challenge, ask children to create new pairs of sentences about Tudor times.

Whiteboard tools
Convert handwriting to text with the Recognition tool.

 Pen tool

 Text editor tool

Highlighter tool

Marquee select tool

 Recognition tool

Plenary
● Invite children to write their sentences on page 5 of the flipchart.
● Look at the sentences, discussing meaning and punctuation.
● Use the children's pictures from the photocopiable sheet to show how the meaning of a sentence can change if the word order is changed.
● Click on the red box to see the sentences written out in the correct order.

Learning objectives
NLS Term 2
● T19: To identify how and why paragraphs are used to organise and sequence information.
● T20: To identify from the examples the key features of explanatory texts.
● T25: To write explanations of a process, using conventions identified through reading.

Resources
'Explanations' flipchart file; printed copy of page 3 of the flipchart for each child; exercise books and pens.

Links to other subjects
Science
QCA Unit 4D 'Solids, liquids and how they can be separated'
● The flipchart file explanatory text links with this unit.

Whiteboard tools
Save the notes made in this flipchart for a suqsequent lesson.

🖨 Print button

✏ Pen tool

📖 Resource library

🖍 Highlighter tool

🔺 Marquee select tool

◉ Activote (optional)

Explanations

Starter
Open page 2 of the flipchart 'Explanations'. Write a *How?* or *Why?* question about a process, linking the question to current work in another curriculum area, such as science or geography. For example: *How are map scales used to calculate distances?* Brainstorm information to answer the question and make notes. Use pictures from the Resource library 📖 where appropriate.

Whole-class shared work
● Display page 3. Do the children recognise the text type? (An explanation.) Point out the title. Explain that a *How?* or *Why?* question is often the title for an explanatory text.
● Draw attention to the verbs. Ask the children what tense is used? (Present.) Point out the use of the passive voice. (*is placed; is changed.*) Explain that in the passive voice the subject of the verb has something done to it. Highlight examples in the text. Check them using the spyglass.
● Ask: *What purpose does the first sentence have?* (It forms an introduction.) Look at the order of the remaining text. The process is explained in sequential steps. Number these steps to highlight the order of the process.
● Highlight the opening words of each step: *The first thing; This means that; After that; As a result.* Establish that the function of these words is to link the paragraphs or steps together. Identify them as connectives.
● Discuss the purpose of organisational devices, such as subheadings, and presentation features, such as diagrams. Agree that they make information more accessible to the reader. Drag the ice cube diagrams into suitable places in the text to illustrate this point. (Move or delete the spyglass if necessary.)
● Go to page 4 to read and discuss the key features of an explanation text.
● Use pages 5 and 6 for two quick questions to check that the children understand the explanatory text.
● Remind the children of question and information from the Starter activity.
● Write the question from page 2 again at the top of page 7.

Independent work
● Ask the children to write an explanation that answers the question.
● Use the notes on page 5 to guide the children in writing their explanations. Provide printouts, if required.
● Display page 2 of the flipchart showing the information they generated in the Starter.
● The children should write the explanation in their exercise books, following the layout of the writing frame and remembering to include key features of explanation texts.
● Less able learners may need help with sequential order.
● As an extra challenge, ask children to set partners a new question to be answered in a written explanation.

Plenary
● Listen to the explanations and use the scanner to view the diagrams.
● Use page 8 to make notes on effective use of diagrams and the types of diagrams that the children chose to use.
● Do children agree that the presentation and diagrams make the written explanations easier to understand? Use Activote devices or alternative voting methods to collect the children's opinions. Record their opinions on page 9.

Common endings

Learning objective
NLS Term 2
● W6: To spell words with the common endings: -*ight*, and so on.

Resources
'Common endings' flipchart file; photocopiable page 50 'Common endings'; individual whiteboards and pens.

Links to other subjects
Citizenship
QCA Unit 9 'Respect for property'
● Ask the children to use some of the following words in a piece of writing suggesting ways to improve a local public space:
through, though, right, obvious, previous, although, ambition, bright, tough, artificial, social, reaction, light, special, partial, serious.

Starter
Say *tough, fiction* and *trivial* out loud and ask the children to spell the words on their individual whiteboards. Open the 'Common endings' flipchart and go to page 2. Compare the children's spellings. Explain that these are words which are difficult to spell. Can any of the children suggest ways to remember the spellings? Share ideas. These may include: pronunciation and letter sounds; common letter strings; the number of syllables in a word; typical patterns of letter strings; a mnemonic. As children suggest a way of remembering, encourage them to explain it.

Whole-class shared work
● Display page 3 of the flipchart. Explain that the bag contains words that are commonly misspelt. Drag the words out of the bag and read them together.
● Ask the children to sort the words into groups on their individual whiteboards. Allow brief thinking time before comparing ideas of how the words could be sorted.
● Delete the coloured box to reveal a table. Place *devious* in one column. Encourage the children to suggest other words which could go in the same group, and why. Guide them towards recognition that *devious, serious* and *obvious* are linked because of their endings (-*ious*). Invite children to move the words together in one column, and write in the heading *ious*.
● In the same way, work with the children to create groups for these word endings: -*ial, -tion, -ight, -ough*.
● Read aloud the *ough* words. Ask the children if they notice anything strange about this group of words. Repeat the words if necessary, until the children focus on pronunciation (-*ough* makes a different sound in each word). Explain that -*ough* is the most unpredictable of these five words endings: it can have a number of different pronunciations.
● Focus on the -*ial* group. In these three words, highlight the letter preceding *ial*. Point out that these words are typical: the letter preceding -*ial* is usually *c* or *t*.
● Talk about word class. What class do the -*tion* words? (Noun.) Which other group is made up of nouns? (-*ight*.) Which endings usually belong to adjectives? (-*ial* and -*ious*.) Which group is most likely to vary? (-*ough*.)

Independent work
● Ask the children to complete the crossword on the photocopiable sheet.
● Emphasise the need to think about spelling.
● Write the common endings of the words used on the whiteboard, if you think the children need this support (-*ial, -ight, -ough, -ious, -tion*).
● Supply less confident children with the opening letters of answers.
● As an extra challenge, ask more able learners to list their answers, finding ways to group them according to pronunciation, word class and spelling patterns.

Whiteboard tools
🖊 Pen tool

Ⓣ Text editor tool

🔦 Marquee select tool

🗑 Delete button

◎ Activote (optional)

Plenary
● Display the crossword on page 4 of the flipchart.
● Invite children to come up and fill in the crossword. Click on the *Clues* button to read the clues in Page notes, if required, and the *Answers* button to see a completed version of the crossword on page 8.
● Identify common spelling patterns and write them on page 5.
● You can use the question on page 6 to check the children's group of common spelling patterns.

Collecting and presenting information

Starter
Look at any charts of information displayed around the classroom. Ask: *Do you think these charts present information effectively? Which do you find easiest to understand? Why? How would you improve these charts?* Share and list ideas on page 10 of the flipchart. Ideas could include:
- less text
- more diagrams
- division of chart into sections
- headings
- numbers.

Whole-class shared work
- Read the text on page 11, which explains how plants make their food.
- Focus on the three main paragraphs describing the process. Highlight the words that begin these paragraphs:
  - *The first thing...*
  - *This means that...*
  - *After that...*
- Explain that you want to make a chart about the process. Start by identifying the main information in each paragraph.
- Model how to summarise each paragraph. Highlight key words and phrases.
- On page 12, type a sentence for each paragraph, each in its own separate text box. Agree on a title and type this in a separate text box. For example:
  > **How plants make their food**
  > *The plant absorbs water and air.*
  > *The plant gets energy from the Sun.*
  > *The plant makes its food through photosynthesis.*
- Would the children find this a helpful chart? Agree on the need for a better format. Suggest a flow chart format.
- Delete the box on the left-hand side of the screen. The numbered parts of the flow chart represent the three steps in the process.
- Move the phrases next to the correct part of the flow chart.
- Discuss what else to add, for example, diagrams. Let the children comment critically on the proposed chart.

Independent work
- Give each child a printout of page 3 of the flipchart, *The process of change*.
- Ask the children to plan a diagram or chart using the printout.
- They should focus on the three main paragraphs highlighted earlier.
- Remind them to highlight key words before summarising each of the three paragraphs in a short sentence or phrase.
- Their planning should include headings and diagrams.
- The charts can be completed in another session.
- Support less able learners by helping them to identify key words.
- As an extra challenge, ask the children to think of how they could make a circular chart, by showing how water can be turn back into ice.

Plenary
- Scan and display the children's flow diagrams onto page 13.
- Ask the children who produced circular diagrams to explain them to the rest of the class.

Prefixes

Starter

Display page 7 of the flipchart 'Suffixes and prefixes'. Ask the children how the words on the whiteboard could be grouped. Share sorting ideas before recognising the relevance of the prefix in each word. Move the words into the three boxes: *always, almost; affect, afflict; adjective, adverb, advent.* Highlight the prefixes.

Whole-class shared work

● Remind the children of what a prefix is: a sound unit added to the beginning of a word.
● List the three prefixes used in the Starter: *ad-, af-, al-*. Do the children know their meanings? Define them:
  ● *ad-* means 'forwards'
  ● *af-* means 'tending towards'
  ● *al-* is a shortened form of 'all'.
● Using these definitions, investigate the meanings of the groups of words in the Starter. Ask: *How does the prefix's meaning contribute to the meaning of the word? How would you define the word?*
● Let the children check in dictionaries to see if a prefix's meaning is ever contained in the definition of the words.
● Ask the children to work in pairs. Give them time to skim through dictionaries to find words to add to these groups.
● Share the results of this exercise, allowing the children to add words to the whiteboard.
● Encourage the children to look carefully at the additions. Do they think the new words keep to the meaning of the prefix? Delete words that do not relate to the prefix's meaning.
● Use the term *root words*. Explain that the root is a word before the prefix is added. Point out that the addition of the prefix sometimes involves spelling changes in the root word. Investigate these changes:
  ● *af-* the *f* is doubled
  ● *ad-* no change
  ● *al-* the prefix loses its second *l*.
● Display page 8 of the flipchart. Gradually move the filled shapes to reveal the words beginning with the prefix *a-*.
● Highlight the prefix *a-*. Explain that it means *in a state of*.

Independent work

● Ask the children to use the list of *a-* words to write a story, of about 120 words, entitled *Sea Battle*.
● Reduce the number of *a-* words and the length of the story for less confident children.
● As an extra challenge, ask children to include words from another prefix group.

Plenary

● Scan and view some of the children's stories, inviting the authors to read them to the class.
● Use page 9 to compare the way in which *a-* words have been used. Investigate the meanings of the *a-* words, asking the children to involve *in a state of* in their definitions.

Writing poetry

Learning objectives
NLS Term 3
● T15: To produce polished poetry through revision.
● S1: To understand that some words can be changed in particular ways and others cannot.

Resources
'Another world' flipchart file; one copy of photocopiable page 51 'A Seaside Trip'; individual whiteboards and pens.

Links to other subjects
Speaking and listening
Objective 44: Identifying the ways presentational features contribute to message and impact.
● This lesson links well to this objective.

Whiteboard tools
To deconstruct words: enable Design mode; right-/ barrel-click on the word you want to remove; select Deconstruct word from the pop-up menu. Click on the page number to view the page thumbnails in the Tool tray. Drag objects to a page thumbnail with the Marquee select tool to copy or move them to that particular page.

🖊 Pen tool

🔍 Marquee select tool

🕵 Design mode

⌨ Floating keyboard

🔊 Sound recorder (optional)

Starter
Read the poem on the photocopiable sheet to the children. (Do *not* display the words.) Discuss what the poem is about and what made it enjoyable to listen to. (Length of lines, rhythm, vocabulary.) Read the poem again. Ask the children to write on individual whiteboards the words or phrases that stick in their mind. Compare results, writing popular words and phrases on page 9. Suggest that for a poem to be successful when read aloud, it needs to contain evocative and memorable words and phrases.

Whole-class shared work
● Open page 10 of the flipchart. Discuss what is meant by *themes*.
● Investigate the text. Identify and circle evocative words that convey the first theme. For example: *speeding, fleeting glimpses, plunged*.
● Deconstruct the text (see Whiteboard tools, below) to separate these words and drag them into the appropriate box.
● Repeat the process for the second theme (for example, *the twisting line; unfamiliar countryside*) and the third theme (for example, *sinister dream; threatening landscape; twisted trees; menacing branches*).
● Copy the words you have deconstructed on to page 11.
● Switch back to Presentation mode.
● Explain that you want the children to write a performance poem (a poem that is written to be read aloud). Click on the button at the bottom of the page to read the important features of a performance poem in Page notes. Add more features if the children have any further ideas of performance poems. (Click on the T in the top left corner of the Page notes window to access the Floating keyboard ⌨ in the Text editor tool tray.)
● Discuss how to achieve these aims in a performance poem about the strange train journey. Ideas could include: a quick rhythm (to match train); short, jerky lines; evocative words.
● Close Page notes. Suggest that the words and phrases taken from the passage could form the basis of a performance poem. Move these words to the edges of the screen, leaving the central area free.
● With the children's input, use the central area to write sample lines. Introduce new vocabulary, as well as dragging words from the edges of the screen into your lines of poetry.
● Start to build up a poem with the class. Demonstrate making revisions: delete and substitute words, reorganise words and lines, and experiment with figurative language.

Independent work
● Ask the children to write a performance poem about the train journey, using some of the words chosen from the narrative.
● Encourage revision of rough drafts, before producing a polished poem.
● Less able learners could work with partner. You could also provide them with the opening lines.
● As an extra challenge, ask more able learners to write another performance poem on a different subject.

Plenary
● Invite the children to perform their poems. Which words and phrases do listeners remember? Write good examples on page 12.
● If a microphone is available, use the Sound recorder to record and add the performances to page 12.

Word roots

Learning objective
NLS Term 3
- W7: Collect/classify words with common roots.

Resources
'Common roots' flipchart file; photocopiable page 52 'Word webs' for each child; etymological dictionaries.

Links to other subjects
History
QCA Unit 6A 'Why have people invaded and settled in Britain in the past?'
- Investigate words with Latin origins.

Starter
Look at page 2 of the flipchart 'Common roots'. Allow thinking time as the children identify what the words have in common. Explain that they have a common root. Use the Highlighter tool to identify the root (*mono*). Explain that it is from the Greek for *alone*.

Use dictionaries to define the words, using *alone* in the definitions. Ask the children if they can add a word to your collection. Make sure that the meaning of a new word relates to the meaning of the root.

Whole-class shared work
- Activate the Reveal tool . Display page 3 of the flipchart. Explain that you are going to show the children some sentences containing words with a common root. Reveal the sentences one at a time. Allow time to think about each sentence, and to write the words on individual whiteboards. Compare answers before highlighting the two words.
- Investigate the identified words. Ask: *What is the root?* Underline the roots.
- Investigate further, by asking children to use etymological dictionaries to find the meaning and origin of each root. Make sure that the children recognise how the meaning of the root affects the meaning of the word.
- Go to page 4 of the flipchart, and click on the *Common roots* activity. Explain the page: each definition must be matched to a root word.
- Allow thinking and partner discussion time before agreeing on an answer. Invite children to the whiteboard to match the roots and labels. Check answers by clicking *Am I correct?* The answers are given on page 5.
- On page 6, make a word web together for one of the roots from the flipchart. Add extra lines if necessary.

Independent work
- Ask the children to complete the word webs on the photocopiable sheet.
- Encourage the use of a dictionary, but remind the children to check the meanings of the words they use.
- Reduce the number of spaces to fill in for each web to support less confident children.
- As an extra challenge, ask children to add another word or two to each web.

Plenary
- Use pages 7 to 14 to go through the Independent work.
- Invite the children to fill in the webs with the words they have found.
- Use page 15 to check the children's answers and to see some examples of words which contain the relevant roots.

Whiteboard tools
Use the Reveal tool to display one sentence at a time in the Whole-class shared work. Use the Lines tool to add extra lines to the word webs if necessary.

 Pen tool

Reveal tool

 Highlighter tool

Lines tool

Punctuation

Learning objective
NLS Term 3
● S2: To identify the common punctuation marks.

Resources
'The dilemma' flipchart file; printouts of pages 6 and 7 for each child; individual whiteboards and pens.

Links to other subjects
History
QCA Unit 6A 'Why have people invaded and settled in Britain in the past?'
● Link the text to information about Roman Britain.

Starter
Read the following text aloud. Make sure that punctuation is clear in the way that you read, but do not supply it. Ask the children to record on individual whiteboards the number of sentences they hear:

Titus was a Roman, but he was living in Britain. As a centurion, he had charge of 100 men. Although he tried to treat his men well, he knew they missed home. The north of England was unwelcoming. The landscape was bleak; the terrain was hard-going. The thing his men hated most was the weather. It was cold and rainy.

Compare answers. Read the text out loud again, this time asking the children to record if, what and where punctuation marks are needed. Display the paragraph on page 3 of the flipchart. Ask the children to punctuate it by dragging up punctuation and capital letters from the bottom of the page.

Whole-class shared work
● Move the spyglass over the text to reveal the correct punctuation.
● Discuss the use of commas. Point out that writers' use of commas is very variable; some writers would leave some of these commas out.
● Revise the function of capital letters, full stops and commas.
● Go to page 4. Explain that it is possible to link two sentences with colons and semi-colons.
● Explain the use of a colon: to introduce further information. Ask the children to show you a place where a colon could be used in the first sentence: *The thing they hated most was the weather: it was cold and rainy.* Invite a volunteer to drag the colon into position, and use the spyglass to see whether they are correct.
● Explain the colon's value: it emphasises the link between two statements, the second one now beginning with a small letter.
● Point out the semi-colon. Explain its use: it can replace a full stop to link two sentences that are related in meaning and are equally balanced. Ask the children where they could use a semi-colon in this paragraph. (*The landscape was rough; the terrain was hard-going.*) Again, demonstrate, using the spyglass to check.
● Tell the children that semi-colons can also be used to separate items in a list, if they have been introduced with a colon.
● Use the text on page 5 to revise the rules for speech marks: where they are placed, how spoken and unspoken words are separated and how new paragraphs are used for each speaker.
● Invite volunteers to add the punctuation. Move the spyglass over the text to show the correct punctuation.

Independent work
● Give each child a copy of pages 6 and 7 of the flipchart. Ask them to add the missing punctuation marks.
● Encourage the children to read sentences aloud to themselves.
● Support less able learners by letting them work with a partner, and by reducing the text.
● As an extra challenge, ask more able learners to write more text using semi-colons, colons and speech marks.

Whiteboard tools

● Pen tool

● Highlighter tool

● Print button

● Eraser tool

● Marquee select tool

● Activote (optional)

Plenary
● Invite volunteers to edit the text to add the punctuation on pages 6 and 7. Pull the tab across over the text to check that they are correct.
● Emphasise the possibility of different punctuation in some instances.
● Use page 8 to assess the children's understanding of punctuation.

33

Summaries

Learning objective
NLS Term 3
● T20: To summarise a sentence or paragraph by identifying the most important elements and rewording them in a limited number of words.

Resources
'The dilemma' flipchart file; access to computers or a copy of page 13 of the flipchart, one per child. (Microsoft Word is required to view the embedded text documents in the flipchart.)

Links to other subjects
History
QCA Unit 6A 'Why have people invaded and settled in Britain in the past?'
● Link the text to information about Roman Britain.

Starter
Open 'The dilemma' flipchart and display page 9. Give the children some oral instructions, making them deliberately long-winded. For example:
Look very closely and carefully at the whiteboard. Check absolutely before you go further that you can see properly. Take out just about all the equipment you could possibly need for this lesson.
Ask the children to comment on your language. (Using unnecessary words.) Encourage suggestions as to how these instructions could be given more briefly. Continue this game, one child giving a wordy instruction, somebody else shortening it. Stress the need to retain important meanings.

Whole-class shared work
● Go to page 10 of the flipchart. Ask the children to help you identify and highlight words that are key to meaning. Identify words that can be deleted, using a different highlighter colour, until you have simpler sentences.
● Erase the blue marks to reveal the sample answers beneath each sentence.
● Read the sentence on page 11. Identify and highlight the keywords: *whiteboard; seen.*
● Discuss the message: whiteboards need to be in the right place to be viewed.
● Type suggestions to summarise the sentence in 12 words or less. For example:
  ● *Whiteboards, put in a good spot, can be seen by all.*
  ● *Whiteboards in a good spot can be seen by all.*
● Investigate the shortened sentences. Identify the words that were left out. Point out where sentence construction has changed.
● Suggest that new vocabulary can help with summaries. Reveal the final sentence: *Well-positioned whiteboards give good visibility.*
● Point out that *good visibility* (two words) expresses the same meaning as *can be seen by all* (five words).
● Go to page 12. Explain to the children that you want to reduce the paragraph from 41 words to 20 or less.
● Work together to edit the text in the white box using the Edit text tool. Focus on one sentence at a time, reminding them to think about key words and main messages. For example:
  ● *Titus agreed and disagreed. The camp would run out of special supplies if everyone ate them. What should he do?*

Independent work
● Go to page 13. Print a copy of this text for every child or open the editable documents and make the text accessible on the children's computers. (The embedded editable document is supplied on page 13.)
● The paragraph has 61 words. Ask the children to reduce it to a summary of about 40 words.
● Give less able learners a target number of words for each sentence.
● As an extra challenge, ask children to summarise the text from page 6.

Plenary
● Invite the children to read their summaries out loud.
● The text may be summarised in a variety of ways. Display the children's edited documents or ask them type their versions on page 14.
● Stress the need to retain important elements.

Whiteboard tools
Use the Edit text tool in the Object edit toolbox to delete words in the Whole-class shared work.

▲ Pen tool

▣ Print button

Ⓣ Edit text tool

▨ Highlighter tool

▨ Eraser tool

Ⓣ Text editor tool

▢ Desktop mode

▦ Return to main screen

Its and it's

Learning objective
NLS Term 3
● W10: To distinguish the two forms: *its* and *it's*.

Resources
'Its and it's' flipchart file; copy of page 7 of the flipchart for each child.

Links to other subjects
Science
QCA Unit 4B 'Habitats'
● Link the Independent work to this unit by asking children to list common observable features in birds, reptiles and mammals (for example, *birds have feathers and beaks*).

Starter
Play an oral game, asking the children simple questions. Encourage informal answers, but in sentences. Use questions containing *is it* or *is* + a singular noun, for example: *What day is it? What time is it? What on earth is wrong with this picture? Whose pen is this?*

Extend the game to the children asking you questions. Make a point (without mentioning it) of using *it's* instead of *it is* in the answers. Invite the children to write a sentence to answer the questions on page 2 of the flipchart.

Whole-class shared work
● Display page 3 of the flipchart. Can the children spot a difference between the language of each question and its answer? Listen to the children's ideas. Guide them towards noticing that every question word is written in full. Ask: *Is this true of the answer?* (No.)
● Point out the highlighted *it's* in the two answers. Ask the children to name the punctuation mark that has been used here. (Apostrophe.) Establish the reason for its use. (To show that a letter has been omitted.)
● Revise this use of apostrophes. Explain that we often run words together in speech, dialogue or informal writing do the same. An apostrophe marks the letter(s) left out.
● Look at the page again and ask: *Which letter is missing in it's?* (i) *What would be the full form?* (it is.)
● Point out the highlighted *its* in the two sentences on page 4. Enquire as to whether an apostrophe is needed here. Guide the children towards recognition that no letter is missing. Discuss the meaning of *its* here? Agree on the answer *belonging to it*.
● Go to page 5. The sentences from pages 3 and 4 have been repeated for comparison. Ensure that the children understand why *its* or *it's* has been used in each case.
● Display page 6. Ask the children to decide and then drag the correct word (*its* or *it's*) to complete the sentences. Move the spyglass over the text to check the correct words.
● Challenge children to provide sentences using *its* and *it's* and write them on the board. Highlight the *its* and *it's*.

Independent work
● Display page 7 and give a printout of the page to each child.
● Ask the children to fill the spaces with either *it's* or *its*.
● Emphasise thinking about what the word means in each sentence.
● Encourage less able learners to focus on part of the text at a time, advising them of how many of each form to look for.
● As an extra challenge, ask more able learners to add more text with *it's* or *its* sentences.

Whiteboard tools
Write sentences with the Pen or Recognition tools.

● Pen tool

● Recognition tool

● Highlighter tool

● Marquee select tool

● Print button

● Activote (optional)

Plenary
● Review the Independent work using page 7 of the flipchart.
● Work on one sentence at a time, reading it aloud, and discussing the meaning of the missing word.
● Drag the *its* or *it's* into the spaces on the flipchart to complete the sentences. Use the spyglass to check the answers.
● Use the sentences on pages 8 and 9 to assess the children's understanding of *its* and *it's*.

Word endings and classes

Starter
Open the 'Word classes' flipchart. Activate the Reveal tool 🖥 to hide the entire screen. Go to page 2 and pull the screen down but keep the last sentence hidden. Discuss the word classes with the children: *noun, verb, adjective* and *adverb*. Then erase the red marks to reveal the definitions.

Give oral practice, asking children to identify classes of words you use in sentences. Say: *The teachers talked to their classes.* Ask: *Which words are the nouns?* (teachers; classes.) *Which word is the verb?* (talked.) Invite them to add an adjective, such as *patient* or *quiet,* and an adverb, such as *loudly.* Reveal the last sentence on the page. Ask volunteers to add their suggested adjective and adverb using the Edit text tool. They should then highlight the different word types, using the same colours that are used in the definitions.

Whole-class shared work
● Display page 3 and switch to Design mode 🛠.
● Point out the words *dined* and *served* and ask: *What do they have in common?* (Both are verbs and end in *-ed.*)
● Extract *dined* and *served* from the text using the Deconstruct word function. Invite a child to drag the words into the correct column of the word classes table.
● Explain that endings can give clues about word class. Elicit the typical ending of a verb. (-ed.) Put *-ed* under the heading *Verb.*
● Identify endings typical of the other word classes. Label the headings:
  ● Noun (plurals end in): *-s, -es*
  ● Verb: *-s, -es, -ed, -ing*
  ● Adjective: *-er, -est*
  ● Adverb: *-ly*
● Point out where endings are typical of more than one word class.
● Investigate further by finding words to agree with the headings, extracting them from the text and moving them into the correct columns.
● Point out that links between word endings and word classes are only generalisations and there are many exceptions. For example, waiter ends in *-er* but it is not an adjective. Ask: *What word class is it?* (noun.)
● Switch back to Presentation mode and display page 4 of the flipchart. Draw attention to the fact that the two sentences use the same root word repeatedly but in different forms, with different endings and in different word classes.
● Drag the highlighted words into the correct column on the table. Point out that *actor* and *buzzer* are nouns.
● Make up more sentences like these. Say the sentences out loud and invite the children to write the words in the chart.

Independent work
● Give out the photocopiable sheet and ask the children to complete the poem.
● Emphasise that the poem does not have to make much sense!
● Less confident children could work with a partner.
● Extend children by asking them to write a second poem of the same type.

Plenary
● Talk about the varied forms of some words used in their poems, making notes on page 5.
● Let children read their poems aloud.

Spelling compound words

Learning objective
NLS Term 3
● W11: To investigate compound words and recognise that they can aid spelling even when pronunciation obscures it.

Resources
Photocopiable page 54 'Compound words'; two flipchart pages showing words that can be moved separately – page 1: *pot, life, class, guard, tea, room*; page 2: *dust, bin, grand, parent, bath, room, sand, bag, wind, mill, ship, yard, cart, wheel, rattle, snake, frost, bite, band, stand, rasp, berry, pine, apple, foot, ball, card, board*.

Links to other subjects
History
QCA Unit 6A 'Why have people invaded and settled in Britain in the past?'
● Demonstrate Roman influence on the English language with compound words which reveal Latin influence (for example, *porcupine, porcelain, portfolio, portmanteau*).

Whiteboard tools
 Text editor tool

 Floating keyboard

Highlighter tool

Marquee select tool

Starter
Display the first page of your prepared flipchart. Ask the children to find pairs of words that make a new word. Allow one or two minutes before letting them make suggestions. Encourage them to explain their pairings.
Move words on the whiteboard into these pairs:
● *tea   pot*
● *class   room*
● *life   guard*
Join each pair to create three single words: *teapot; classroom; lifeguard*. Explain that these are compound words. Compound words occur when words join to form a new word.

Whole-class shared work
● Explain that the separate parts forming a compound word can help you to spell the word correctly.
● Type *cupboard* on the whiteboard. Say it aloud and ask the children what they notice about your pronunciation. Repeat the word a few times until the children notice that *p* is not heard. Thinking of the word in two parts, *cup + board*, makes it easier to remember to include this letter.
● Consider other examples of compound words where a letter's sound may be difficult to hear because of the way the word is pronounced. Each time:
  ● Write the compound word on the whiteboard.
  ● Ask the children to look at it as you pronounce it.
  ● Encourage them to note on their individual whiteboards a letter they found hard to hear.
  ● Compare children's answers.
● Suitable words might include: *postman, scrapbook, earring, goldfish, football*.
● Type *grand* and *mother*. Elicit that the compound word is grandmother.
● Add these sentences to the whiteboard:
  ● She is a *grand mother* to her daughter.
  ● She is a *grandmother* to her daughter's children.
● Discuss with the children how the meaning of the compound word is not always the same as the meanings of the separate words.
● Point out that some compound words show historical changes. For example, *cloakroom* dates from a time when people usually wore cloaks instead of coats.

Independent work
● Tell the children that they are going to create compound words using the photocopiable page 'Compound words'.
● They should underline three examples of letters not always heard.
● To support less able learners, divide the words into first-half and second-half lists.
● As an extra challenge, ask children to add examples of their own.

Plenary
● Display page 2 of your prepared flipchart. Invite children to move the words to make compound words: *dustbin, grandparent, bathroom, sandbag, windmill, shipyard, cartwheel, rattlesnake, frostbite, bandstand, raspberry, pineapple, football, cardboard*.
● Encourage children to read the words aloud as others look and listen. Are letters hidden in the pronunciation? Highlight these. Emphasise that remembering original separate parts helps with spelling.

Sentence types

Learning objective
NLS Term 3
● S3: To understand how the grammar of a sentence alters when the sentence type is altered.

Resources P
Photocopiable page 55 'Questions and answers'; individual whiteboards and pens.

Links to other subjects
History
QCA Unit 18 'What was it like to live here in the past?'
● Encourage children to think of questions about their own area, that they could put to an older person.

Starter
Type the following words and punctuation marks up on a blank flipchart page in separate text boxes.

The   area   been   has   changing   .   ?

Make two sets. Use one set to demonstrate making a statement:

The area has been changing.

Use the other set to demonstrate making a question:

Has the area been changing?

Ask what the children notice about the sentences. Establish that the words used are the same, but that word order and punctuation have changed.

Whole-class shared work
● Use the Reveal tool 🖬 to hide the question and focus on the statement.
● Ask what the verb is here. Identify and highlight *has been changing.* Explain that this is a *verb string.*
● Explain that a verb string has a main verb and other helping verb(s). Ask: *Which is the main verb?* (*changing.*) *Which are the helping verbs?* (*has* and *been.*) Label these types of verb.
● Introduce and define the term *auxiliary verbs*: verbs that are used together with other verbs. In the statement, *has* and *been* are auxiliary verbs.
● Now display the second sentence: *Has the area been changing?*
● Ask: *Which is the main verb?* (*changing.*) *Which are the auxiliary verbs?* (*has* and *been.*) Label these types of verb.
● Discuss what has happened to the verb string? (It has been split up.)
● Now type a new sentence on the whiteboard: *The area changed.*
● Do the children know what type of sentence is this? (A statement.) What is the verb? (*changed.*)
● Let the children try to make a question from the statement. (It is impossible.) Explain that a statement that contains a verb string can be changed into a question by re-ordering the words. When a statement uses only a main verb, auxiliary verbs are needed to make the question.
● Now try the task again, asking the children to think of auxiliary verbs to help form the question. For example: *Has the area changed? Did the area change?* (Notice that *changed* has become *change.*)

Independent work
● Ask the children to complete the photocopiable sheet.
● Remind the children that they may need to add auxiliary verbs,
● Highlight the starting words for each question to support less able learners.
● As an extra challenge, ask more able learners to add five new statements and their questions.

Plenary
● Type some of the statements on the board. Ask children to identify verb strings.
● Let children demonstrate on the whiteboard how words can be re-ordered to become a question.

Whiteboard tools
Use the Reveal tool to reveal sentences one at a time.

🖊 Pen tool

⌨ Floating keyboard

🖌 Highlighter tool

🖬 Reveal tool

Advertisements

Learning objectives
NLS Term 3
● T19: To evaluate advertisements for their impact, appeal and honesty, focusing in particular on how information about the product is presented.
● T25: To design an advertisement.

Resources
'Advertisement' flipchart file; individual whiteboards and pens.

Links to other subjects
Science
QCA Unit 4C 'Keeping warm'
● Link the advertisements to science experiments on insulation.

Starter
Go to page 2 of the flipchart. Give the children a minute to think of an advertisement for a product. Ask: *Which advertisement comes most quickly into your mind?* Share results, recording some on the whiteboard.

Focus on one advertisement, particularly if the same one has been thought of by a few children. Ask the children to think of a reason why this advertisement should have been thought of by more than one of them. Allow thinking and partner discussion time before they write a reason on individual whiteboards.

Whole-class shared work
● Share the reasons children came up with for why this advertisement was remembered. List interesting points on page 3 and add points of your own. The points can be placed in order of importance. Click on the blue button to read possible reasons in Page notes.
● Refer to other advertisements that illustrate some of these points. For example, a memorable slogan: *Have a break. Have a KitKat;* or wordplay: *Beanz meanz Heinz.*
● Talk about what an advertiser is trying to achieve. Agree that they are:
  ● making you read about the product
  ● making you remember its name
  ● making you want to try the product.
● Display page 4 and give the children time to read the advertisement.
● Discuss what the product is. Then ask the children to write on individual whiteboards the first thing that attracts their attention in the advertisement. Compare their answers.
● Investigate the advertisement further, identifying devices and approaches that it uses to achieve its aims. Point out and label:
  ● bold capitals to grab attention
  ● appealing layout
  ● mixture of text and illustration
  ● audience involvement (questions to answer; repeated use of word *you*)
  ● clever product name: magimitt is a mixture of *magic* and *mitt* (mitten)
  ● varied font
  ● product name in large, bold capitals
  ● repetition of product name
  ● exaggerated claims (permanently hot)
  ● dramatic punctuation (exclamation marks).
● Would the children have done this advertisement differently? If so, how?

Independent work
● Ask the children to carry out one of the following tasks:
  ● Design a new advertisement for this same product or a different one to keep something warm.
  ● Design an advertisement for a product to keep something cold.
● Less confident children could work with a partner.
● As an extra challenge, ask the children to design two advertisements for the same product but aimed at different audiences.

Plenary
● Use the scanner to view a selection of designs.
● Let the children present their ideas to the class.
● Go to page 5 and use voting methods to evaluate how easy or difficult the children found the task of designing advertisements.

Whiteboard tools

 Pen tool

 Highlighter tool

Recognition tool

Marquee select tool

Activote (optional)

Connectives

Learning objective
NLS Term 3
● S4: The use of connectives to structure an argument.

Resources
'Connectives' flipchart file; copy of page 4 of the flipchart file per child; writing materials.

Links to other subjects
Citizenship
QCA Unit 11 'In the media – what's the news?'
● Link the Independent writing activity to an argument of local interest.

Starter

Revise and define the term *clause*: a group of words that make sense on their own. Display the top part of page 2 of the flipchart 'Connectives', keeping the words in the white box hidden with the Reveal tool . Discuss ways to link the clauses. Reveal the words at the bottom of the page, and invite the children to use them to join the two sentences. Remind them that they will need to change some letters to capitals, and full stops to commas. For example:

*I was hot **but** the weather was cold.*
***Although** I was hot, the weather was cold.*
*The weather was hot. **On the other hand**, I was cold.*
*The weather was hot. **However**, I was cold.*

Explain that the words in red are called connectives.

Whole-class shared work

● Investigate the connectives used in the Starter activity. Explain that
  ● *But* is a **conjunction,** linking clauses within one sentence.
  ● *Although* is a **conjunction** linking clauses within one sentence.
  ● *However* is a **connecting adverb,** connecting ideas, but keeping separate sentences.
  ● *On the other hand* is a **connecting adverbial phrase,** connecting ideas, but keeping separate sentences.
● Write these three terms on the whiteboard beneath the examples.
● Point out the commas in the linked examples.
● Display page 3. Investigate one or two lines at a time, asking the children to identify the connectives. Use the spyglass to reveal them.
● Explain that connectives help when writing a point of view.
● Display page 4 of the flipchart. Click on the Page notes icon in the top-right corner to see what the children have to write in each box:
  ● Paragraph 1: arguments against the supermarket and in favour of village shops.
  ● Paragraph 2: counter arguments against village shops and in favour of the supermarket.
  ● Paragraph 3: a decision.
● Encourage the children to identify sentences that are relevant to paragraph 1.
● Copy the original sentences and the children's ideas for paragraph 1, placing the copy in the relevant box. Ask for volunteers to experiment with linking the sentences. For example: *The village shops are in the village centre and they are convenient.*
● Look briefly at the sentences that are relevant to the second paragraph.

Independent work

● Hand out the printouts of page 4 and ask the children to write the second paragraph. They will need to add ideas, and then link clauses using connectives.
● Provide less able learners with linking words and phrases to choose from.
● As an extra challenge, ask the children to plan and write the final paragraph.

Plenary

● Ask children to write their paragraphs on page 4 and read them out.
● Invite other children to identify the connectives used and highlight them.
● Use voting methods to assess the children's learning with pages 5 to 7.

Whiteboard tools
Use the Reveal tool to hide the connectives on page 2 of the flipchart.

 Text editor tool

 Highlighter tool

 Print button

Reveal tool

Edit text tool

 Duplicate

Activote (optional)

Now and then

Now I eat curry.

Then I ate rusks.

Now I suck my pencil.

Then I _____

Now I sleep in a bed.

Then I _____

Now I wear _____

Then _____

Now I sing _____

Then _____

Now I drink _____

Then _____

Now I have _____

Then _____

Now I am _____

Then _____

The meeting

■ There was a lively meeting of the class council that week. Year 4 children were discussing class rules, and they had a lot to say.

"Play time is too short," Matt called _____.

"_____," Miss Bramble replied
_____.

"_____," he continued _____
_____.

"_____," Rafael muttered
_____.

Jez spoke _____: "_____"

"_____," Miss Bramble answered
_____.

One girl said _____, "_____
_____"

One boy asked _____, "_____
_____?"

"_____,"Matt interrupted
_____.

"_____," Miss Bramble said
_____.

◄ SCHOLASTIC
www.scholastic.co.uk

Story planning

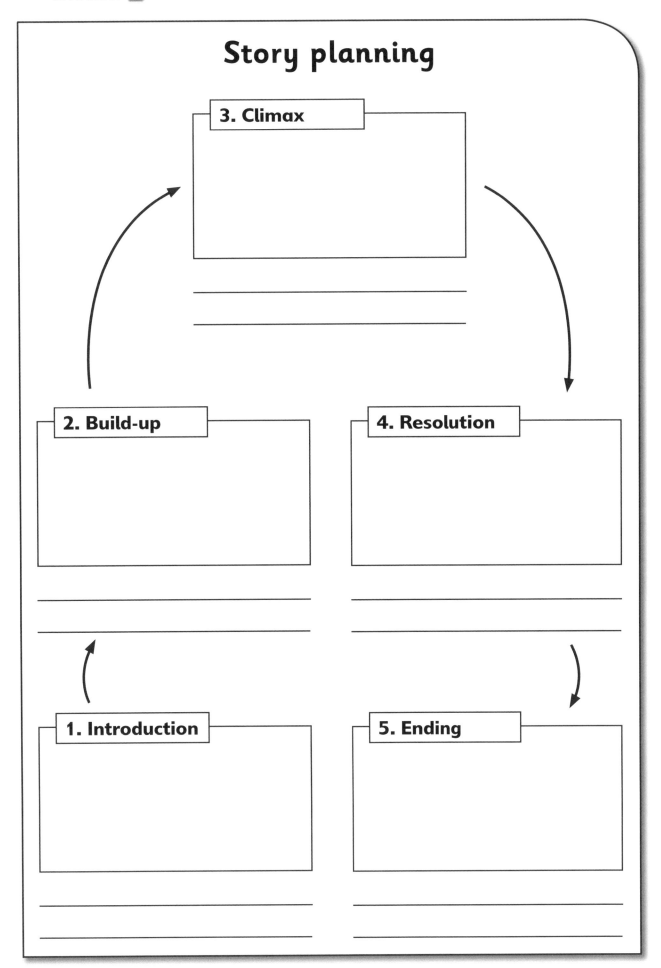

3. Climax

_____

_____

2. Build-up

4. Resolution

_____

_____

1. Introduction

5. Ending

_____

_____

Alphabetical order

■ Put the 'c' section of the school handbook into alphabetical order.

■ Remember to look at second, third and fourth letters.

cloakroom	1. _____
classroom	2. _____
class	3. _____
calculator	4. _____
cleaner	5. _____
choir	6. _____
canteen	7. _____
cash	8. _____
cheque	9. _____
chewing gum	10. _____
chickenpox	11. _____
chocolate	12. _____
crisps	13. _____
clipboard	14. _____
comics	15. _____
conkers	16. _____
cricket	17. _____
circle-time	18. _____
camcorder	19. _____
conduct	20. _____
cross-country	21. _____
concussion	22. _____
child-minder	23. _____
celebrations	24. _____
chairs	25. _____
carpet	26. _____

Story summaries

The Conch Bearer
by Chitra Banerjee Divakaruni (published by The Chicken House)

Anand wants his life to change: he was a happy 12-year-old before ill luck forced him to work on the streets of his home in India. His chance comes the day he meets a strange and ragged old beggar. But who is he? What does he want?

The old man needs Anand's help to protect a treasure of immeasurable value – a tiny, beautiful conch shell. But this is no ordinary conch, it has a potent magical force and must be returned to its rightful home, many hundreds of miles away.

Anand and the old man set out and are soon joined by Nisha, a headstrong but resourceful young sweeper girl. Together they must travel across burning plains and turbulent rivers, facing evil spirits and fantastical creatures, to reach the mountainous Silver Valley. And all the time a dangerous thief, who can sense the force of the conch, is never far behind them.

Buster Bayliss: Night Of The Living Veg
by Philip Reeve (published by Scholastic Children's Books)

Buster Bayliss is being forced to stay at his Fake Auntie Pauline's house in the flowery spare bedroom while his mum's away – it's a fate worse than death. Probably. Anyway, Buster is just about to find out for sure, as Smogley is being overrun with giant, man-eating, alien vegetables. Is Buster too weakened by the wallpaper torture to resist the alien advance?

The Stunning Science Of Everything
by Nick Arnold (published by Scholastic Children's Books)

Taking a journey from the very small, to the very big, readers will be taken on a glorious tour of everything in science from the smallest thing ever to the horribly huge universe.

Individual chapters cover atoms, molecules, light and sound, microbes, diseases, bugs, humans and the body, animals, the earth and outer space.

And it's all in glorious full colour!

Letter from Britain

▪ Use the words from the Homophones box to complete the letter.

_____ Mother,

_____ can't imagine how cold it is

_____! I have _____ warm clothes.

Tomorrow we march north to Eburacum. From _____

we go to a _____ near the dreaded Picts. It will

_____ even colder there, I am told. We

_____ freeze. I am going to help build a wall as

high as _____ men. We will guard it day and

_____: the Roman _____ will watch

everywhere. The enemy will not get _____ our

defence. It will be _____ difficult!

    Only _____ years to go before I return across

the _____ to Italy. I can't _____

– what a _____ celebration there will be when we

get back! _____ to me with the news from home.

Your loving _____,

Titus

Homophones

their/there/they're	plaice/place	deer/dear
to/two/too	mite/might	weight/wait
no/know	for/four	threw/through
eye/I	sun/son	grate/great
bee/be	knight/night	ewe/you/yew
see/sea	right/write	hear/here

A strange shopping list

■ Wilf is a sorcerer's apprentice. The sorcerer asks him to write a shopping list for a spell – but Wilf does it all wrong! The sorcerer needs more than one of everything.

■ Help Wilf by writing a new shopping list.

One spellbook shelf	*Five spellbook shelves*
One loaf of magibread	_____
One cat's life	_____
One spare shirt cuff	_____
One starry scarf	_____
One dragon knife	_____
One plum duff	_____
One green elf	_____
One dandelion puff	_____
One Indian chief	_____
One golden calf	_____
One falling leaf	_____

■ Write the spell that the sorcerer is going to make.

_____

_____

_____

_____

_____

Animal possessions

The giraffe's neck is a useful ladder,

The kangaroo's pouch is the baby's cot,

The _____

The _____

The _____

The _____

The _____

The _____

The _____

The _____

The _____

The _____

◣**SCHOLASTIC**

w w w . s c h o l a s t i c . c o . u k

Illustrations © Jim Peacock / Beehive Illustration

Name _____

Changing order – changing meaning

▪ Use each row of words to make two different sentences.

1. everyone the remembers Henry VIII name of

a _____

b _____

2. six Henry had wives divorces and some

a _____

b _____

3. the king eventually to Pope the spoke selfish

a _____

b _____

4. Pope order asked Henry the for permission in to the law break special

a _____

b _____

5. Pope's unfortunately the to request answer was no

a _____

b _____

6. Catherine the in Henry end sent away

a _____

b _____

▪ Draw two pictures to go with one of your pairs of sentences:

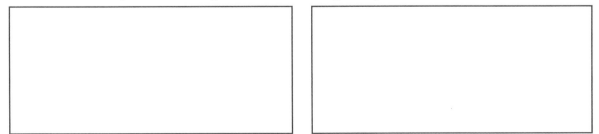

Name _____

Common endings

Across:

4. When a plane is in the sky it is in _____.

5. I don't walk under ladders because I am _____.

8. Another word for branch is _____.

9. The man in the badge and uniform looks _____.

10. 'Two plus two' is an _____ sum.

11. Harry had a sore throat and a tickly _____.

12. Our cat is very _____ and always wants to know what's going on.

13. After the day comes the _____.

Down:

1. Pigs eat their food from a _____.

2. This is a _____ day for me because it's my birthday.

3. The farmer uses a _____ to turn over the earth in his field.

6. Ella didn't go to school in case her illness was _____.

7. 'Five take away three' is a _____ sum.

A seaside trip

A seaside trip

is the best of treats because you can

> bake hot
>
> cool off
>
> surf waves
>
> slurp drinks
>
> lick lollies
>
> scale rocks
>
> tunnel under
>
> slide dunes
>
> see shells
>
> sail boats
>
> enjoy sun
>
> have fun

at the beach side, seaside.

(by Eileen Jones)

Illustrations © Jim Peacock / Beehive Illustration

Word webs

◢ Complete these word webs.

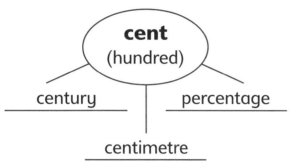

cent
(hundred)

century   percentage

centimetre

port
(carry)

tri
(three)

aqua
(water)

audi
(hear)

tele
(far)

dent
(tooth)

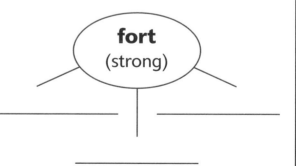

fort
(strong)

100 Activprimary™ WHITEBOARD LESSONS • YEAR 4

◤ SCHOLASTIC
www.scholastic.co.uk

Same word – different endings

Finish this poem using the same words but with different endings.

The player, playing, played in plays.

The sailor sailed in a sailing ship with sails.

The worker _____

_____, skipping, _____

_____, _____, _____ in some shops.

_____

_____

_____

_____

_____

_____

_____

_____

_____

_____

_____

_____

Helpful words

play	work	shop	skip	hop	look	teach
farm	sail	look	act	help	fish	write
speak	care					

Helpful word endings

-er	-s	-es	-ing	-ed	-ly	-ful

Compound words

foot	**Separate words**	**Compound words**
grand	tea + spoon	teaspoon
dust		
sand		
wheel		
frost		
wind		
yard		
bite		
bath		
band		
board		
ball		
rattle		
room		
cart		
card		
tea ✓		
apple		
berry		
bag		
bin		
parent		
rasp		
stand		
snake		
ship		
spoon ✓		
pine		
mill		

Questions and answers

- Kerry has to prepare some questions. She has to ask her gran what the local area was like when she was young.

- Help Kerry by turning these statements into questions. The first one has been done for you.

1. You did live here in the past.

Did you live here in the past?
_____

2. You did like this area.

_____

3. The windmill was working.

_____

4. Prefabs were built in Sheep Street.

_____

5. Children did walk to school.

_____

6. You did go to Sunday school.

_____

7. Children did not wear a uniform.

_____

8. The town centre looks the same.

_____

9. You can remember the old cinema.

_____

10. You did have supermarkets.

_____

11. Most people walked to the shops.

_____

Mathematics

This chapter provides 30 lessons based on the objectives taken from the National Numeracy Strategy framework, covering all the strands and key objectives. The whiteboard can enhance all three parts of the mathematics lesson, allowing you to demonstrate concepts to the class and model strategies. The children will become actively involved by highlighting, writing and dragging the particular elements of each lesson.

Essential mathematical concepts, such as place value and number bonds, can appear on screen from a Resource library. A bar chart can take minutes to draw (allowing time to interpret and discuss); interactive rulers can be turned, dragged and adjusted to demonstrate to the whole class how to use the equipment; picture images allow children to experience mathematics outside the context of the classroom, linking it to real life scenarios or objects.

On the CD-ROM you will also find links to relevant DfES *Interactive Teaching Programs* (ITPs). The whiteboard is an ideal medium for making the most of these exciting and interactive resources.

Lesson title	Objectives	What children should know	Cross-curricular links
Term 1			
Lesson 1: Place value ⬤ 🅿	• Read and write whole numbers to at least 10 000 in figures and words, and know what each digit represents. • Partition numbers into thousands, hundreds, tens and ones.	• Reading and writing numbers in figures and words to at least 1000.	**History** QCA Unit 8 'What were the differences between the lives of rich and poor people in Tudor times?'
Lesson 2: Using the symbols < and > 🅿	• Read and write the vocabulary of comparing and ordering numbers. • Use symbols correctly, including less than (<), greater than (>), equals (=).	• Comparing two- and three-digit numbers and saying which is more and less.	**Citizenship** QCA Unit 9 'Respect for property'
Lesson 3: Estimating and approximating ⬤	• Read and write the vocabulary of estimation and approximation. • Make and justify estimates up to about 250 and estimate a proportion.	• Estimating up to about 100 objects.	**Art and design** QCA Unit 4C 'Journeys'
Lesson 4: Counting patterns	• Recognise odd and even numbers up to 1000, and some of their properties, including the outcome of sums or differences of pairs of odd/even numbers.	• Recognising odd and even numbers to at least 100.	**History** QCA Unit 9 'What was it like for children in the Second World War?'
Lesson 5: Make 100 ⬤ 🅿	• Derive quickly: all number pairs that total 100 (for example, 62 + 38, 75 + 25, 40 + 60).	• Being able to use mental calculation strategies for addition of two two-digit integers.	**Geography** QCA Unit 25 'Geography and numbers'
Lesson 6: Pictograms ⬤	• Solve a problem by collecting quickly, organising, representing and interpreting data in tables, charts, graphs and diagrams, including those generated by a computer, for example: pictograms – symbol representing 2, 5, 10 or 20 units.	• Making pictograms, using a symbol to represent two units.	**ICT** QCA Unit 4D 'Collecting and presenting information: questionnaires and pie charts'
Lesson 7: Reading scales ⬤ 🅿	• Record estimates and readings from scales to a suitable degree of accuracy.	• Reading scales to the nearest half unit.	**Design and technology** QCA Unit 4A 'Money containers'

Mathematics ▢ Chapter 2

Lesson title	Objectives	What children should know	Cross-curricular links
Lesson 8: Telling the time ◉ 🄿	• Read the time from an analogue clock to the nearest minute, and from a 12-hour digital clock.	• Reading the time to five-minute intervals.	**Geography** PoS (2c) To use maps and plans at a range of scales.
Lesson 9: Polygons ◉ 🄿	• Classify polygons using criteria such as number of right angles, whether or not they are regular, symmetry properties.	• Describing 2D shapes using appropriate mathematical vocabulary.	**Art and design** QCA Unit 3B 'Investigating pattern'
Lesson 10: Identifying angles ◉ 🄿	• Begin to know that angles are measured in degrees and that: one whole turn is 360° or 4 right angles; a quarter turn is 90° or one right angle; half a right angle is 45°. • Start to order a set of angles less than 180°.	• Recognising right angles and identifying these in shapes and the environment.	**ICT** QCA Unit 4B 'Developing images using repeating patterns'
Term 2			
Lesson 11: Using *Counter*	• Add/subtract 1, 10, 100 or 1000 to/from any integer, and count on or back in tens, hundreds or thousands from any whole number up to 10,000.	• Adding/subtracting 1, 10 or 100 to any two- or three-digit number.	**Geography** QCA Unit 16 'What's in the news?'
Lesson 12: Multiplying and dividing by 10 and 100	• Multiply or divide any integer up to 1000 by 10 (whole-number answers), and understand the effect. • Begin to multiply by 100.	• Multiplying single-digit and decade numbers by 10, and single-digit numbers by 100.	**Design and technology** QCA Unit 4A 'Money containers'
Lesson 13: Rounding ◉	• Round any positive integer less than 1000 to the nearest 10 or 100.	• Rounding two-digit numbers to the nearest 10 and three-digit numbers to the nearest 100.	**Geography** QCA Unit 18 'Connecting ourselves to the world'
Lesson 14: Fractions	• Use fraction notation. • Recognise simple fractions that are several parts of a whole (such as $\frac{2}{3}$ or $\frac{5}{8}$), and mixed numbers (such as 5 ¾). • Recognise the equivalence of simple fractions (such as fractions equivalent to ½, ¼ or ¾).	• Recognising units simple unit fractions and beginning to recognise simple fractions that are several parts of a whole, such as ¾.	**ICT** QCA Unit 4B 'Developing images using repeating patterns'
Lesson 15: Difference	• Find a small difference by counting up.	• Finding differences by counting up, eg where the two integers lie either side of 100, such as 97 and 103.	**English** NLS Term 1 S5: To practise using commas to mark grammatical boundaries within sentences
Lesson 16: Remainders	• Find remainders after division.	• Deriving division facts from 2, 3, 4, 5 and 10 multiplication tables.	**Design and technology** QCA Unit 4B 'Storybooks'
Lesson 17: Number puzzle	• Solve mathematical problems or puzzles, recognise and explain patterns and relationships, generalise and predict. Suggest extensions by asking 'What if...?'	• Using hundred squares; recognising and explaining number patterns.	**ICT** QCA Unit 4D 'Collecting and presenting information: questionnaires and pie charts'
Lesson 18: Bar charts ◉	• Solve a problem by collecting quickly, organising, representing and interpreting data in tables, charts, graphs and diagrams, including those generated by a computer, for example: bar charts – intervals labelled in 2s, 5s, 10s or 20s.	• Making bar charts where intervals are labelled in twos.	**Citizenship** QCA Unit 6 'Developing our school grounds'
Lesson 19: When? ◉ 🄿	• Read simple timetables and use this year's calendar.	• Reading a simple calendar.	**ICT** QCA Unit 4D 'Collecting and presenting information: questionnaires and pie charts'

Mathematics — Chapter 2

Lesson title	Objectives	What children should know	Cross-curricular links
Lesson 20: Reflections	• Sketch the reflection of a simple shape in a mirror line parallel to one side (all sides parallel or perpendicular to the mirror line).	• Recognising lines of symmetry in simple shapes.	**ICT** QCA Unit 4B 'Developing images using repeating patterns'
Term 3			
Lesson 21: Negative numbers	• Recognise negative numbers in context (for example, on a number line, on a temperature scale).	• Counting and ordering whole numbers, and using a number line.	**Geography** QCA Unit 24 'A passport to the world' **Science** QCA Unit 4C 'Keeping warm'
Lesson 22: Multiples	• Recognise multiples of 2, 3, 4, 5 and 10 up to the tenth multiple.	• Knowing 2, 5 and 10 multiplication tables.	**Art and design** QCA Unit 3B 'Investigating pattern' **ICT** QCA Unit 4B 'Developing images using repeating patterns'
Lesson 23: Money	• Understand decimal notation and place value for tenths and hundredths, and use it in context. For example: order amounts of money; convert a sum of money such as £13.25 to pence.	• Recognising all coins and notes.	**History** QCA Unit 9 'What was it like for children in the Second World War?'
Lesson 24: Totalling multiples of ten	• Add three two-digit multiples of 10, such as 40 + 70 + 50.	• Totalling quickly three single-digit numbers.	**English** NLS Term 1 S5: To practise using commas to mark grammatical boundaries within sentences; link to work on editing and revising own writing.
Lesson 25: Using + and – mental strategies	• Use known number facts and place value to add or subtract mentally, including any pair of two-digit whole numbers.	• Bridging through a multiple of ten and adjusting.	**Science** QCA Unit 4B 'Habitats'
Lesson 26: Solving word problems	• Choose and use appropriate number operations and appropriate ways of calculating (mental, mental with jottings, pencil and paper) to solve problems. • Develop and refine written methods for column addition and subtraction.	• Using informal methods of recording; beginning to use column addition and subtraction.	**Citizenship** QCA Unit 04 'People who help us – the local police'
Lesson 27: Venn diagrams	• Solve a problem by collecting quickly, organising, representing and interpreting data in tables, charts, graphs and diagrams, including those generated by a computer, for example: Venn diagrams (two criteria).	• Using Venn diagrams to sort data; one criterion.	**Science** QCA Unit 4B 'Habitats'
Lesson 28: Carroll diagrams	• Solve a problem by collecting quickly, organising, representing and interpreting data in tables, charts, graphs and diagrams, including those generated by a computer, for example: Carroll diagrams (two criteria).	• Using Carroll diagrams to sort data; one criterion.	**Science** QCA Unit 4B 'Habitats'
Lesson 29: Finding positions	• Recognise positions and directions: for example, describe and find the position of a point on a grid of squares where the lines are numbered.	• Using coordinates which label spaces, such as a square on a grid.	**Geography** QCA Unit 10 'A village in India'
Lesson 30: Using compass directions	• Use the eight compass directions N, S, E, W, NE, NW, SE, SW.	• Using the four compass points N, S, E and W.	**Geography** QCA Unit 8 'Improving the environment'

Place value

Starter

Explain that you will say a whole number up to 1000. Ask the children to write it, using numerals, on their individual whiteboards and show you. Write the whole number on page 2 of the flipchart 'Place value' to confirm how it should be written. Invite a volunteer to write the same whole number in words on the flipchart page.

Repeat this process and include examples where zero is a place holder for tens and/or units, such as *650; 605*. Ask the children questions such as: *What does the zero stand for? What digit is in the hundreds/tens/units* place?

Whole-class shared work

● Extend the number range from the Starter to include thousands. Write an example on the whiteboard using figures and words, such as *4256* and *four thousand two hundred and fifty-six.*
● Provide further examples for the children to try for themselves, such as *9043; 7360*. Extend to whole numbers greater than 10,000, writing an example on page 3. For each example, ask: *What does ... stand for? Which place does the digit ... hold?*
● Display page 4 of the flipchart. Ask a child to drag a number from the box at the bottom of the screen into the *Whole number* column in the table.
● Invite the children to suggest how to fill in each of the columns. Ask a volunteer to drag and drop each digit into place using the numbers at the bottom of the table. Repeat for seven more four-digit numbers dragged from the number box.
● Page 5 can be used to investigate whole numbers greater than 10,000. This can be done as part of this lesson or in a later lesson.

Independent work

● Ask the children to work in pairs. Provide each pair with a set of 0 to 9 numeral cards, and a copy of the photocopiable sheet 'Partitioning'. The members of each pair take turns to pick four numeral cards. Both children make a four-digit whole number using the cards. They should try to make their integers different. Each children records their whole number on the photocopiable sheet.
● Decide whether to limit the range to three-digit integers for less able learners by blanking out the thousands column on the sheet.
● Challenge more able learners to extend the range to five-digit integers. They can draw their own table to complete the work.

Plenary

● Use page 6 of the flipchart to invite children to take turns to say one of their whole numbers. Write their whole number in the whole number column of the table. Invite other children to drag and drop, or write, the appropriate digits in the partitioning columns.
● Ask questions such as: *Which digit represents thousands/hundreds/tens/ units? What would the whole number be if you changed over the tens and hundreds digits?*

Using the symbols < and >

Learning objectives
● Read and write the vocabulary of comparing and ordering numbers.
● Use symbols correctly, including less than (<), greater than (>), equals(=).

Resources P
Photocopiable page 90, 'Using the symbols < and >' for each child; a set of 0-9 number cards for each pair.

Links to other subjects
Citizenship
QCA Unit 9 'Respect for property'
● Follow up this work by asking children to compare crime statistics for two local areas, using newspaper and Internet sources. Encourage them to use < and > to compare the statistics.

Starter
Remind children that < means *is less than* and > means *is greater than*. Use the Dice tool to generate pairs of three-digit integers on a blank flipchart page, leaving a gap between the two integers. Invite children to say which is larger and write in < or > correctly. If necessary, highlight digits to help the children to see which integer is smaller or larger. Repeat this for other pairs. Over time, extend to four-digit integers.

Whole-class shared work
● Write the following on a blank flipchart page: 430 < ☐
● Ask for suggestions for the missing number.
● Repeat this, using the Dice tool to generate four-digit integers. Use both < and >.
● Write 1234 < ☐ < 1563. Invite suggestions for the missing numbers.
● Discuss the range of integers that will fit in each box. Which will not fit?
● Type five four-digit integers on to the whiteboard, out of number order. Make sure they are in separate text boxes so that they can be moved independently. Invite the children to re-order these, smallest first. Ask them to insert < between each integer.
● Repeat for another set, this time writing the largest first and inserting > between each integer.

Independent work
● Ask the children to work in pairs. Each pair needs a set of 0 to 9 number cards. Hand each child a copy of the photocopiable sheet and some scrap paper.
● In their pairs, the children take turns to choose four number cards.
● They each make six different four-digit integers using their chosen cards. They should make a note of these numbers on the scrap paper.
● Next they should record the numbers on to the sheet, making sure that they put the numbers in the correct order.
● Decide whether to ask less able learners to choose three cards to make HTU integers.
● More able learners can be challenged to choose four digits from 1 to 9 (not zero) and to find all possible four-digit integers (24 possibilities).
● As the children work, challenge them to tell you which sign would fit between sets of two integers, and why.

Plenary
● Write the following on the whiteboard: 6435 < ☐ > ☐
● Ask the children to suggest integers that will fit into the boxes. Encourage them to suggest a range of integers that will fit each box. Repeat for another example, such as 2004 > ☐ < ☐.

Whiteboard tools
Use the Floating keyboard to type integers in separate text boxes. Use the Dice tool in the Special tools menu to generate random numbers

 Highlighter tool

 Pen tool

 Floating keyboard

 Marquee select tool

Dice tool

Estimating and approximating

Starter
Display page 2 of the 'Estimating' flipchart. Show the image for about five seconds and invite the children to estimate how many counters there are. Hide the screen with the Reveal tool 🔲. Ask the children to record their estimates on their individual whiteboards and invite them to share their estimates. Reveal the screen again and ask: *How shall we count these to check?* Invite a child to demonstrate by counting in fives or tens. The counters can be dragged and grouped into sets. Reveal the answer at the top of the page.

Reset the page and delete some of the counters. Repeat the estimating activity.

Whole-class shared work
● Display page 3 of the flipchart. Ask: *How many snails do you estimate there are? How did you make your estimate?*
● The children could use voting methods to vote on the estimated number of snails.
● Invite a child to demonstrate how they made their estimate, such as counting a small number of snails and multiplying up.
● Repeat this for pages 4 and 5.
● Now show the children the prepared containers. Tell them to work quickly in small groups to make estimates of how many counters there are. Allow about five minutes for this.
● Bring the class back together. Compare and discuss estimates and how these were made. Invite children to check their estimates by counting the counters in their container.
● Hide the containers, and remove half or a quarter of the counters from each. Show each container in turn and ask the children to about how many counters have been removed, and to express this as a fraction.

Independent work
● Children should work in pairs with about 250 counters in a container and a large paper plate.
● They take turns to spread some of the counters out on the plate. They both estimate how many counters there are.
● They record their estimate. Challenge them to think of a quick way to count the counters. They then record the actual number. The children should repeat the activity ten times.
● Limit the maximum number of counters to 100 for less able learners. Extend more able learners by increasing the number to 300.

Plenary
● Display page 6 of the flipchart, and ask the children to estimate how many triangles are on the page. Invite them to explain how they worked this out.
● Repeat this for page 7.
● Invite a child to estimate half of the circles on page 7 by selecting approximately half of the circles and deleting them.
● Then ask another child to estimate half of what is left in the same way. Ask: *What portion is left?* (a quarter.) *Do you agree? Why do you think that?*
● Repeat for other quantities, asking children to remove estimates of quarters and halves.

Counting patterns

Learning objective
● Recognise odd and even numbers up to 1000, and some of their properties, including the outcome of sums or differences of pairs of odd/even numbers.

Resources
Counter software (available on the CD-ROM in the *Using ICT to support mathematics in primary school* training pack, DfES references: DfES0260/2000 for entire training pack; DfES0267/2000 for CD-ROM only - also available through the DfES website: **www.standards.dfes.gov.uk** Set Step to +2 for counting up, and then –2 for counting back. Set 361 in the memory.

Links to other subjects
History
QCA Unit 9 'What was it like for children in the Second World War?'
● Ask the children to collect information about rationing. They can use their knowledge of sums of odd and even numbers to determine how many items of food children had in a week, month and year, and whether these are odd or even numbers.

Starter
Set *Counter* to begin to count in twos from 500 to 600. Invite the children to join in the count, keeping a regular counting pace. Repeat, counting back in twos. Ask: *If you count in twos from 500, do you say odd or even numbers? How can you tell whether a number is odd or even?* Repeat for counting in twos starting on an odd number, such as 531.

Whole-class shared work
● Recall the memory in *Counter* (MR button). Ask the children if 361 is an odd or even number. How can they tell?
● Begin the count in twos from 361. Can the children tell you if *Counter* is showing odd or even numbers now. Stop *Counter* and check if they know what would need to be added to the displayed number to make it even.
● Agree the rules for recognising odd numbers (unit digit is 1, 3, 5, 7 or 9), and for even numbers (unit digit is 0, 2, 4, 6 or 8).
● Ask the children questions such as: *Will 4 add 2 give an even or odd sum? What about 6 add 8? And 10 add 14? Do you think that an even plus an even number will always be even? Why do you think that?*

Independent work
● Tell the children that they are going to work in pairs to investigate the sums and differences of odd and even numbers.
● Write the following on a blank flipchart page:
  ● odd + odd = ?
  ● even + even = ?
  ● odd + even = ?
  ● even + odd = ?
● Explain to the children that you would like them to decide, in each case, whether the sum is odd or even and to give some examples to demonstrate their findings.
● Work with less able learners as a group, using small numbers to demonstrate examples for each of the above sums.
● Extend more able learners by challenging them to explain why, for example, the sum of two odd numbers is always even.

Plenary
● Review each of the above generalised addition sentences, writing appropriate number sentences on to the whiteboard, and agree whether the sum is odd or even in each case.
● Ask the more able learners to explain why the sum of two odd numbers is always even. (An odd number can always be expressed as one more than an even number: for example, 3+3 = 2+1+2+1. So there are always two ones to total to make the sum even.)

Whiteboard tools
Launch Activprimary before starting *Counter* and work in Desktop mode. This enables use of the Desktop toolbar.

🖊 Pen tool

🔍 Desktop mode

🔍 Return to main screen

Make 100

Learning objective
● Derive quickly: all number pairs that total 100 (for example, 62 + 38, 75 + 25, 40 + 60).

Resources
'Make 100' flipchart file; photocopiable page 91 'Make 100', one copy for each pair; two different coloured pencils for each pair.

Links to other subjects
Geography
QCA Unit 25 'Geography and numbers'
● Children can use number pairs to 100 to help them compare distances between towns.

Starter
Explain that you will say a small number. Ask the children to call out, together, the number that adds to your number to make a total of 20. So, if you say 13, the children call out seven. Keep a good pace to this to encourage rapid recall.

Alternatively, you can drag random numbers from the *Numbers* box on page 2 of the flipchart if the children find it easier to see the number. If children falter for any responses, reveal the hundred square on the *Number grid* ITP and use this to demonstrate the answer by counting up in appropriate groups.

Whole-class shared work
● Go to page 3 and display the *Number grid* ITP. Explain that the children will be finding pairs of numbers that total 100, quickly and easily.
● Begin with the easier pairs, using what is already known: 9 + 1 = 10; 90 + 10 = 100, and so on. Click on the pairs to highlight them, to mark these numbers so that the children can see which pairs have been found.
● Now move to other pairs and ask: *How did you work out the answer?* Praise those who *knew* it. Spend about five minutes on finding other pairs.

Independent work
● Ask the children to work in pairs on photocopiable page 91 'Make 100'.
● Invite the children to take turns to choose a start number for their partner. The partner finds the other number to total 100. The first child can challenge if they think their partner is wrong, and must find a way to demonstrate that they are correct. Children score a point for a correct answer. Encourage them to colour each pair of numbers, each child using a different colour.
● They should continue until they have found all pairs.
● Work with less able learners as a group. Invite them to take turns to say a pair that they think totals 100. Discuss strategies for finding answers.
● When the more able learners have finished playing the game, ask them to write some strategies for finding solutions quickly.

Plenary
● Go to page 4 and open the *Number grid* ITP.
● Put the class into four teams, appoint a captain to each team, and play *Finding pairs to make 100* as a class game.
● Invite the more able learners to suggest strategies for finding solutions quickly.
● List these strategies on page 4, and invite all the children to think of which pairs could be made using that strategy. Strategies could include: using decade numbers, using numbers which end in five and using number bonds to ten to find the unit digit of the missing number.

Whiteboard tools

 Pen tool

 Marquee select tool

Pictograms

Learning objective
● Solve a problem by collecting quickly, organising, representing and interpreting data in tables, charts, graphs and diagrams, including those generated by a computer, for example: pictograms – symbol representing 2, 5, 10 or 20 units.

Resources
'Pictogram' flipchart file.

Links to other subjects
ICT
QCA Unit 4D 'Collecting and presenting information: questionnaires and pie charts'
● This lesson links directly to ICT. Use the other data collected to repeat this lesson so that children become proficient with using and interpreting pictograms where the symbol represents several units.

Starter
Go to the second page of the flipchart. Write in a survey question, such as: *What pets do you have?* Agree how to collect the data, for example, by recording the number of children who have dogs, cats or rabbits. Draw a simple data collection chart and enter the information using tallies. Go to page 3 of the flipchart and repeat for another question, such as: *How do you come to school?*

Whole-class shared work
● Put the children into mixed ability groups of about four. Tell them that they are going to gather data from other children. (The quantity of data needs to be large, so agree with other teachers that children can come to their classes in small groups to ask their questions.)
● Display page 4 of the flipchart. Encourage each group to think of a survey question, for example, month of birth or number of brothers or sisters. Write notes and suggestions on the flipchart if required.
● Discuss and agree how the children should collect their data. They should make a tally chart and agree the fields (or headings) before they begin.

Independent work
● Children should collect their data and total it for each field. Encourage more able learners to provide support for those who are less able, if necessary.

Plenary
● Pick one of the groups to share their data.
● Go to page 5 of the flipchart.
● Click on the button to open the pictogram. Discuss what the headings for each row should be and type these in.
● Discuss how many items one symbol should stand for. Explain that you can't use a symbol to represent every single item. For example, in many pictograms a symbol represents ten or even twenty items.
● Ask the children to calculate how many symbols are needed for each heading and input these. Discuss how to complete the row where the items do not divide exactly by the number of units chosen for each symbol.
● Fill in the key box.
● Use the Camera tool to insert a screen shot of the finished pictogram on to the current flipchart page.
● Minimise the pictogram.
● Ask questions about the data, such as: *How many more ... are there than ...? Which is the most/least popular? How can you tell that?*
● Encourage children to speculate about their data. Ask: *How accurate do you think this data is? Why do you think that? How could we improve on our data collection?*
● Use the data collected by other groups in subsequent lessons.

Whiteboard tools
Use the Lines tool to draw charts, the Pen tool to enter the tally and the Floating keyboard to add headings to the empty pictogram.

 Highlighter tool

 Lines tool

Pen tool

Text editor tool

Camera tool

Floating keyboard

Reading scales

Learning objective
● Record estimates and readings from scales to a suitable degree of accuracy.

Resources ⊙ ℗
'Reading scales' flipchart file; photocopiable page 92 'Reading scales' for each child.

Links to other subjects
Design and technology
QCA Unit 4A 'Money containers'
● When planning and making items, encourage children to use their measuring skills and to make decisions about estimating and rounding measurements.

Starter
Display page 2 of the flipchart 'Reading scales'. Ask the children to look at the first ruler and to say what measurement they see on it. Discuss the scale, and how it is marked. Ask the children to read the scale. Repeat this for the other scales, ensuring that children understand that for some of the rulers they will need to estimate how many millimetres there are between the markings.

Whole-class shared work
● Display page 3 and discuss the scale, noting that the markings between each centimetre are in millimetres.
● Invite children to make estimates of the readings and then to look carefully to check the readings. Encourage them to do this accurately. Discuss whether to round up or down to the nearest half centimetre, and why this may be appropriate. Check that the children understand that millimetres can be expressed as a decimal fraction of a centimetre.
● Display page 4 and discuss how the containers are marked, and how to read the scale.
● Ask the children to read the water levels, and to make estimates where necessary. Encourage them to explain their estimates.
● Go to page 5. Again, discuss the scale and invite the children to estimate the readings. Repeat this for page 6.
● Display page 7, which shows three lines. Select the Ruler tool ⊖ from the Special tools menu. Invite a child to move the ruler until it lines up with the line. Discuss how to make the measurement to the nearest half centimetre.
● Repeat for the other two lines.

Independent work
● Give each child a copy of the photocopiable page 'Reading Scales' to complete.
● As children work, discuss how they make their estimates, and how accurate they think these are.
● Less confident learners could be asked to read to the nearest cm, nearest 100ml and nearest 10kg. More confident learners can be challenged to read to the nearest mm, nearest 25ml and nearest 5kg.
● When the children have completed the sheet, ask them to draw some lines, using a ruler on the back of the sheet. They should work with a partner to measure the lines to the nearest half centimetre.

Plenary
● With the children watching, draw some more thick lines onto page 8 of the flipchart using the Lines tool ❙. Invite individuals to take turns to move the ruler into place so that it lines up with the drawn line.
● Invite children to read, from the ruler, the length of the line to the nearest half centimetre. They could try using a real ruler as well, to check that the measurements are the same.
● Ask: *How do you decide whether to round a measurement up or down?*

Whiteboard tools
Use the Ruler tool to measure the lines. Add lines to the page with the Lines tool.

 Pen tool

 Ruler tool

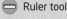 Lines tool

Telling the time

Learning objective
● Read the time from an analogue clock to the nearest minute and from a 12-hour digital clock.

Resources
Flipchart file, 'Telling the time' Photocopiable page 93 'How long?', one for each pair

Links to other subjects
Geography
PoS (2c) To use maps and plans at a range of scales.
● Use string to measure approximate distances on a map. You will also need to talk about the issue of scale when you do this.

Starter
Display page 2 of the flipchart. Select the XY origin tool ⊕ in the Special tools menu and place the XY origin icon in the centre of the clock. Write a time, in words, at the top of the page, and invite a pair of children to place the hands on the analogue clock in the correct place, and write the correct digits into the digital clock. Use times of five-minute intervals, for example twenty past six, quarter to ten. Invite the other children to check that they agree.
  Reset the page and invite another pair to try the activity. Repeat for several more pairs.

Whole-class shared work
● Reveal the pair of clocks on page 3 of the flipchart. Ask: *What time does the first analogue clock show?* Invite a child to write this time on the digital clock. Repeat for the second clock.
● Repeat this for the clocks on page 4. For the second clock ask: *How many minutes past the hour does the clock show?* Invite the children to count the minutes as you point to the minute marks on the clock. Ask: *So what is the time?* Invite a child to write in the time on the digital clock to match.
● Repeat this for the next pairs of clocks on pages 5 to 8.
● Look at the pair of clocks on page 9. Read the problem next to the clocks. Encourage answers and write the answer in the space provided.
● Challenge the children to make up time word problems for the next two pairs of clocks on page 10, and answer them. This page shows a mixture of analogue and digital clocks.

Independent work
● Distribute the photocopiable sheets and ask children to complete them, working cooperatively.
● Work with the less able learners in a group. Say the time on each clock together, counting the minutes where necessary. Encourage the children to suggest a word problem for each.
● Provide analogue and digital clock templates for more able learners. Challenge them to use them to write some times, and to create word problems to go with them. These can be scanned into the computer for the Plenary.

Plenary
● Display the pair of clocks on page 11 of the flipchart.
● Ask the children to say the difference between the times and suggest a time sentence to go with them. For example, a suitable sentence might be: *The meal started at 12.37 and finished at 1.41 so it lasted for one hour and four minutes.*
● Repeat this for the pair of clocks on page 12.
● Invite the more able group to reveal one of their scanned-in time word problems for other children to solve. Repeat for the other time word problems.

Whiteboard tools
Use the XY origin tool (in the Special tools menu) to alter the centre of rotation of an object. This means that an object will rotate around a given rotation point. Select the Teacher tools menu and the Page reset button to erase any unsaved changes.

⊕ XY origin tool

◤ Marquee select tool

✎ Pen tool

↻ Page reset button

Learning objective
● Classify polygons using criteria such as number of right angles, whether or not they are regular, symmetry properties.

Resources
'Polygons' flipchart file; photocopiable page 94 'Polygons' for each child (you may wish to enlarge the sheet); scissors; shape tiles; paper and glue.

Links to other subjects
Art and design
QCA Unit 3B 'Investigating pattern'
● Provide examples of patterns from other cultures. Invite the children to describe the shapes they see and to explain how each pattern is made. They can search for polygons, explain whether or not these are regular, and why they think that.

Whiteboard tools
Use the Shapes tool for the Starter. Click on the Point-to-point button in the Pen tool tray to create irregular polygons with straight sides.

⬚ Shapes tool

◤ Marquee select tool

▯ Pen tool

⦂ Point-to-point button

⬬ Ruler tool

Polygons

Starter
Open the flipchart 'Polygons' and go to page 2. Describe a polygon (for example: *I am thinking of a shape that is regular. It has four right angles*). Ask the children to guess what it is (for example, a square). Use the Shapes tool ⬚ to place the shape on the page, so that children can see if they were right. Encourage them to check the shape against your description. Repeat for different polygons.

Whole-class shared work
● Display page 3 of the flipchart. Discuss the definition of a polygon: *a closed, flat shape with three or more straight sides.*
● Discuss the definition of a regular polygon: *a closed, flat shape with three or more straight sides, and all sides and angles equal.*
● Go to page 4 and tell the children you want them to sort the shapes. Point out the title of the Carroll diagram: *Sorting polygons.*
● Point out the headings: *Triangles; Quadrilaterals; Regular; Not regular.*
● Ask the children to suggest how to sort the shapes and to explain why each shape belongs in its specific place. Invite a volunteer to drag the shapes into the Carroll diagram as they are discussed.
● Point out the shapes that do not fit into the Carroll diagram. Ask the children to explain why they don't belong in the diagram. Emphasise that the remaining shapes are neither triangles nor quadrilaterals because they have more than four sides; however, they are all polygons.
● Use page 5 to discuss the definitions for equilateral (all sides and angles equal), isosceles (two sides and angles equal) and right-angled (one right angle) triangles.
● Complete the polygon sorting activities on pages 6 and 7. Use the Ruler tool ⬬ if necessary, to measure the sides of the shapes.

Independent work
● Give each child a copy of the photocopiable sheet.
● Ask them to cut out the sets of triangles and to separate them into isosceles, equilateral and right-angled triangles. They should then use the sets to make patterns. The shape tiles in their patterns must touch, leaving no gaps (tessellation).
● When the children have produced patterns they are happy with, these can be stuck on to paper to preserve them.
● Decide whether less able learners should use plastic shape tiles, and work as a group. Encourage the children to describe the properties of the shapes.
● Provide more able learners with some assorted shape tiles. Which shapes tessellate and which do not?

Plenary
● Review the patterns that children have made. Discuss the properties of the shapes.
● Ask questions such as: *Are these shapes polygons? Regular polygons? Is a circle a polygon? Why not?*
● Record the children's observations on page 8 of the flipchart.
● Invite the more able learners to explain which of the tiles they have been given will tessellate, and to explain why this is so.

Identifying angles

Learning objectives
● Begin to know that angles are measured in degrees and that: one whole turn is 360° or 4 right angles; a quarter turn is 90° or one right angle; half a right angle is 45°.
● Start to order a set of angles less than 180°.

Resources
Flipchart file, 'Angles' Photocopiable page 95, 'Identifying angles', one for each pair of children; 45° and 60° set squares, one of each for each pair of children.

Links to other subjects
ICT
QCA Unit 4B 'Developing images using repeating patterns'
● When re-sizing images on screen, ask the children to consider whether the angles of the shape have changed, and in what way.

Starter
Display page 2 of the flipchart 'Angles'. Ask the children to stand up and face the front of the classroom. Explain that you will say an angle and would like them to turn in the direction that you say. Say, for example: *Turn a right angle to the right. Turn two right angles to the right. Now turn another right angle to the right. How many right angles have you turned? And where have you finished? So how many right angles are there if you turn through a complete circle?*
   Repeat with left, and more right, turns, and using 30°, 60°, as well as 90°.

Whole-class shared work
● Display page 3. Ask the children to look carefully at the angles and to say their size. Agree and check with the Protractor tool 🌗 that these are all 90° angles.
● Go to page 4 and explain that two different types of angles are shown. Ask for volunteers to measure the angles on the page.
● Demonstrate how to record and read the angles in degrees.
● Now display page 5 and ask the children to decide which is the smallest angle, the next smallest, and so on.
● Use the Marquee select tool to drag and drop the angles into order from smallest to largest. Pick up the angles by the middle rather than either end.
● Use the Protractor tool, if necessary, to measure the angles.

Independent work
● Ask the children to work in pairs.
● Provide each pair with a 45° and 60° set square.
● Ask each pair to complete the photocopiable page 'Identifying angles'.
● Decide whether to work with less confident children as a group, with an A3 enlargement of the photocopiable sheet and the board set squares.
● If more able learners complete the work quickly, suggest that they use the set squares to construct some triangles with angles of 45° and 60°.

Plenary
● Use page 6 of the flipchart to draw an angle, using either the Pen tool or the Lines tool.
● Ask the children whether the angle you have drawn is larger or smaller than a right angle.
● Repeat this for other angles, comparing them with 45° and 60° and using the protractor to check.

Whiteboard tools
Use the Pen tool or the Lines tool to draw angles. Use the Protractor tool in the Special tools menu to measure them.

🖊 Pen tool

🢔 Marquee select tool

🌗 Protractor tool

▮ Lines tool

Learning objective
● Add/subtract 1, 10, 100 or 1000 to/from any integer, and count on or back in tens, hundreds or thousands from any whole number up to 10,000.

Resources
Individual whiteboards and pens; *Counter* software: set the Start number to 54. Set Step to +1 for counting up in ones, and then -1 for counting back in ones (CD-ROM containing the *Counter* software is available from *Using ICT to support mathematics in primary school* training pack (DfES references: DfES0260/2000 for entire training pack; DfES0267/2000 for CD-ROM only); four sets of 0-9 number cards for each pair.

Links to other subjects
Geography
QCA Unit 16 'What's in the news?'
● Search newspapers for numerical information, such as numbers attending football matches. Discuss what happens if there are 1/10/100 more or fewer.

Using *Counter*

Starter
Decide upon the number range, such as up to 1000/5000/10,000, and explain that you will say a number and ask the children to write it, using numerals, onto their whiteboards. Keep the pace sharp. Ask questions such as: *What does the first/second/third/digit stand for? What number would you have if you removed the ... digit?*

Whole-class shared work
● Explain that you have set *Counter* to count on from 54 (or any number under 100). Begin the count and ask the children to count with *Counter*. Stop the count and ask them what the next number would be.
● Set the Step to -1 and begin the count again. Stop the count. Ask: *What would the next number be? And the next? So how could we describe the count?*
● Repeat this for counting on and back in tens, then in hundreds.
● Write on a blank flipchart page *546* (or any number under 1000). Ask: *What is one more or less than this? What is ten/hundred more or less than this?*
● Repeat this for other starting numbers, up to 10,000.
● Discuss which digits change when adding/subtracting 1, 10 and 100. Highlight the changed digits on the whiteboard.

Independent work
● Provide each pair with number cards. Ask them to generate a starting number, then to write the +1, -1, +10, -10, +100 and -100 number.
● The children can record their work by making a simple table like this:

Start number	+1	-1	+10	-10	+100	-100

● Provide three sets of number cards for less able learners and ask them to make starting numbers with three digits.
● Provide five sets of cards for more able learners and challenge them to make integers with five digits, and to add/subtract 1000 to each integer.
● Encourage the children to explain which digit will change as they add and subtract, and why other digits remain unchanged.

Plenary
● Review starting numbers from each group and ask the children to say the numbers which are one, ten and one hundred more or less than this number. Write on to the whiteboard the numbers that the children say. Ask: *Which digits could change when we add/subtract one/ten/hundred? Why is that?*

Whiteboard tools
Launch Activprimary before starting *Counter*.

 Highlighter tool

 Pen tool

 Desktop mode

 Return to main screen

Multiplying and dividing by 10 and 100

Starter
Open your prepared flipchart and reveal the two cakes. Explain that you have nine people coming to tea and you need to multiply the cakes by ten to have enough for everyone (including yourself). Write the number sentences on the whiteboard ($2 \times 10 = 20$; $20 \div 10 = 2$) and ask the children to multiply and divide by ten. Reveal the 20 cakes on the right. Go to a new page and repeat the process of writing a digit on the board and asking the children to multiply and divide by ten. Next, use decade numbers (for example, 20 or 40) and multiply and divide by 100. Keep the pace of this sharp. Discuss the effect of multiplying and dividing by 10 and 100.

Whole-class shared work
● Write the numbers 1 to 9, well spaced, and highlight them.
● Under each number, write the result when it is multiplied by 10 (10 under 1, 20 under 2 and so on).
● Ask: *What has happened to these numbers? What is the pattern? Suppose I multiplied by one/two/100? What would I write then?* On the next line down, write the children's suggestions: 100, 200 and so on.
● Now ask the children what would happen if you multiplied by 1000. Invite them to take turns to complete the next row of this table.
● Challenge the children to say what will happen if you divide by ten. (1000 becomes 100, 100 becomes 10 and 10 becomes 1.)
● Discuss the place value of each zero in the thousands row, and the effect on the digits in each integer of multiplying/dividing by 10 or 100.

Independent work
● Working in pairs, children should generate two-digit numbers using number cards and record the effect of multiplying by 10 then by 100. One group of children could use the Dice tool to generate numbers, recording results in a table.
● Challenge children to write a list of four-digit numbers that can be divided by both 10 and 100.
● Less able learners should generate unit numbers, and write three-digit numbers that can be divided by both 10 and 100.
● More able learners should generate three-digit numbers, and write five-digit numbers which can be divided by both 10 and 100.

Plenary
● Ask questions such as: *How many times larger is 350 than 35? How many £1 coins are there in £25, £250, £2500? How many 10p coins in each amount? How did you work that out?* Write the multiplication and division by 10, 100 and 1000 as appropriate for each of these questions.

Learning objective
- Round any positive integer less than 1000 to the nearest 10 or 100.

Resources
'City distances' flipchart file.

Links to other subjects
Geography
QCA Unit 18 'Connecting ourselves to the world'
- Children can use maps and the internet to find places in the world and compare distances between them.

Rounding

Starter

Display page 2 of the flipchart. Agree the rules for rounding to the nearest ten: unit digit of five to nine rounds up; unit digit of one to four rounds down. Write the rules on to the flipchart. Explain that you will say a two-digit number. Ask the children to decide whether to round it up or down to the nearest ten. If it rounds up, ask them to point up; if it rounds down, they point down. Keep the pace of this sharp.

Whole-class shared work

- Go to page 3. Explain that you will write a three-digit number on to the table. Challenge the children to round it up or down to the nearest ten, then the nearest hundred, recording the answers in the appropriate columns.
- Display page 4 of the flipchart. Ask: *To round these distances, is it more sensible to round to the nearest 10 or 100 miles? Why do you think that?*
- Delete the box with the heading *Round to 10 or 100?* to reveal the heading *Rounded to nearest 10.*
- Invite the children to round some of these distances to the nearest ten. Move the spyglass over the answers column to reveal the correct answers.
- Repeat for the map and distances on page 5.

Independent work

- This should take no longer than ten minutes. Allow extra time for the Plenary.
- Display page 6 of the flipchart, showing the larger distances for Europe. Ask: *Is it more sensible to round the distance between ... and ... to the nearest 10 or 100? Why do you think that?*
- Explain that you will use this page to look at distances between London and various cities in Europe. Tell the children to write down the cities and the distances.
- Now ask them to round these distances to the nearest 10 miles and 100 miles and to record their results.
- Work with the less able learners to check that they understand the rounding rules. Challenge the more able learners to undertake a web search to find further distances for the Plenary.

Plenary

- Review the roundings from the Independent work. Discuss which would be more sensible: rounding by 10 or by 100 for each distance.
- Use page 7 to round by both 10 and by 100 to observe the effect. Write the rounded distances in the first column under each heading.
- Move the spyglass over the second column under each heading to reveal the answers. For each example, ask: *Would it be more sensible to round by 10 or by 100? Why do you think that?*

Whiteboard tools

 Pen tool

 Marquee select tool

 Recognition tool

Fractions

Learning objectives
● Use fraction notation.
● Recognise simple fractions that are several parts of a whole (such as $2/3$ or $5/8$), and mixed numbers (such as $5\ 3/4$).
● Recognise the equivalence of simple fractions (such as fractions equivalent to $1/2$, $1/4$ or $3/4$).

Resources
Centimetre-squared paper and pens.

Links to other subjects
ICT
QCA Unit 4B 'Developing images using repeating patterns'
● Children can follow up this work by using the shapes made by their fractions to create repeating patterns.

Starter
Use the Fraction creator tool ⓵ to write $1/2$ on a blank flipchart page. Ask the children to suggest another fraction that is equivalent to this, for example, $2/4$. Now write $1/10$ and ask them how many tenths make one whole. Repeat this for other fractions, such as $1/4$, $1/5$ or $1/8$. Write $3/10$ and ask: *How many more tenths do I need to make one whole?* Repeat for other fractions such as $2/5$ or $7/8$.

Whole-class shared work
● Draw an empty number line on to the whiteboard. Label one end 0 and the other 1. Invite a child to write in where they estimate $1/2$ should go. Now ask where $2/4$ will go. Agree that $1/2$ and $2/4$ are equivalent.
● Repeat this for other pairs of fractions, such as $1/5$ and $2/10$; $1/4$ and $2/8$; $3/4$ and $6/8$.
● Draw a set of eight triangles using the Shapes tool 🔷. Ask: *How many triangles are there? So how many would $5/8$ be? What about three-quarters?* Allow the children to drag and drop the shapes to count them if necessary. Repeat for other sets of shapes.
● Extend to mixed numbers, such as $2\ 3/4$, by drawing two sets of four shapes, and then three more.

Independent work
● Explain that you will write some fractions on to the whiteboard. Challenge the children to draw the fraction, using centimetre-squared paper. For example, if you wrote $1/4$, the children would draw a shape with four squares and shade one square. Then ask them to draw a shape for, and write, an equivalent fraction. For example, they could draw a shape with twelve squares and shade three of them, and write the equivalent fraction $3/12$.
● Write up the following fractions: $1/4$, $1/3$, $2/3$, $1/5$, $3/5$, $1/8$, $5/8$, $1/10$ and $7/10$, using the Fraction creator tool. Ask the children to continue the exercise using these.
● Decide whether less able learners should work as a group. The children could model each fraction using counters.
● Challenge more able learners by extending the range of fractions to include ninths and twelfths.

Plenary
● Review each fraction. Ask the children to suggest equivalents. These can be drawn on to the board using shapes made of squares with the fractions shaded using the Fill tool 🪣.
● Say: *Tell me an equivalent fraction for $2/6$; $4/6$; $4/8$* and so on. Insert an empty number line and mark one end 0 and the other 1. Say: *Where does $1/2$; $1/4$; $3/8$; $5/10$ (and so on) fit?* Invite a child to mark up the fractions.
● Encourage the children to suggest some fractions that are greater than $1/2$ and to write these on to the number line.

Whiteboard tools
Use the Fraction creator (from the Special tools menu), the Shapes and Fill tools to demonstrate fractions. Find a number line in the mathematics folder in the Resource library.

⓵ Fraction creator tool

🔷 Shapes tool

🔲 Marquee select tool

✏ Pen tool

🪣 Fill tool

📖 Resource library

Difference

Learning objective
● Find a small difference by counting up.

Resources
Individual whiteboards and pens.
Prepare a flipchart file. Use the Rubber stamp tool to insert 22 birds from the Resource library on to the page. Insert text: *22 birds are in a pet shop. 18 are bought in a week, so how many are left.* Prepare two more problems with text only. Use differences of nine or less.

Links to other subjects
English
NLS Term 1 S5: To practise using commas to mark grammatical boundaries within sentences
● Ask the children to incorporate difference problems within sentences, using commas appropriately.

Whiteboard tools
Use the Clock tool's Count down function to keep the pace brisk in the Starter. Select a number line from the mathematics folder in the Resource library.

🖉 Pen tool

🔖 Rubber stamp tool

📖 Resource library

⏱ Count down tool

Starter
Display the first page of your prepared flipchart. Talk the children through the problem. Ask them to write the difference on to their whiteboards, and, when you say *Show me,* hold up their boards for you to see. Limit their response time by setting the Count down tool ⏱. Repeat using the following pages of your prepared file, showing problems without illustrations. Ask how children worked out each answer and discuss the strategies used.

Whole-class shared work
● Explain that you will be using the whiteboard to model finding small differences between pairs of numbers. Insert an empty number line (from the Resource library) on to the board and write *95 – 88 = ?*
● Ask: *How can we use the empty number line to help us to work this out?* Agree this:

● Repeat for other pairs of two-digit and three-digit integers, such as 97 and 106, 388 and 407, or 9000 and 8994.
● Now ask the children to work out mentally the differences between pairs of numbers that you say. Encourage them to count up in the same way that they have done with the empty number line. They can write their answer on to their whiteboards and hold these up for you to see.

Independent work
● Write the following integers on a blank flipchart page: 106; 507; 631; 5000; 6994. Ask the children to find the integers that have a difference of 8, 12 and 15 with these numbers. So, for 106 they would write: 98 and 114; 94 and 118; 91 and 121.
● Ask the children to choose a pair of numbers with a small difference and write a word problem using these numbers.
● For less able learners, provide a separate list of two-digit integers.
● Challenge more able learners to choose their own pairs of four-digit integers with a difference of 14.
● Encourage the children to use a mental, rather than written, number line where possible.

Plenary
● Review the children's answers. Discuss how they calculated, and whether they used a mental or written number line.
● Invite a child from each ability group to read out their word problem for the others to solve. Establish how they solved the problem. Discuss how, by counting up, it is possible to find small differences quickly and easily.

🗔 **73**

Remainders

Learning objective
● Find remainders after division.

Resources
Two sets of 0 to 9 number cards for each pair; exercise books and pens.
Prepare a flipchart file. Use the Rubber stamp tool to insert 23 pictures of sheep.
Write: *A farmer sorts 23 sheep into 4 pens. He wants the same number of sheep in each pen. How many sheep will be left over?*

Links to other subjects
Design and technology
QCA Unit 4B 'Storybooks'
● Ask the children to work out how many book pages they can cut from a piece of card. Encourage them to use division to find the answer.

Starter
Explain that you will ask some division questions. Ask the children to use their multiplication table facts to help them to find the answers. Ask, for example: *What is 40 divided by 5? 30 divided by 3? 45 divided by 9?* Ask questions where there is no remainder. If any children are unsure of the answer to a question, use an empty number line from the Resource library to demonstrate counting up in equal groups. (For example, for 56 divided by 8, count up 7 × 8 times to reach 56.)

Whole-class shared work
● Display your prepared flipchart with the 23 sheep. Write on the board 23 ÷ 4 and ask for the answer. Agree that 4 × 5 = 20, so the answer is 5 remainder 3.
● Repeat for other examples but without using illustrations. If any children are unsure, use near table facts and empty number lines to demonstrate the nearest multiple.
● Extend this to questions which lie outside the normal range of table facts, such as 63 ÷ 5 or 46 ÷ 3. Ask the children to give the multiplication each time, such as 63 ÷ 5=12 remainder 3; 63 = (12 × 5) + 3.
● Over time, extend to include division of three-digit integers.

Independent work
● Ask the children to work in pairs. Explain that you would like them to generate two-digit integers using the number cards. Each integer should be divided by 2, then 3, 4, 5, 6, 7 and 10. Ask the children to record each division on paper, and show any remainders. Encourage them to generate at least five numbers and write the divisions.
● Decide whether to limit the range of divisions to those by 2, 3, 4, 5 and 10 for less confident learners.
● Challenge more able learners to include divisions by 8 and 9.

Plenary
● Ask the class to work in pairs. Explain that you will say a remainder. Challenge each pair to write five different division sentences that contain this remainder.
● Give the children a couple of minutes and then ask each pair, in turn, to come to the whiteboard and write up one of their divisions.
● Explain that each division must be different from any that have gone before. When the children have run out of ideas, repeat the activity for a different remainder.

Whiteboard tools
Display empty number lines from the Resource library to explain the mental strategy. Use the Rubber stamp tool to duplicate images.

 Pen tool

 Rubber stamp tool

Resource library

Number puzzle

Learning objective
● Solve mathematical problems or puzzles, recognise and explain patterns and relationships, generalise and predict. Suggest extensions by asking *What if...?*

Resources
Monty (available from the DfES website: **www. standards.dfes.gov.uk**). For the Starter: set to grid 1 and a ten seconds delay. For Whole-class shared work: set to grid 3 and a 120 seconds delay. For Independent work: reduce the time to about 20 seconds delay. Paper and pencils.

Links to other subjects
ICT
QCA Unit 4D 'Collecting and presenting information: questionnaires and pie charts'
● When children collect numerical data, ask them to search for any number patterns in the data.

Starter
Explain that the children should look at the *Monty* grid and identify the way the numbers are ordered. They will have ten seconds to do this. Click on the box next to the word *Monty* to start, and after a few seconds click anywhere on the screen. Invite the children to suggest which numbers *Monty* is concealing and use your computer keyboard to type these into the box at the top of the screen. Encourage the children to explain their thinking. Repeat, clicking on Start to use another grid 1.

Whole-class shared work
● Display grid 3. Explain that the children will have 120 seconds to look at the grid and understand how the numbers work.
● Start *Monty* and when he stops, invite the children to say which numbers the snake is covering and to explain their thinking. Type the numbers into the box.
● Reveal the grid again, by clicking on Grid. Children can check if they identified correctly where their chosen numbers are.
● Repeat this for another grid 3.
● Now show a different grid 3 and let *Monty* start. Click on the screen to stop him.
● Encourage the children to explain carefully why they think that particular numbers are under *Monty*. Ask: *Why do you think the number ... is under Monty? Do you all agree? Why/why not?*
● Repeat this for other grid 3s.

Independent work
● Ask the children to work in pairs. They will need paper and pencils.
● Display another grid 3. Ask them to agree the number range and to try to spot the pattern.
● Stop *Monty* and invite the pairs to discuss and write down all the numbers that they think are under him.
● Take feedback, asking questions such as: *How did you work out that ... was under Monty? Does this give us a clue about other numbers that are under Monty? Tell me some numbers that you are sure are not under Monty. How do you know that?*
● Reveal the grid again, by clicking on Grid. Children can check if they identified correctly where their chosen numbers are.
● All children can tackle this task. Less able learners can work as a group with an adult. More able learners can be challenged to explain in further detail how they made their decisions.

Plenary
● Display a grid 5, counting in ones. This is more difficult, and will give a diagonal pattern of numbers, starting in the top-right corner.
● Invite the children to say how the number pattern is displayed.
● Repeat the *Monty* activity, again asking children to suggest what numbers are hidden by *Monty*.
● Ask questions such as: *Tell me some numbers that are not under Monty. Where do you think these numbers will be?*
● Reveal the grid again, by clicking on Grid, to show the answers.

Whiteboard tools
Run the program *Monty* while in Desktop mode.

 Desktop mode

Return to main screen

 Marquee select tool

Learning objective
● Solve a problem by collecting quickly, organising, representing and interpreting data in tables, charts, graphs and diagrams, including those generated by a computer, for example: bar charts – intervals labelled in twos, fives, tens or twenties.

Resources
'Bar charts' flipchart file; small safety mirrors; large sheets of sugar paper.

Links to other subjects
Citizenship
QCA Unit 6 'Developing our school grounds'
● Follow up this work by undertaking a school-wide survey about opinions on changes that could be made to the school grounds. They can record data using tally charts and create bar charts from these.

Whiteboard tools
Use the Highlighter tool to draw attention to data in the bar charts. Use the Marquee select tool to alter the height of the bars in the bar chart. Double-click on text and select the Edit text button in the Object edit toolbox to amend the headings and labels for the bar chart.

 Highlighter tool

 Pen tool

 Marquee select tool

 Edit text tool

 Page reset button

Bar charts

Starter
Open page 2 of the flipchart and prompt the children with questions to analyse the bar chart and the data that it represents:
- *What is the title of this bar chart? What do you think it will tell us?*
- *What is the scale?*
- *How many children went on holiday to ...?*
- *Which was the most/least popular destination?*
- *How many fewer/more children went to ... than ...?*
- *If everybody went on holiday, how many children are in the school?*

Whole-class shared work
- Discuss the survey question on page 3 of the flipchart.
- Give each child a small safety mirror. Ask them to count their own teeth and make a note of the result.
- Discuss how to gather the data. Children could put their hands up if they have 20 teeth, 21 teeth, and so on.
- When the data has been gathered, reveal the blank bar chart on page 4. Ask children to suggest the title and axes headings.
- Discuss what scale should be used, and why. (This is likely to be in twos or fives, but will depend upon the data gathered.)
- Edit the headings and complete the bar chart. Discuss any data that needs a fraction of a bar and how this can be represented.
- Discuss the data and highlight comparisons. Ask questions such as: *How many children have ... teeth? Are there more/fewer children with ... teeth than ...?*

Independent work
- Ask the children to work in mixed ability groups of four or five. Each group will collect data about the colour of the family car from a different class in the school. (You will need to agree this with the relevant teachers beforehand).
- Children should agree how to collect the data and what the headings on their tally chart should be.
- Once they have collected the data, they should use it to make a bar chart on large sheets of sugar paper. They should agree the scale, the title and the axes headings.
- Allow one group to use the bar chart file on page 4 of the flipchart.
- Encourage more able learners to support those who are less able.

Plenary
- Invite each group, in turn, to show their data.
- Reset the bar chart on page 4 to compile a collective bar chart, using all of the data that the children have collected.
- Invite the children to suggest axes headings, scale and title.
- Ask questions about the data, such as: *How many more red than blue cars are there? Which is the most popular colour? How would the chart look if we changed the scale to ...? Would this be helpful? Why/Why not? Is the data from each class the same? Why not?*
- Make a note of the children's observations on page 5.

When?

Learning objective
● Read simple timetables and use this year's calendar.

Resources ●
'Calendar and timetable' flipchart file; photocopiable page 96 'When?' for each child. (Microsoft Excel is required to view the embedded calendar spreadsheet in the flipchart.)

Links to other subjects
ICT
QCA Unit 4D 'Collecting and presenting information: questionnaires and pie charts'
● Ask the children to collect dates and of birthdays from friends and family. They can then use this year's calendar to find out the day each birthday will fall upon.

Starter
Display page 2 of the flipchart 'Calendar and timetable'. Remind the children of the months of the year and, together, arrange them in the correct order.

Whole-class shared work
● Display the month of January on page 3 and ask: *What day of the month is the seventh of January? How many days has January? How many Sundays are there in this month?* Ask the children to come up and highlight some of the answers. Continue asking questions about January and its dates, to check that the children can read the calendar for a month correctly.
● Go to another month (the months of the year are on pages 3 to 14) and ask children to highlight different dates. Ask questions such as: *What date is the third Tuesday in April? How many Wednesdays are there in September?... How many days between ... and ...? How many weeks between ... and ...?*
● Some days have special symbols on them. Ask: *What is this symbol? Why does this day have a special symbol? What special day is it?*
● Some symbols have been supplied at the bottom of the relevant pages. Invite the children to drag the symbols to the correct day on the calendar. The symbol can be duplicated if the celebration lasts for several days.
● Click on the text on page 15 to open the calendar in a spreadsheet format. Explain that this shows the same year, but in a different format. Ask questions about the composition of the year: number of months, weeks, days. Discuss leap years and how and why these have an extra day.
● Go to page 16 of the flipchart. Can children explain how to read the bus timetable?
● Ask questions about the data. For example: *How long does it take to get from ... to ...? Which bus should I catch if I want to get the train that leaves at 10.48?*

Independent work
● Explain that the individual work is in two parts and that you will give the children ten minutes for each part. Provide each child with the photocopiable sheet.
● Provide the children with printouts of the calendar to help them with answering the calendar questions.
● After ten minutes change to the bus timetable for the children to answer the rest of the questions.
● Decide whether to work with less able learners as a group. Check that the children can read and interpret calendars and simple timetables.
● Challenge more able learners to make up further questions about the calendar.

Whiteboard tools
Use the Highlighter tool to highlight relevant dates and times. Use the Clock tool's Count down function to time the first part of the Independent work.

 Marquee select tool

 Pen tool

 Highlighter tool

 Count down tool

 Duplicate

Return to main screen

Plenary
● Review each of the questions from the photocopiable sheet. Display the calendar or timetable as appropriate, and invite children to point to the relevant information.
● Highlight relevant data, such as, for question 3, all the Mondays in July.
● Invite more confident learners to read out their further questions for the other children to answer. Again, highlight relevant data on the calendar.
● Go to page 17 to access hyperlinked pages that show the answers.

Reflections

Starter

Explain that you will be asking the children to draw the reflection of an image. Display page 2 of the flipchart. Discuss what a reflection is and how you would draw one. Ask the children to draw the image on page 2 on to squared paper, using the lines to help, and to put in the mirror line. Invite individual children to describe lines of the image using vocabulary such as *horizontal* and *vertical.* Then ask the children to draw the reflection of the image on their squared paper. Ask them to show you this, then invite them to explain how the reflection is the same as, and different from, the original image. Invite individuals to come up and draw the reflective image on to the flipchart page.

Click on the arrow to check the answer. This will take you to the next page, which shows the reflected image of the shape. Repeat for the shape on the next page of the flipchart (page 4), checking the reflected image on page 5.

Whole-class shared work
● Go page 6 of the flipchart.
● Invite the children to draw the image on squared paper and then to sketch its reflection.
● Ask individuals to come up and draw the reflection on the whiteboard. Click on the arrow to reveal the correct reflection on the next page.
● Use the squares on the grid or the Ruler tool 📏 to compare the distances between the mirror line and points on the image, and the mirror line and the reflected point.
● Encourage the children to do the same with their rulers.
● Discuss how equivalent points on the image and its reflection are the same distance from the mirror, or line of symmetry.
● Repeat for the next images on pages 8, 10 and 12 (the correct reflections are on pages 9, 11 and 13).

Independent work
● Provide each child with a copy of photocopiable page 97, a ruler and a safety mirror.
● Ask them to complete the sheet individually, but say that they can compare and discuss what they are doing with a partner.
● Decide whether to bring less able learners together as a group and to discuss what they see on the sheet. Encourage them to use the vocabulary of symmetry as they describe shapes and lines.
● Challenge more able learners to work in pairs. Using squared paper they can draw an image of their own, then swap sheets and draw the reflection of their partner's image.

Plenary
● Invite individuals to come up and draw their images on page 14. Ask another child to draw the reflected image.
● Reset the page and repeat this several times.

Negative numbers

Learning objective
● Recognise negative numbers in context (for example, on a number line, on a temperature scale).

Resources
'Thermometer' flipchart file; today's newspaper; photocopiable page 98 'Negative numbers' for each child.

Links to other subjects
Geography
QCA Unit 24 'A passport to the world'
● Follow up your work on negative temperatures by looking at an area in the world that is cold (below 0°C).
● Encourage children to compare the temperatures of home and the chosen area.
Science
QCA Unit 4C 'Keeping warm'
● Talk about how weather affects body temperature – what do you need to do to maintain body temperature.

Starter
Ask the children to count in ones from 10 to 100 and back again. Continue the exercise, counting up from 0 to 10, then back beyond 0. If children find counting back beyond zero difficult, use the empty number line on page 2 of the flipchart, writing the numbers on the line as they say them.

Repeat this for other starting and finishing numbers which use both positive and negative numbers.

Reset the page and invite children to estimate and write on the number line where 10 would go, and then 4, 0, -3 and so on.

Whole-class shared work
● Display the thermometer on page 3 and introduce the concept of temperature.
● Move on to discuss where children have seen negative numbers used, such as on thermometers, and the temperatures in colder climates.
● Go to page 4, activating the Reveal tool beforehand to focus on the first thermometer. Ask the children to read the temperature. Agree that the temperature is marked in degrees Celsius and that the top of the alcohol line marks the temperature.
● Reveal the next thermometer and repeat, drawing attention to the negative numbers.
● Display the thermometers on page 5. Adjust the shape on the alcohol line and mark in two readings, such as -4 on one and +6 on the other. Invite the children to find the difference between the two readings. Reset the page and repeat for other pairs of readings where one is negative and one positive.

Independent work
● Provide each child with a copy of the photocopiable sheet. Ask them to use what they know about reading and comparing temperatures to find the answers to the thermometer problems and word problems. Suggest that children draw their own number line to help, if necessary.
● Work with less confident learners as a group. Use the empty number line on page 2 to act as an aid. Mark in 0 and the negative and positive temperatures.
● Challenge more confident learners to find out about world temperatures from today's newspaper, and to find the difference in temperature between London and the coldest and hottest places.

Plenary
● Review the answers to the questions on the photocopiable sheet. Invite children to explain how they worked out the answers, such as using an empty number line, or mental counting up.
● Invite the more confident learners to give the maximum and minimum temperatures that they have found in the newspaper for others to find the difference.

Whiteboard tools
Use the Reveal tool to show the thermometers one at a time.

 Reveal tool

 Pen tool

Marquee select tool

Page reset button

Multiples

Learning objective
● Recognise multiples of 2, 3, 4, 5 and 10 up to the tenth multiple.

Resources P
Number grid Interactive Teaching Program, set numbers 1–100; photocopiable page 99 'Hundred square', one for each pair; coloured crayons; individual whiteboards and pens.
Counter software: set to count in twos, threes, fours, fives and tens, starting from zero, with Controls not showing. Then set the count to start from a small number. (*Counter* software is available on the CD-ROM in the *Using ICT to support mathematics in primary school* training pack (DfES references: DfES0260/ 2000 for entire training pack; DfES0267/2000 for CD-ROM only).

Links to other subjects
Art and design
QCA Unit 3B 'Investigating pattern'
● Follow up this work by getting children to create a patchwork pattern based on the patterns they have created in their hundred squares.
ICT
QCA Unit 4B 'Developing images using repeating patterns'
● Challenge children to recreate and repeat the patterns they find in hundred squares, for different multiples, using the computer.

Whiteboard tools
 Highlighter tool

 Activities explorer

 Marquee select tool

 Desktop mode

 Return to main screen

Starter
Begin with multiples of two. Explain that *Counter* will make a number pattern. Ask the children to identify what the next number will be, and the next, and so on. Ask them to say which multiplication table the pattern belongs to. Repeat for other tables. Then repeat, but this time starting from a different number.

Whole-class shared work
● Go to Activities explorer and select KS2 DFES NNS ITP. Display the *Number grid* ITP.
● Ask the children to identify multiples. Begin with multiples of two, set the Highlighter tool to green, highlight the multiples as the children say these, or ask individuals to come up and highlight them. Go up to 30.
● Repeat for multiples of three, up to 30, this time highlighting in pink. Invite the children to suggest which multiples will be common to both the two- and three-times tables.
● Repeat for multiples of five, highlighted in red, and ten, in yellow.
● Ask: *Which numbers are in both the two- and three-times tables? The two- and five-times tables? The three- and five-times tables? Which number is in all of these tables?* (30.)
● Ask the children to write on their individual whiteboards all the table facts with a product of 30. Discuss how one integer can be formed from different multiples.

Independent work
● Ask the children to work in pairs and give each pair a copy of the photocopiable sheet.
● Tell them they are going to continue the multiplication patterns from 30 to 100. Explain that they should use the same colours for the multiples as used on the hundred square on the whiteboard.
● Before they start, ask the pairs to make a list of the numbers that they think will be products in all of the two-, three-, five- and ten-times tables (60 and 90).
● Challenge the more able learners to continue the patterns beyond 100. (Note that the ITP can be set to start from any number you wish.)
● Work with the less able learners as a group, using the hundred square on the whiteboard. Discuss how to count on to find the next multiple using the hundred square.

Plenary
● Ask the children questions about the number patterns that they have found. For example
  ● *Which numbers are multiples of two and three? two and five? two, three and five?*
  ● *Which numbers did you predict would be products in all of the two-, three-, five- and ten-times tables? Did you make a good prediction?*
  ● *Which number do you think will be the next product that is in the two-, three-, five- and ten-times tables?* (120.) *How did you work that out?*

Money

Learning objective
● Understand decimal notation and place value for tenths and hundredths, and use it in context. For example: order amounts of money; convert a sum of money such as £13.25 to pence.

Resources
Toy Shop software (Available on the CD-ROM in the *Using ICT to support mathematics in primary school* training pack, DfES references: DfES0260/2000 for entire training pack; DfES0267/2000 for CD-ROM only. Also available through: **www.standards.dfes.gov.uk).** Set to the third level (up to £2.49); name the players Team 1 and Team 2. Individual whiteboards and pens.

Links to other subjects
History
QCA Unit 9 'What was it like for children in the Second World War?'
● Children can use what they have learned in this lesson to find out about the cost of different types of food in the Second World War, and compare to today's prices.

Starter
Write: *£12, £15, £8, 40p, 70p, 90p, 3p, 8p, 1p* on a blank flipchart page. Point to one amount for pounds, then one for tens of pence, then one unit pence and ask the children to write on their whiteboards how much this comes to in total, using the £ and decimal point signs. When you say *Show me,* the children show you their boards. Repeat for other examples, including some where there are no unit pence, and others where there are no tens of pence.

Whole-class shared work
● Play the *Toy Shop* game in two teams. A toy is selected and the price displayed. The teams take it in turns to tender a coin to buy a toy. The team who offer the coin that makes up the correct price win. You need to click on *New game* to get a new item.
● Discuss how the amounts of money are displayed, using the £ sign and the decimal point.
● Keep a list of toys and amounts of money paid.
● When you have finished playing the game, choose two of these amounts and ask how they would total these.
● Demonstrate some of the methods, including formal pencil and paper methods.
● Repeat, this time asking for totals and change from £10.

Independent work
● Ask the children to work in pairs and to take turns in the following activity.
● One child says an amount of money. The other child first counts it out using as few coins as possible. Then he or she finds the change for the amount from £15. The amount of money should be recorded as a decimal fraction of £s. The change from £15, and the method used to work it out, should also be recorded.
● Give more able learners a maximum of £20 and less able a maximum of £5 or £10.
● Discuss with different pairs what they are doing. Ask: *How do you know you have found the least number of coins? How did you calculate the change*

Plenary
● Play the *Toy Shop* game again and keep a points score of which team wins each round. Play six rounds and keep a list of the amounts of money.
● Challenge the children to work in pairs to find a way to total these amounts and to calculate the change from £20. Ask questions such as: *How did you calculate the total? How did you calculate the change? Ask the children to demonstrate their methods.*

Whiteboard tools
Run the *Toy Shop* game when in Desktop mode.

⬚ Desktop mode

▣ Pen tool

▦ Return to main screen

Totalling multiples of ten

Learning objective
● Add three two-digit multiples of 10, such as 40 + 70 + 50.

Resources
A set of 1-9 number cards for each pair; *Number grid* Interactive Teaching Program (ITP); exercise books and pens.

Links to other subjects
English
NLS Term 1 S5: To practise using commas to mark grammatical boundaries within sentences; link to work on editing and revising own writing
● When children write down their word problems, encourage them to use commas correctly, and to revise and edit their work.

Starter
Ask questions about adding tens to make a total of 100. For example: *What is 30 add 70? What is the difference between 100 and 80?* Keep the pace sharp. If children are unsure, model the question using an empty number line from the Resource library, or the *Number grid* ITP. (Go to Activities explorer 🔘 and click on KS2 DFES NNS ITP.)

Whole-class shared work
● Write 5 + 2 + 4 and ask for the total. Now write 50 +20 + 40 and ask: *How can we find the solution to this?* Remove the zeros to demonstrate the link with the first question. Children may suggest totalling 50 and 40, then adding 20. Use the empty number line to demonstrate the addition.
● Compare the two totals of 11 and 110. Remind the children that, when totalling multiples of tens, they can check by totalling just the tens digit and multiplying by ten.
● Repeat for other examples and time children's responses using the Count down tool 🔘. Use the empty number line to model each example.
● Make up a word problem. Ask the children to solve the problem and to explain how they found the answer. Repeat for another word problem.

Independent work
● Ask the children to work in pairs with a set of 1 to 9 number cards.
● They should choose three cards, multiply each number by ten, write down these decade numbers and find the total. For each addition, they write a word problem. Give them time to write five or six word problems. One group of children can use the Dice tool 🔘 to generate their numbers on the whiteboard.
● Now ask the children to work in fours, but not with their partner. They must take turns to say one of their word problems for the others to solve.
● Give each group of four a couple of minutes to invent another two word problems, using addition of multiples of tens.
● Provide less able learners with empty number lines to model the additions.
● More able learners can try adding four two-digit multiples of ten.

Plenary
● Invite each group to ask the whole class to solve one of their problems. Encourage them to explain how they found the answer? Model this, as necessary, using an empty number line.
● Repeat, until all the word problems have been tried by the other children.
● Challenge the children to total four decade numbers and to explain how they worked this out. Try, for example, 40 + 70 + 60 + 20. (40 + 60 = 100; 70 + 20 = 90; 100 + 90 = 190.)

Whiteboard tools
Select number lines and number buttons from the mathematics folder in the Resource library to demonstrate the addition. Use the Clock tool's Count down function to put a time limit on children's responses.

🔘 Count down tool

🔘 Pen tool

🔘 Dice tool

🔘 Resource library

🔘 Activities explorer

🔘 Recognition tool

Using + and - mental strategies

Learning objective
● Use known number facts and place value to add or subtract mentally, including any pair of two-digit whole numbers.

Resources
Photocopiable page 100 'Add and subtract' for each child.

Links to other subjects
Science
QCA Unit 4B 'Habitats'
● Children can use mental methods to find the overall total of different organisms they find in a given area.

Starter
Invite a child to use the Dice tool 🎲 to generate a teen number. Ask children to suggest addition and subtraction sentences with this integer as the answer (for example, 17: 19 - 2 = 17 and 9 + 8 = 17) and write them up. When several number sentences are on the board, ask the children to use these to find others. Ask: *How did you use what you can see to find this?*

Whole-class shared work
● Explain that the children will use mental methods to total pairs of two-digit whole numbers. Begin by totalling decade numbers, such as 50 + 70.
● Ask children how this might be calculated and record their suggestions. For example: 50 + 50 + 20 = 120.
● Discuss why the methods work. Repeat for other examples. Include subtraction, such as 160 - ☐ = 90.
● Move on to examples where one number is a decade and the other not, such as 43 + 60 and ☐ - 60 = 43. Discuss different methods. If children are unsure, demonstrate with an empty number line.
● If children are confident with the above, then extend to adding or subtracting any pair of two-digit numbers, such as 56 + 39 and 95 - ☐ = 39. Record methods and, where necessary, use the empty number line to demonstrate a mental method of counting up or back.

Independent work
● Provide each child with the photocopiable sheet. Ask them to think about how they solve the questions and to be ready in the Plenary to explain their chosen methods.
● Remind the less able learners that they can draw empty number lines to help them to work mentally.
● More able learners can write a set of four number sentences for each of the open questions at the end of the photocopiable sheet, using the same numbers for each set. This will produce two add and two subtract sentences.
● Target children to ask for explanations of the mental methods they choose to use for specific questions.

Plenary
● Review the photocopiable sheet together. Invite individual children to write up their addition sentences and to explain their mental methods.
● Repeat this for the subtraction sentences.
● Ask questions such as: *How did you work this out? Who used a different method? Do you think that one of these methods is better? Why do you think that?*

Whiteboard tools
Use the Dice tool in the Special tools menu to generate random numbers.

⛏ Highlighter tool

▢ Pen tool

📖 Resource library

🎲 Dice tool

⌨ Floating keyboard

Recognition tool

Learning objectives
● Choose and use appropriate number operations and appropriate ways of calculating (mental, mental with jottings, pencil and paper) to solve problems.
● Develop and refine written methods for column addition and subtraction.

Resources 💿 🅿
'Word problems' flipchart file; photocopiable page 101 'Word problems', one for each child.

Links to other subjects
Citizenship
QCA Unit 04 'People who help us – the local police'
● Invite a police spokesperson to talk about their role. Set some further word problems which relate to police work in the community.

Solving word problems

Starter
Display page 2 of the flipchart. Read the question out loud and ask the children for the answer. Invite them to share their answers and count the legs to check. Repeat this for pages 3 and 4.

Explain that you will now ask a series of simple word problems for the children to solve mentally, without pictures. They should state the answer and explain their mental method. Say, for example: *I think of a number. I add 22 to it, and the answer is 44. What was my number?* or: *Jodie has 42 felt-tipped pens. Dilshad has half as many. How many has Dilshad?* Write the answers as number sentences on page 5.

Whole-class shared work
● Explain that the children will be solving complex word problems involving multi-step operations.
● Reveal the next problem on page 6. Ask: *What information does this give us? What do we need to find out? How can we do this?*
● Ask the children how they would complete the first step in the problem. They will need to total the books on the top and bottom shelves. Invite them to suggest which method to use. Use a pencil and paper method, writing this on the flipchart page.
● Discuss what the next step should be (subtracting the total for the two shelves from the overall total). Again, record this on the whiteboard using a pencil and paper method.
● Click on the *Answer* button to check that you are right.
● Repeat this for the other problems on pages 7 and 8.

Independent work
● Provide each child with a copy of the photocopiable sheet. Ask them to work individually to solve the first problem. They should then compare their method with a partner and discuss which method, if there is a difference, is more appropriate, and why.
● They should repeat this for the other three problems.
● Decide whether to work together as a group with less able learners. Demonstrate recording methods on paper or on the whiteboard. Ask children to write down the recording method on their sheets.
● More able learners could invent their own word problem, which should have multiple steps.

Plenary
● Review each problem from the photocopiable sheet. Invite children from each ability group to explain how they worked out the answer. Ask: *Which method do you think is best? Why do you think that?*
● Invite one child to demonstrate how they recorded by writing on page 9 of the flipchart.
● Discuss the recording method chosen and its suitability.
● Use pages 10 to 13 to check the answers and methods.
● Invite the more able learners to take turns to read out their invented word problems for the others to try to solve.

Whiteboard tools
 Pen tool

 Marquee select tool

 Recognition tool

Venn diagrams

Learning objective
● Solve a problem by collecting quickly, organising, representing and interpreting data in tables, charts, graphs and diagrams, including those generated by a computer, for example: Venn and Carroll diagrams (two criteria).

Resources
A prepared flipchart file: create a large, four-region Venn diagram using the Shapes tool. Paste several copies of the diagram on to separate pages of a prepared flipchart (four or five should be enough). Type the numbers 1 to 50, in separate text boxes, at the top of the first two pages. Individual whiteboards and pens, or pencils and paper.

Links to other subjects
Science
QCA Unit 4B 'Habitats'
● Encourage children to use Venn diagrams to record data about observable features of the organisms being grouped.

Starter
Display the first Venn diagram and write in the headings: *Multiple of 6* and *Not a multiple of 6*; *Multiple of 3* and *Not a multiple of 3*. Ask the children to suggest where each integer from 1 to 40 should fit and invite individuals to drag and drop the integers into the correct position. Discuss where each number fits: for example, twelve is both a multiple of three and six; but eight is a multiple of neither. If time allows, extend to integers up to 60.

Whole-class shared work
● Display the next Venn diagram and explain to the children that they are going to do a class task. You want them to draw a Venn diagram to sort the numbers 1 to 50 into odd numbers and multiples of seven. Help them to decide on a title and labels for the new diagram.
● Give them about five minutes to complete the task on their individual whiteboards, or with pencils and paper.
● Ask individuals to come up and sort the numbers into the Venn diagram on the flipchart.
● Discuss the numbers that fit in the intersection (numbers that are odd and are multiples of seven. For example: 35 is an odd number and it is a multiple of seven.
● Repeat on the next diagram for multiples of four and multiples of nine.

Independent work
● Set another task to sort the integers 50 to 100 into multiples of three and multiples of four.
● Ask the children to work in pairs to draw their own Venn diagrams, writing their own titles and labels.
● Ask less able learners to use the integers 1 to 50.
● Challenge more able learners to also try multiples of seven and multiples of eight for the integers 50 to 100.
● As children work, ask them to explain why particular integers fit where they do.

Plenary
● Review the task together. Go to the next Venn diagram in your prepared flipchart, and invite children to write in their headings and labels.
● Discuss any differences in wording and agree on the best form of wording.
● Discuss which numbers fit in the intersection of the Venn diagram.
● Invite the more able learners to demonstrate their challenge. Ask questions, such as: *Which integers are both a multiple of 7 and 8? What do you think will be the next one? Why do you think that?*

Whiteboard tools
Adjust the transparency of your Venn diagram by enabling Design mode, selecting Properties from the Object edit toolbox, and going to Appearance. Type numbers using the Floating keyboard.

 Highlighter tool

Pen tool

 Shapes tool

Marquee select tool

Design mode

Properties

Floating keyboard

Carroll diagrams

Learning objective
● Solve a problem by collecting quickly, organising, representing and interpreting data in tables, charts, graphs and diagrams, including those generated by a computer, for example:
Venn and Carroll diagrams (two criteria).

Resources
A prepared flipchart file: several copies (about five or six) of an empty Carroll diagram (you could use the Carroll diagrams in the 'Polygons' flipchart file: delete all the shapes and save the file under a new name). Photocopiable page 102 'Carroll diagrams', one for each child.

Links to other subjects
Science
QCA Unit 4B 'Habitats'
● Encourage children to use Carroll diagrams when they study habitats, to record data about where animals live.

Starter
Reveal the first empty Carroll diagram and write in the headings: *Even* and *Not even* (across the top); *Numbers greater than 20* and *Numbers not greater than 20* (down the side). Invite the children to suggest some numbers to fit into each box and to write these in. Continue until there are at least four or five numbers in each box. Ask: *Which number does not fit?* (20) *Why is that?* Repeat, if there is time, using different criteria, such as *Is/Is not a multiple of 5* and *Is/Is not a multiple of 4.*

Whole-class shared work
● Display the next Carroll diagram and group the children in pairs.
● Provide each pair with a photocopiable sheet. Give them the following task: sort the numbers 20 to 60 into *Is/is not even; has/has not three tens.* Remind them that they need to complete the title and region headings boxes.
● Give the children about five minutes to do this. Use the Count down tool 🔲 to time them.
● Invite the children to take turns to suggest what the title should be and what should go in the region headings boxes.
● Now encourage them to suggest which numbers go into which boxes and ask volunteers to come up and write them in.
● Repeat this for another sorting activity, such as *Is/is not a multiple of 6* and *Is less than/not less than 20.* Set the number range as 0 to 60.

Independent work
● Ask the children to continue to work in their pairs.
● Provide them with fresh copies of photocopiable page 102 'Carroll diagram'.
● Provide the criteria for sorting a range of numbers from 0 to 80, for example: *Is/is not odd* and *Numbers that are/are not multiples of 8,* or *Is/is not a multiple of 2 and 3* and *Is/is not a multiple of 4.*
● Allow less confident learners to work as a group and record on the whiteboard. Challenge more able learners to try *Is/Is not a multiple of 12* and *Is/is not a multiple of 9* for the number range 0 to 150.

Plenary
● Review each of the sortings and allow the children to write the numbers on to a fresh copy of Carroll diagram on the flipchart.
● Ask questions such as: *What do you think will be the next number that could go into the box that 'Is ...' and 'Is ...'? What properties must this number have?*
● Invite the more confident learners to show their results for the challenge. They can sort their numbers on to a Carroll diagram on the whiteboard. Challenge them to say what the next number would be that *Is a multiple of 12 and 9* after 108.

Whiteboard tools
Use the Shapes tool and the Lines tool to create Carroll diagrams. Type numbers with the Floating keyboard.

🔲 Pen tool

🔲 Count down tool

🔲 Floating keyboard

🔲 Shapes tool

🔲 Lines tool

🔲 Recognition tool

Finding positions

Learning objective
● Recognise positions and directions: for example, describe and find the position of a point on a grid of squares where the lines are numbered.

Resources
'Position and direction' flipchart file; photocopiable page 103 'Finding positions' for each child; squared paper.

Links to other subjects
Geography
QCA Unit 10 'A village in India'
● Encourage children to use maps with simple coordinate markings when they study other countries. Invite the children to give the position of key towns and cities using the coordinates and to find places from coordinates given to them.

Starter
Display the second page of the flipchart 'Position and direction'. Discuss how positions where lines cross can be written as a coordinate, and the convention for doing this: (row, column). Use a phrase, such as: *Walk along the corridor and then go up or down the stairs*, to help children remember the order. Discuss and show the children how to write the coordinate of the star.

Mark a chosen coordinate, such as (3, 2), with a cross and ask: *What is the coordinate of this point?* Agree how this should be written. Invite a child to write the coordinate in the form (3, 2). Repeat for other coordinates.

Reset the page, and name a coordinate. Invite a child to mark with a cross where it should be. Repeat for other coordinates.

Whole-class shared work
● Display page 3 of the flipchart, showing the map of an island.
● Discuss with the children what they can see on the map.
● Ask for the coordinate of the treasure chest. Invite a child to write this next to the treasure chest icon beside the map.
● Repeat for the other items on the map.
● Now ask the children to identify points where there is nothing on the map.
● The icons on the map can be moved if you wish to check their understanding of coordinates. For example, move the parrot to (5,1).
● Return to page 2 of the flipchart and delete the star.
● Mark a cross at (5, 1) and explain that you want to draw a square, four squares high.
● Ask: *What will the coordinate of the top of the line above (5, 1) be?* Mark the cross and draw the line.
● Repeat for the other two crosses and draw the lines.
● Reset the page and repeat for drawing another shape.

Independent work
● Provide each child with a copy of photocopiable page 103 'Finding positions'.
● Ask them to work individually to note the positions on the map.
● Less able learners could use an A3 enlargement of the photocopiable sheet and work together as a group. Encourage them to say the coordinates out loud, pointing to the row and column position each time.
● Ask more able learners to draw their own map, marking in special places and the coordinates for these.

Plenary
● Display page 4 of the flipchart.
● Explain that you would like to draw a rectangle on to the grid with sides that are three and six units in length.
● Give a starting point of (1, 1) and ask the children to suggest where the other crosses should go.
● Go to page 5, give a starting point of (1, 1) and this time draw a right-angled triangle. The two sides containing the right angle should both be four units in length. Discuss how one side of the triangle is a diagonal line.

Whiteboard tools
Select the Point-to-point option to draw straight lines with the Pen tool. Use the Page reset button to re-use the grid.

Pen tool

Point-to-point button

Page reset button

Marquee select tool

Learning objective
● Use the eight compass directions N, S, E, W, NE, NW, SE, SW.

Resources P
'Position and direction' flipchart file; photocopiable page 104 'Using compass directions'.

Links to other subjects
Geography
QCA Unit 8 'Improving the environment'
● Ask the children to make maps of the school on squared paper and to give coordinates and compass points. The children can use the maps to describe routes around the school and its grounds.

Using compass directions

Starter
Ask if the children can remember the names of the directions of a compass. Display the NSWE compass on page 6 of the 'Finding positions' flipchart and label it. Explain that you will draw lines to show the different angles between the directions. Ask the children to say how many right angles there are between, for example, north and west, north and south, and so on. Let them use the Protractor tool 🌓 if necessary. Delete the lines and repeat for different movements. Include clockwise and anticlockwise turns and ask the children to say in which direction the turn is.

Whole-class shared work
● Reveal the eight-point compass on page 7. Label the points for north, south, east and west.
● Explain that between, for example, north and east there is another direction. This direction is 45° from north and east and is called north-east. Label it on the compass.
● Repeat for the other directions.
● Use lines to mark an angle between north-east and south-east and ask: *How many degrees of turn is this?* Let the children use the Protractor tool if necessary.
● Repeat for other 90° turns.
● Now extend this to include turns of 135°.
● Include turns that are anticlockwise as well as clockwise.
● Reveal the 0 to 10 grid on page 8.
● Draw attention to the eight-point compass. Now ask the children to suggest how to move south-west from coordinate (8, 2) for four units. List all the coordinates and mark the points visited with crosses.
● Repeat for other directions and starting points.

Independent work
● Ask the children to work in pairs on the photocopiable sheet, taking turns to mark in the directions. They could use counters to mark their routes if they like.
● Less confident learners may need to practise using just a four-point compass.
● Suggest to more confident learners that they describe movements that combine two directions, such as south-east for three units, then north-west for four.

Plenary
● Go to page 9 of the flipchart, which shows a forest. The forest is on a grid and some of the squares contain obstacles.
● Point to a coordinate on the map and say: *Give me a route from (9, 1) in a north-westerly direction.* Explain that the children will need to think about how to move around the squares that cannot be used. List the coordinates that they suggest at the side of the whiteboard and put crosses on to the coordinates to mark the route.
● When the route is finished, draw it on to the page.
● Ask: *Was all of the route in a north-westerly direction? Tell me what was not. What direction was the rest in?*
● Reset the page and repeat for other starting coordinates and compass directions.

Whiteboard tools
Use the Point-to-point function in the Pen tool tray to mark in direction arrows on to the compass. Use the Protractor tool, in the Special tools menu, to measure the angles between compass directions.

📱 Pen tool

↥ Point-to-point button

🌓 Protractor tool

⊚ Activote (optional)

Partitioning

- ◨ Work with a partner.
- ◨ You will need a set of 0 to 9 number cards.
  - ☐ Take turns to choose four cards.
  - ☐ Both of you make a four-digit integer with the cards. Try to make your integers different!
  - ☐ Record your integer and its partition in the grid below.
  - ☐ Do this nine more times.

Integer	Thousands	Hundreds	Tens	Units

- ◨ Now write your integers again, this time using words.

1. _____
2. _____
3. _____
4. _____
5. _____
6. _____
7. _____
8. _____
9. _____
10. _____

Using the symbols < and >

- Work with a partner.
- You will need a set of 0 to 9 number cards.
  - ☐ Take turns to choose four cards.
  - ☐ Make six four-digit integers with your cards. Make a note of each number on some scrap paper.
  - ☐ Record your numbers below in the first line. Make sure you put each number in the right place!
  - ☐ Do this nine more times.

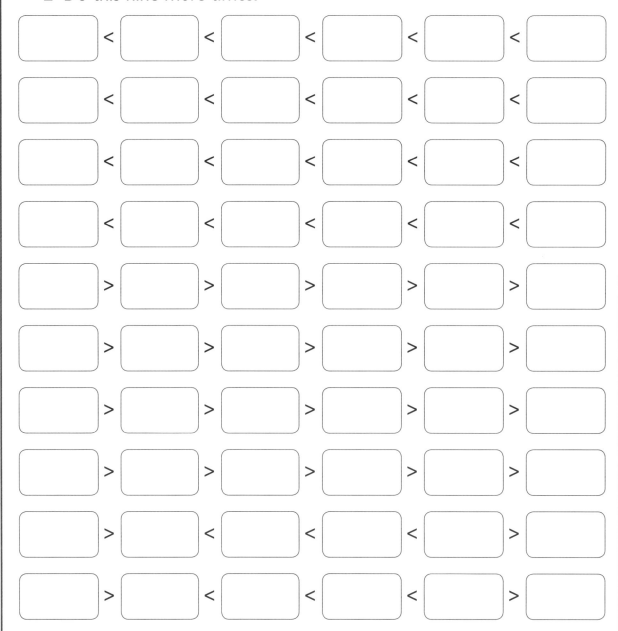

Make 100

- Work with a partner to find pairs of numbers to total 100.
- Colour each pair of numbers. Choose a different colour from your partner.

1	2	3	4	5	6	7	8	9	10
11	12	13	14	15	16	17	18	19	20
21	22	23	24	25	26	27	28	29	30
31	32	33	34	35	36	37	38	39	40
41	42	43	44	45	46	47	48	49	50
51	52	53	54	55	56	57	58	59	60
61	62	63	64	65	66	67	68	69	70
71	72	73	74	75	76	77	78	79	80
81	82	83	84	85	86	87	88	89	90
91	92	93	94	95	96	97	98	99	100

Reading scales

◢ Read the measurement on each ruler. Write the measurement to the nearest 0.5cm.

measurement _____ cm

measurement _____ cm

measurement _____ cm

measurement _____ cm

◢ Read the scale on each beaker. Record the water level to the nearest 50ml.

_____ ml　　　　　_____ ml

◢ Read the bathroom scales. Write the weight to the nearest 10kg.

_____ kg　　　　　_____ kg

How long?

- Work with a partner.
  - ☐ Look at each set of clocks in turn.
  - ☐ Work out how long between the times on the first and second clocks.
  - ☐ Write this in the box at the end of the set.
  - ☐ Write a sentence using all three clock times.

    8.42   The difference is _____

1. _____

    6.48   The difference is _____

2. _____

    12.07   The difference is _____

3. _____

    3.19   The difference is _____

4. _____

    11.24   The difference is _____

5. _____

Polygons

◼ Cut out the shape tiles.

◼ Sort them into three sets.

◼ Use each set to make a pattern. Try to leave no gaps in your pattern.

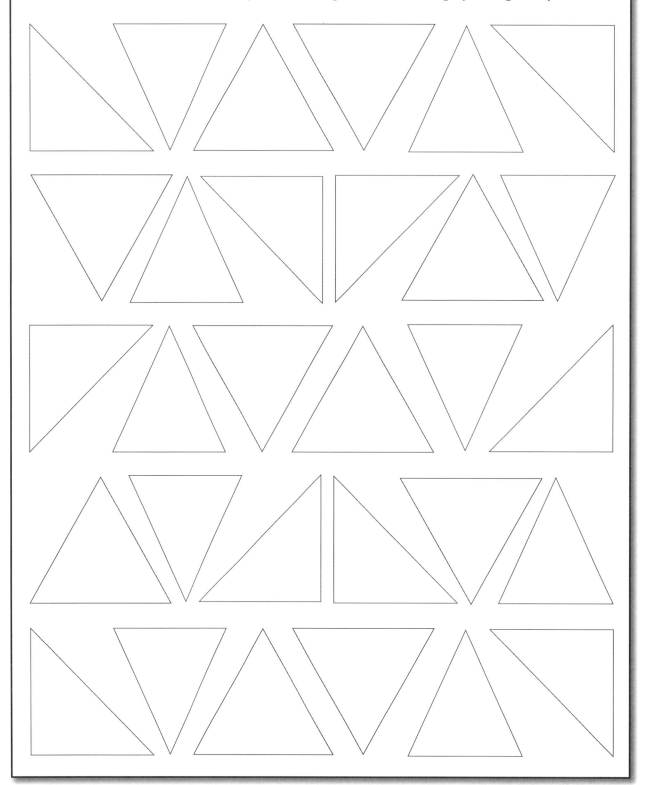

Identifying angles

- ◀ Work with a partner.
- ◀ You will need a 45° set square and a 60° set square.
- ◀ Measure these angles and write their measurements.

Measurement _____

Measurement _____

- ◀ Order these angles from smallest to largest and write their letters in order.

1. a. b. c. d.

smallest _____ largest

2. e. f. g. h.

smallest _____ largest

- ◀ Challenge!
  - ☐ On the back of this sheet, use the set squares to draw angles of 45°, 60° and 90°.

When?

◀ Use the calendar to help you to answer these questions.

1. Which months have 30 days? _____

2. On what day is 2nd August? _____

3. How many Mondays are there in July? _____

4. How many days are there between 3rd June and 24th June? _____

5. Which day of the week is New Year's Day? _____

◀ Use the timetable to help you to answer these questions.

1. How long does it take to get from Esplanade to the train station?

_____

2. How often does a bus leave Low Street? _____

3. I need to be at the bus station by half past ten. Which bus should I catch from High Street? _____

4. The 10 o'clock bus from Esplanade is running ten minutes late. What time will it get to the train station? _____

5. On Fridays the buses all run five minutes earlier than the timetable. Write the times for the buses on Fridays in this timetable.

Esplanade			
High Street			
Low Street			
Bus station			
Train station			

Name _____

Reflections

■ Draw the reflections of these shapes. You can use your ruler to check that the reflection is drawn correctly.

 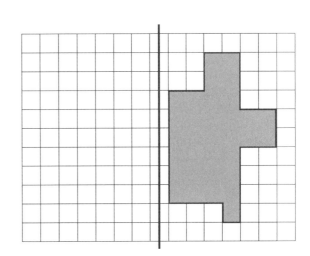

■ Now draw two images of your own. Make sure the lines are vertical or horizontal. Draw the reflection of each of your images.

 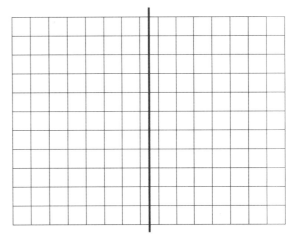

Name _____

Negative numbers

◢ Write the temperature readings for each of these thermometers.

temperature _____

temperature _____

temperature _____

temperature _____

◢ Write the difference in temperatures between these pairs of thermometers.

difference _____

difference _____

◢ The temperature in Greenland last night was –5°C.
The temperature today is 8°C.

What is the difference in temperature? _____

◢ In Ottawa in the winter, the temperature can be as
low as –11°C. Today the temperature is 11°C.

How much warmer is it today than in the winter? _____

▸ S C H O L A S T I C
www.scholastic.co.uk

Hundred square

- ◢ Circle the multiples of 2, 3, 4, 5 and 10 in different colours.
- ◢ Complete the key to record what each colour represents.

Key		multiple of 4
	multiple of 2	multiple of 5
	multiple of 3	multiple of 10

1	2	3	4	5	6	7	8	9	10
11	12	13	14	15	16	17	18	19	20
21	22	23	24	25	26	27	28	29	30
31	32	33	34	35	36	37	38	39	40
41	42	43	44	45	46	47	48	49	50
51	52	53	54	55	56	57	58	59	60
61	62	63	64	65	66	67	68	69	70
71	72	73	74	75	76	77	78	79	80
81	82	83	84	85	86	87	88	89	90
91	92	93	94	95	96	97	98	99	100

Add and subtract

- ◀ Choose a pair of numbers from the grid.
- ◀ Find their total.
- ◀ Write the addition sentence.
- ◀ Cross out your chosen numbers in the grid.
- ◀ Do this nine more times.

45	36	70	90	80	72	15	63	40	52
21	37	69	43	60	20	28	63	44	30

_____   _____   _____

_____   _____   _____

_____   _____   _____

_____

◀ Now write the answers to these subtraction sentences.

1. $90 - 30 = \boxed{}$

2. $45 - \boxed{} = 20$

3. $\boxed{} - 30 = 42$

4. $60 - \boxed{} = 19$

5. $80 - 36 = \boxed{}$

6. $\boxed{} - 37 = 56$

◀ Decide how to complete these number sentences. Make each one different.

1. $\boxed{} + \boxed{} = \boxed{}$

2. $\boxed{} + \boxed{} = \boxed{}$

3. $\boxed{} + \boxed{} = \boxed{}$

4. $\boxed{} - \boxed{} = \boxed{}$

5. $\boxed{} - \boxed{} = \boxed{}$

6. $\boxed{} - \boxed{} = \boxed{}$

Word problems

◢ Read each problem and decide how to answer it.

◢ Write your working out on the back of this sheet.

1.
> I think of a number and subtract 4. Then I multiply by 3.
> The answer is 15. What was my number? _____

Now compare with your partner.

Did you both use the same method? _____

Did you both get the same answer? _____

2.
> There are 234 red cars in the car park. The rest of the cars are silver.
> 48 cars leave. Now there are 295 cars left in the car park.
> How many silver cars were there altogether? _____

Now compare with your partner.

Did you both use the same method? _____

Did you both get the same answer? _____

3.
> There are four stacks of jotters. In the first stack there are 12 jotters.
> The second stack has twice as many as the first stack. The third stack
> has half as many as the first stack. Altogether, there are 58 jotters.
> How many jotters are there in the fourth stack? _____

Now compare with your partner.

Did you both use the same method? _____

Did you both get the same answer? _____

4.
> Sam has half as many CDs as Jon. Jon has half as many CDs as Peter. Peter
> has 48 CDs. How many CDs does Jon have? _____
> How many does Sam have? _____

Now compare with your partner.

Did you both use the same method? _____

Did you both get the same answer? _____

Carroll diagrams

Finding positions

🬀 Write the coordinates of the items on the map.

Treasure chest _____　　Tree _____

Cat _____　　　　　　　Dog _____

House _____　　　　　　Boy _____

🬀 Now put a cross on the map at these coordinates.

(4, 1)　　(4, 4)　　(1, 4)　　(1, 1)

Join the crosses with straight lines.

What shape have you made? _____

🬀 Draw a small rectangle onto the map.

Write its coordinates here. _____

🬀 Draw your own shape on the map.

Write its coordinates here. _____

Using compass directions

- Take turns to give directions to your partner. You must:
  - ☐ Write the starting coordinate.
  - ☐ Write the direction.
  - ☐ Write how many units to move.
- Your partner writes the coordinates.
- Check that you agree.
- Do this until you each have had five turns.

Starting coordinate	Direction	Number of units	Finishing coordinate

Science

The following lessons offer ways to use an interactive whiteboard to teach science, using different whiteboard tools to target different learning styles. Using an interactive whiteboard gives teachers and children a unique opportunity to project, annotate and save large-scale images.

In science lessons, the whiteboard can be used to aid practical activities such as investigations. It can also display experiments and tests that would normally not be considered safe to perform in a classroom. The use of peripherals, such as the digital microscope or the digital camera, adds an extra dimension to lessons: organisms can be observed at close proximity and habitats can be photographed for children to explore.

Using a combination of tools, the whiteboard can assist the children's structured written work: word banks, photographs and video clips can be projected on to the whiteboard as an aide-mémoire; children's results can be shared using data-handling programs and resultant bar charts or line graphs can be projected to encourage class discussions and analysis.

Lesson title	Objectives	What children should know	Cross-curricular links
Lesson 1: Similar skeletons	QCA Unit 4A 'Moving and growing' • That humans (and some other animals) have bony skeletons inside their bodies and to raise questions about different bony skeletons • To make and record relevant observations of bones and skeletons.	• That our skeletons help us to move and that they support our bodies.	**ICT** QCA Unit 4C 'Branching databases'
Lesson 2: Skeleton investigation	QCA Unit 4A 'Moving and growing' • To learn that human skeletons are internal and grow as humans grow. • To identify a question, make a prediction and test it. • To decide and make a body measurement. • To use bar charts to present measurements. • To say what the evidence shows and whether it supports the prediction.	• That our skeletons help us to move. • How to take accurate measurements.	**Mathematics** NNS: Use, read and write metric units; suggest suitable units and measuring equipment to measure length; solve problems by collecting, organising, representing and interpreting data in tables, charts, graphs and diagrams.
Lesson 3: Supporting skeletons	QCA Unit 4A 'Moving and growing' • To learn that the skeleton supports the body.	• That a skeleton protects the soft, delicate parts of an organism.	**English** NLS Term 1 S3: Identify the use of powerful verbs. NLS Term 1 S4: To identify adverbs.
Lesson 4: Muscles and bones	QCA Unit 4A 'Moving and growing' • To learn that animals with skeletons have muscles attached to the bones. • To learn that a muscle has to contract (shorten) to make a bone move. • To learn that muscles work hard when you exercise. • To make observations and comparisons relating to exercise and rest.	• That bones do not move freely on their own.	**PE** PoS (4a) How exercise affects the body in the short term; (4b) To warm up for different activities.
Lesson 5: Different organisms	QCA Unit 4B 'Habitats' • To group organisms according to observable features. • To use keys to identify plants or animals.	• That groups of organisms share similarities.	**ICT** QCA Unit 4C 'Branching databases'

Lesson title	Objectives	What children should know	Cross-curricular links
Lesson 6: Food chains ⦿ P	**QCA Unit 4B** 'Habitats' • To identify the structure of a food chain in a specific habitat. • That animals are suited to the habitat in which they are found. • That most food chains start with a green plant.	• That different animals are found in different habitats.	**Geography** QCA Unit 10 'A village in India'
Lesson 7: Different habitats	**QCA Unit 4B** 'Habitats' • That different animals are found in different habitats. • To make predictions of organisms that will be found in a habitat. • To learn that animals are suited to the environment in which they are found.	• That all organisms need a habitat, and that all habitats are different.	**Geography** QCA Unit 8 'Improving the environment' **History** PoS (2a) To learn about characteristic features of periods and societies studied.
Lesson 8: Changing habitats	**QCA Unit 4B** 'Habitats' • To recognise ways in which living things and the environment need protection.	• That all organisms need a habitat, and that all habitats are different.	**Geography** QCA Unit 21 'How can we improve the area we see from our window?' **English** NLS Term 3 T23: To present a point of view in writing.
Lesson 9: Temperature and thermometers ⦿	**QCA Unit 4C** 'Keeping warm' • That the sense of touch is not an accurate way of judging temperature. • To use a thermometer to make careful measurements of temperature. • That something hot will cool down and something cold will warm up until it is the same temperature as its surroundings. • To explain temperature and temperature changes using scientific knowledge and understanding.	• That temperature is a measure of how hot or cold things are. • The importance of accurate measurements.	**Mathematics** NNS: Record estimates and readings from scales to a suitable degree of accuracy.
Lesson 10: Keeping things cold ⦿ P	**QCA Unit 4C** 'Keeping warm ' • To turn an idea about how to keep things cold into a form that can be investigated. • To decide what evidence to collect. • To make a table and record results in it. • To draw conclusions from their results.	• What happens to food when it is taken out of the freezer.	**Geography** QCA Unit 24 'Passport to the world' **English** NLS Term 3 W7: Collect/ classify words with common roots.
Lesson 11: Keeping warm ⦿ P	**QCA Unit 4C** 'Keeping warm ' • To make careful measurements of temperature at regular time intervals. • To record results in a table and to use these to draw conclusions. • Some materials are good thermal insulators.	• How they keep themselves warm during the cold winter months.	**Geography** QCA Unit 24 'Passport to the world'
Lesson 12: Flowing materials ⦿ P	**QCA Unit 4D** 'Solids, liquids and how they can be separated' • To make careful observations and measurements of volume recording them in tables and using them to draw conclusions. • That liquids do not change in volume when they are poured into a different container. • That solids consisting of very small pieces behave like liquids in some ways.	• That liquids will run freely into a space when poured or pushed.	**Mathematics** NNS: Measure and compare using standard units (l, ml).

Lesson title	Objectives	What children should know	Cross-curricular links
Lesson 13: Mixing solids and liquids ⊙	QCA Unit 4D 'Solids, liquids and how they can be separated' • That changes occur when some solids are added to water. • To make careful observations, recording results in tables and make comparisons.	• What happens when they mix a drink such as coffee, hot chocolate, or milkshake.	**Art and design** PoS (2b) Pupils should be taught to apply their experience of materials and processes.
Lesson 14: Sieving and filtering solids	QCA Unit 4D 'Solids, liquids and how they can be separated' • That when solids do not dissolve or react with the water they can be separated by filtering. • To choose apparatus to separate an undissolved solid from a liquid.	• That when materials are mixed, a change occurs.	**ICT** QCA Unit 4D 'Collecting and presenting information'
Lesson 15: Dissolving solids	QCA Unit 4D 'Solids, liquids and how they can be separated' • That some solids dissolve in water to form solutions and that although the solid cannot be seen it is still present. • To predict whether sugar can be separated from a solution by filtering and to test the prediction. • To decide what apparatus to use. • When it is safe to taste things to test them.	• The properties of solids and of liquids.	**PSHE** PoS (3a) To consider what makes a healthy lifestyle.
Lesson 16: In a spin 🄿	QCA Unit 4E 'Friction' • That air resistance is a force that slows objects moving through air. • To plan a fair test saying what to change, what to keep the same and what to measure. • To make measurements of time. • To identify a pattern in the results and to explain it in terms of air resistance.	• That all objects when dropped from a height will fall, but that all objects do not necessarily fall in the same way.	**ICT** QCA Unit 4D 'Collecting and presenting information'
Lesson 17: Complete circuits ⊙ 🄿	QCA Unit 4F 'Circuits and conductors' • To learn that a circuit needs a power source. • To learn that a complete circuit is needed for a device to work.	• How to construct a simple circuit.	**PE** PoS (4b) To warm up and prepare appropriately.
Lesson 18: Circuits and switches ⊙	QCA Unit 4F 'Circuits and conductors' • To understand that a circuit needs a power source. • To know that a complete circuit is needed for a device to work. • That a switch can be used to make or break a circuit to turn things on or off (using batteries or mains).	• How to construct a simple circuit.	**Design and technology** QCA Unit 4E 'Lighting it up'
Lesson 19: Using switches ⊙	QCA Unit 4F 'Circuits and conductors' • To know that a circuit needs a power source and needs to be complete for a device to work. • To understand that a switch can be used to make or break a circuit to turn things on or off. • To construct a circuit with a switch.	• How to construct a simple circuit. • How switches are used in everyday life.	**English** NLS Term 1 T25: To write clear instructions. NLS Terms 1–3 T25: Identify phonemes. **Design and technology** PoS (5c) Design and make assignments using a range of materials.
Lesson 20: How bright?	QCA Unit 4F 'Circuits and conductors' • To make predictions about the effect of including additional batteries in a circuit, and check whether results support the prediction made. • That bulbs can burn out if components in a circuit are changed. • How to change the brightness of bulbs in a circuit. • To plan to change one factor and keep others constant.	• That components need power in order to work.	**Design and technology** QCA Unit 4E 'Lighting it up'

Similar skeletons

Learning objectives
QCA Unit 4A 'Moving and growing'
● That humans (and some other animals) have bony skeletons inside their bodies and to raise questions about different bony skeletons.
● To make and record relevant observations of bones and skeletons.

Resources
'Bones' flipchart file; examples of animals bones, thoroughly cleaned and sterilised (if available); photocopiable page 128 'Similar skeletons?' one for each child; pictures of different skeletons, enough for two per group; large pieces of sugar paper; white paper; pencils; glue.

Links to other subjects
ICT
QCA Unit 4C 'Branching databases'
● Challenge children to create a branching database to identify their two skeletons.

Whiteboard tools
Use the Lines tool to link written ideas on the concept map. Delete objects by selecting Delete in the Object edit toolbox.

🖉 Pen tool

📏 Lines tool

🔦 Marquee select tool

🗑 Delete button

📺 Activities Explorer

Starter
Display page 2 of the flipchart 'Bones' and build a concept map with the children to find out what they know about bones. Ask: *Why do we have bones? Are bones all the same size? Where do you have/can you feel bones in your body? Can you name any of the bones?* Label any bones that the children know. The activity *Boneyard Bill* in Activities Explorer 📺 (in 'KS1_2 Science') can be used to look at the names of major bones in the human body.

Whole-class shared work
● Together, read pages 3, 4 and 5 and answer the questions. Double click on the panels and click the Delete button 🗑 in the Object edit toolbox to reveal the answer. Discuss any new and interesting facts.
● If possible, show examples of the bones to the children. Explain where these bones are from and which part of the (animal) body they are from.
● Go to page 6. Look carefully at the picture of the skeleton and ask the children what they notice. What type of skeleton do they think is shown here? How does it compare to a human skeleton? What type of animal does it belong to? Click on the *What is it?* button to find the answer. Are the children surprised by the answer?
● Repeat this process for the skeleton on page 7.
● Remind the children of the bone words collected during the Starter. Can they identify different bones in the skeletons on pages 6 and 7? Add their suggestions to the flipchart.

Independent work
● Give each child a photocopiable sheet to complete as they carry out the following activity.
● Put the children into small, mixed-ability groups. Give each group two pictures of different skeletons or examples of bones, a large piece of sugar paper, white paper, scissors, pencils and glue.
● Ask the groups to make two sets of labels using the words in the word bank. They should then put the skeleton pictures in the middle of the sugar paper and arrange the labels around the outside to identify the different parts of the skeletons. When they are satisfied with the result they can stick the pictures and labels down.
● As the children work, encourage them to notice similar parts of each skeleton, for example the skull, and to discuss how they are the same or different.
● Ask the children to write down the similarities and differences between the two skeletons, for example: one had longer arm bones than the other; both skeletons had the same number of ribs.
● If there is enough time, ask the children to draw pictures of the skeleton or bones on the back of the photocopiable sheet or on separate sheets of paper.
● Mixed-ability groups should support less able learners. Monitor the groups to ensure that everyone contributes to the task.

Plenary
● Show the children pictures of bones and ask them to think of adjectives to describe them, for example, *long, thin, smooth, fragile, tough, hard.* Make a note of the words that they suggest on page 8.
● Show the children the X-ray photographs of a human ankle and knee on page 9 and ask them to describe what they see. Ask: *Has anyone had an x-ray? Why did you have one? What was used to take the x-ray? How do you think the machine works?*

Skeleton investigation

Learning objectives
QCA Unit 4A 'Moving and growing'
● To learn that human skeletons are internal and grow as humans grow.
● To identify a question, make a prediction and test it.
● To decide and make a body measurement.
● To use bar charts to present measurements.
● To say what the evidence shows and whether it supports the prediction.

Resources
'Skeleton investigation' flipchart file; photocopiable pages 129 and 130 'Investigation report 1' and '2'; one of each for each child; tape measures and rulers. (Microsoft Excel is required to view the embedded spreadsheet in the flipchart.)

Links to other subjects
Mathematics
NNS: Use, read and write metric units; suggest suitable units and measuring equipment to measure length; solve problems by collecting, organising, representing and interpreting data in tables, charts, graphs and diagrams.
● The children should record the body measurements accurately and use bar charts to present their results.

Whiteboard tools
Use the Lines tool to draw a simple table. Change to Desktop mode when working with the spreadsheet. Use the Handwriting tool to enter data into the spreadsheet.

 Pen tool

 Highlighter tool

 Recognition tool

▯ Lines tool

▢ Desktop mode

Handwriting tool

Return to main screen

Starter
Display page 2 of the flipchart and ask the children to compare the size of their forearm with their neighbour's. Ask: *What do you notice about the size of your neighbour's forearm? Whose arm is bigger? Why do you think this is?* Make notes of the children's ideas.

Whole-class shared work
● Go to page 3. Ask: *Who has the biggest head size in the class? Do you think my head will be the same size, bigger or smaller as yours? Why? How could we find out?*
● Demonstrate how to measure your head size using a tape measure. Ask for a suitable unit of measurement. (Centimetres.) Encourage the children to predict what the measure will be.
● Compare the measurement of your head size with a child's head size and discuss whether the children's predictions were correct.
● Explain that our bones grow as we grow, so adults have longer or bigger bones than children. Ask: *Does this mean that all the children in this class are the same size?*
● Go to page 4 of the flipchart. Ask the children whether the boys and girls in their class are the same size. Explain that, as a class, they will design an investigation to find this out. Invite them to suggest what they could measure, for example, head size, hand span, or forearm length. Make notes on the board.
● Give the children the 'Investigation report' photocopiable sheets to help them write up their investigation. Work through pages 5 to 8 of the flipchart with them, adding their suggestions to the board.

Independent work
● Organise the children into groups of four or five.
● Display page 9 of the flipchart. Discuss how they will record results. Draw a table, using the Lines tool ▯ for them to copy on to their photocopiable sheet.
● Allow the children enough time to take measurements of their chosen bone, filling in their sheets as they do so.
● Provide less able learners with adult support in measuring bones.

Plenary
● Go to page 10, click on the icon to open the *Measurement investigation* spreadsheet. (This will automatically take you into Desktop mode.) An *EXAMPLE Table* and *EXAMPLE Chart* have been provided to illustrate how the children can record data and use it to create a suitable bar chart.
● Fill in the data fields on the *Table* worksheet.
● Ask the children to predict what the bar chart will look like.
● Bring up the *Chart* worksheet and ask the children questions about the bar chart, for example: *Which group of people had the smallest head? How do you know?*
● Use the other headings on page 11 to discuss how to write the conclusion to, and evaluation of, the investigation. The children can finish their reports as follow-up work.

Supporting skeletons

Learning objective
QCA Unit 4A 'Moving and growing'
● To learn that the skeleton supports the body.

Resources
'Supporting Skeletons' flipchart file; a range of reference books containing information about different invertebrates.

Links to other subjects
English
NLS Term 1 S3: Identify the use of powerful verbs.
NLS Term 1 S4: To identify adverbs.
● Encourage the children to think about how invertebrates move and to use powerful verbs, such as slithered. More able children will also be able to add adverbs to describe the movement.

Whiteboard tools
Select Delete in the Object edit toolbox to remove them. Write or add text with the Pen or Text editor tools.

🔍 Marquee select

🗑 Delete button

🖊 Pen tool

T Text editor tool

◎ Activote (optional)

Starter
Play the video clip on page 2 of the flipchart. Ask: *What do you notice about how this animal moves? How quickly does it move? Does it move in a certain way? Do you think this animal has a backbone or not?*

Whole-class shared work
● Show the children page 3 and ask them what the animal is. (A jellyfish.) Reveal the right answer. What do the children notice about the jellyfish? Encourage them to point out the structural differences between this animal and a mammal.
● Ask the children to think about how their own skeletons support their bodies: they would not be able to stand if they had no leg bones! Go to page 4 to show how the skeleton acts as a framework for the human body.
● Go to page 5, and ask the children to work in pairs to discuss where they think each animal should go. Invite pairs to the board to drag pictures into the correct space, giving reasons for their choices.
● Explain that animals with a skeleton are called *vertebrates* because they have a backbone, which is the supporting column of the body. Ask the children: *What does having a backbone enable you to do? What does it not allow you to do?*
● Explain that the animals without an internal skeleton are called *invertebrates*.

Independent work
● Display page 6. Ask the children to work in pairs to create a fact file about an animal without an internal skeleton. They should choose one invertebrate and find out information about it, using the questions on the board as a guide: *How does it move without a skeleton? What shape is it? How does it protect itself?* Encourage the children to think of further questions.
● Provide them with a selection of reference books that give information about different invertebrates.
● Mixed-ability pairs should provide support for less able learners. Monitor pairs to ensure that they both contribute to the task.
● Challenge more able learners to think about how they want to present their information in a fact file.

Plenary
● Ask the children to share what they have discovered about their chosen invertebrates. Display page 6 and add interesting facts that the children have gathered about how these animals support or protect themselves.
● Children should understand that all bodies need some sort of support, but not all animals have an internal structure to do this. Point out that animals without an internal skeleton often have strong muscles to help them to move, whereas other animals, like spiders, have an *exoskeleton* (a skeleton on the outside of the body).
● Go to page 7 and summarise what the children have learned.
● If time is available the children can use Activote devices or alternative voting methods to vote on the most interesting facts that they have learned.

Muscles and bones

Starter
Ask the children to find a space in the room. Tell them to pick up a book and lift it up and down. What helps them to do this? Is it their bones alone? Explain that muscles are attached to their bones, and that these help to support their movements. Ask the children to point out any muscles that they know. Add a picture of a person to a blank flipchart page and annotate with the children's suggestions about muscles.

Whole-class shared work
● Ask the children to discuss in pairs what they think muscles do. Allow three to five minutes' thinking time.
● Invite the children to share their ideas and note them down on a new flipchart page.
● Explain that muscles help us to move parts of our bodies. Every movement we make involves muscles, for example, smiling, writing and clapping. Ask the children to try a few of these movements and to identify where muscles are being used.
● Ask the children to roll up their sleeves then stretch one arm right above their head. Tell them to bend their arm slowly and to look at it while they perform this action. Ask: *What do you notice when you bend your arm? What do you think is happening inside your arm?*
● Tell the children that muscle contraction is an active process and that muscles work in pairs. Ask them to feel their upper arm as they flex their arm. The biceps contracts (it gets rounder and harder) and the triceps relaxes as the arm is flexed.
● Tell the children that they will be doing some short exercises and, as they do so, you'd like them to think about the muscles they are using.

Independent work
● Move to a room where there is space for the children to move around.
● Ask the children to organise themselves into pairs and find a space.
● Give each pair paper and a pencil.
● They should list the following five activities in a column on the left:
    ● sit ups
    ● marching
    ● stretching out arms and touching shoulders
    ● running on the spot
    ● star jumps.
● Using the stopwatch, time the children as they carry out each of the five activities for 60 seconds.
● After each activity, ask the children to write which muscles they think they used. They do not need to know the specific names, but should be able to identify whether they are using their leg, arm, shoulder muscles and so on.

Plenary
● Go back to the classroom and go through the exercises and muscles used on the board. Ask the children how they feel after the exercises.
● Explain that their muscles are working a lot harder when they move around than when they are sitting still. That is the reason why it is important to warm up before they take part in longer exercises, so that their muscles are ready for the movement.

Different organisms

Learning objectives
QCA Unit 4B 'Habitats'
● To group organisms according to observable features.
● To use keys to identify plants or animals.

Resources
'Grouping and identifying organisms' flipchart file, photocopiable page 131 'Organisms cards' cut up and made into cards – each group of children will need one set of cards.

Links to other subjects
ICT
QCA Unit 4C 'Branching databases'
● Ask the children to create their own branching databases for sorting organisms, using a suitable software package and a bank of clip art.

Starter
Display the pictures on page 2 of the 'Grouping and identifying organisms' flipchart and ask children to discuss in pairs how they would sort them. There is no single correct way but it is important to think about the similarities and differences. Children should look at the features of each organism, such as the legs, wings, eyes and colours. Invite pairs to sort the animals on the board and ask them to explain their reasons for sorting them in a particular way.

Whole-class shared work
● Provide groups of three to four children with a set of 'Organisms' cards, made from the photocopiable sheet.
● Go to page 3. Give children five to ten minutes to group similar organisms together. Use the Count down tool 🕐 to time them.
● Invite groups to explain how they sorted the organisms and what criteria they used. Write their ideas on page 3.
● Explain that they have sorted these organisms based on similarities, or features that the organisms shared.
● Ask the children to sort one of the groups into two smaller groups. What would happen if they took one of the groups and sorted it, and then did it again and again? (They should eventually end up with a single organism.)
● Enable the Reveal tool 🖥 and go to page 4. Explain that this page shows a key to identify the animals that they looked at during the Starter. They will be asked questions to sort the animals into two groups, and then into two groups again, and so on until they are left with one animal in each group.
● Pull the blind down from the top of the screen. Read and discuss the questions one at a time.
● When the full screen is revealed, demonstrate how each question sorts the animals.
● Tell the children that a key provides an easy way to identify an organism. It is like a sign-posted diagram; at each post you can either go one way or the other.

Independent work
● In pairs, ask the children to shuffle the organism cards and place them upside down. They should then choose six cards and create their own key for this group of animals.
● Less able learners can choose four cards; more able learners can create a key for eight animals.

Plenary
● Display page 5. Tell the children that there is an animal hidden behind the box on the left. Can they guess what it is?
● Pull a question from the red box and place it in the white area to read it. Then drag it onto the blue box to reveal the yes or no answer. Encourage the children to guess the animal. Delete the box on the right to reveal the animal.
● Finish the lesson by asking the children what kind of yes or no questions they could ask to identify a human being. For example: *Can it talk? Can it fly? Can it crawl? Can it walk? Does it stand on two legs?*

Whiteboard tools
Remove objects by selecting Delete in the Object edit toolbox. Use the Clock tool's Count down function to time the sorting activity. Hide and reveal parts of the screen with the Reveal tool.

🔦 Marquee select tool

🗑 Delete button

🖊 Pen tool

🕐 Count down tool

🖥 Reveal tool

Food chains

Learning objectives
QCA Unit 4B 'Habitats'
● To identify the structure of a food chain in a specific habitat.
● That animals are suited to the habitat in which they are found.
● That most food chains start with a green plant.

Resources
'Food chains' flipchart file; photocopiable page 132 'Food chains' for each child; scissors; glue.

Links to other subjects
Geography
QCA Unit 10 'A village in India'
● Find out about animals that are native to India and construct a variety of food chains. Are some animals and plants only found in India?

Starter
Remind the children of the word *habitat*. Ask: *What does the word habitat mean? How many types of habitat can you name? Which habitat do we live in?* Write their suggestions on page 2 of the flipchart.

Whole-class shared work
● Go to page 3. Ask the children to match the organisms to their correct habitat. Choose a few animals and ask the children what those animals eat. Are some of the foods in the picture?
● Enable the Spotlight tool ⬤ and go to page 4 of the flipchart. Focus on one of the words at the top of the page using the spotlight. Ask the children to think about what it means. Allow them some quiet thinking time. Do the same for the other word.
● Encourage the children to share their ideas.
● Reveal the whole screen and point out the producers and consumers on the page. Tell the children that the word *producer* means *maker*. The producers are usually plants, and they make their own food. The word *consumer* means *eater* or *drinker*. The consumers are usually animals. They either eat plants, or other animals.
● Use the Marquee select tool to match the producers on the page with the correct consumers.
● Repeat this process for the words *predator* and *prey* on page 5, asking children to share ideas first and then explaining what the words mean. The words predator means *an animal that hunts other animals for food* and the word prey means *an animal that is hunted for food*. Explain that more than one predator can hunt for the same prey.
● Go to page 6. Ask the children to group pictures together that illustrate a producer and consumer (a plant and one animal), or a producer, prey and predator (a plant and two animals). Invite children to the board to demonstrate their choices and their reasons.
● Emphasise the arrows and the direction in which they are pointing. What does it mean if you rotated the arrow to face the other direction?

Independent work
● Provide the children with a copy of the photocopiable sheet. Ask them to cut out the pictures, labels and arrows and use them to create food chains.
● The less able learners could pair together a producer and a consumer. The more able learners will be able to create a complete food chain and identify, using the labels, the predator, prey, consumer and producer.

Plenary
● Ask the children to talk about the examples of food chains that they have created.
● Go to page 7 and, as a class, create a fact file for a human being and an owl. Use the Resource library to choose suitable *foods*.

Whiteboard tools
Use the Spotlight tool to focus on words on the screen. Use the Resource library to find suitable animals and plants for a food chain.

 Pen tool

 Marquee select tool

 Spotlight tool

 Resource library

Floating keyboard

Different habitats

Learning objectives
QCA Unit 4B 'Habitats'
● That different animals are found in different habitats.
● To make predictions of organisms that will be found in a habitat.
● To learn that animals are suited to the environment in which they are found.

Resources
Prepared flipchart file showing a habitat and some animals that might live there (the animals should be hidden behind shapes); individual whiteboards and pens; digital camera (if available); video clips or images of different types of habitat (copyright permitting), such as fresh water, seaside, woodland; picture of a local habitat – if possible, organise a visit to this habitat to collect organisms (alternatively focus on the habitat of the school grounds).

Links to other subjects
Geography
QCA Unit 8 'Improving the environment'
● Investigate litter problems around the school and think about how this affects the habitat of creatures that live on the school grounds.
History
PoS (2a) To learn about characteristic features of periods and societies studied.
● Use a similar technique to prompt children to guess the purpose of artefacts placed on an historical background.

Whiteboard tools
Create a habitat using resources from Backgrounds and the Resource library. Use shapes to hide the animals.

🔲 Backgrounds tool

📖 Resource library

🔳 Shapes tool

🖊 Pen tool

🔍 Marquee select tool

Starter
Show the prepared flipchart to the children and ask them to guess what animals are living in this habitat. They can only ask ten questions for each animal and you can only answer *yes*, *no* or *sometimes*. Reduce the size of the shape to reveal each animal, or drag them out from their hiding places.

Whole-class shared work
● Ask the children to organise themselves into groups of three. Provide each group with an individual whiteboard and pen to record their decisions.
● Tell the children that they are going to play a game called *Who lives here?* You will show them a habitat. They have to identify the habitat and predict what kind of animals would live there. They also need to think of good reasons for their choices.
● Show your pictures and/or video clips of different habitats. Ask the children to tell you what kind of habitats they saw and what kind of animals would live in them. How would they describe the habitats? Why did they choose these animals? Would those animals be able to live in any of the other habitats? They should write their suggestions on individual whiteboards.
● Annotate the children's suggestions around the images.

Independent work
● Put a heading on a new flipchart page, *Our class field trip*, and show a picture of a local habitat.
● Explain that the children will be going on a field trip to this place to collect animals. Emphasise that this must be done with care, to ensure that the animals are not damaged.
● Tell the children you want them to make some notes to prepare for their field trip. Ask them to:
  ● predict the different types of organisms they might find in the habitat that they are going to visit, and explain their predictions
  ● suggest equipment for collecting the animals, and explain why the equipment is appropriate and necessary
  ● suggest what information they should plan to collect, and how they will collect it.
● Suggest that a digital camera could be used to take pictures of the organisms and the location(s) in which they were found. Another idea is to design a table to collect information about the conditions in which each organism is found. (For example: How much light/shade did the organism have? Was the organism found near water? What type of soil was it found in? How hot or cold was the place where it was found?)

Plenary
● Discuss the children's ideas, making notes on the flipchart page.
● Explain the importance of returning any animal collected to their original habitat.
● Discuss with the children why we should respect an animal's habitat.

Changing habitats

Learning objective
QCA Unit 4B 'Habitats'
● To recognise ways in which living things and the environment need protection.

Starter
Ask the children if they have ever moved house or stayed in a place away from home. How did it feel to be somewhere different? How long did it take for them to get used to it? Did it feel strange that things they were used to weren't there any more? Write their responses on a blank flipchart page.

Whole-class shared work
● Show the prepared scene to the children. Ask them to describe this habitat and the animals living in it.
● Tell the children that the wood has been sold to a construction company to build houses on the land. Delete the trees one at a time until only the animals should remain. Ask them what will happen to the habitat and the animals.
● Explain that organisms are affected when changes occur in their habitat.
● Ask the children to imagine that a local pond is going to be drained and covered over, so that a new playground can be built on it.
● Ask: *Is it so bad to fill in the pond if it means that children will have somewhere to play?*
● Tell the children to discuss with a partner what the effects would be, and why the habitat is important to the organisms and to the local area. Ask: *What do plants give back to people that we need? What will happen to the plant life and animals if the pond is drained?* Note down their suggestions on the flipchart.

Resources
Prepared flipchart page showing a busy woodland scene, using a plain countryside background and trees and animals from the Backgrounds tool and the Resource library; presentation software, such as Microsoft PowerPoint (optional).

Links to other subjects
Geography
QCA Unit 21 'How can we improve the area we see from our window?'
● Study the local area and identify good places to site a pond.
English
NLS Term 3 T23: To present a point of view in writing.
● Write a formal letter of complaint about the pond.

Independent work
● Split the class in two. In pairs, one half of the class will prepare notes on why the change you have been discussing is bad. (For example, the pond provides a valuable habitat for plants and animals, and a valuable resource for humans.) The other half will argue why this change is good. (For example, it will improve the habitat of humans by giving children somewhere safe to play.)
● At the end of the lesson, the two groups will take turns to debate why this is a good or bad change, giving reasons for their argument.
● Mixed-ability pairs should provide support for less able learners. Challenge more able learners to prepare a presentation using appropriate software, such as Microsoft PowerPoint, if resources are available.

Plenary
● Seat the two groups on opposite sides of the room. Invite pairs from each group to speak in turn, stating their argument.
● Encourage the opposing group to respond to the statements. Tell them they must abide by the rules: no interruptions!
● Make a note of the children's arguments on a new flipchart page.
● Conclude the lesson by asking all the children to vote on whether they believe the change is good or bad. They do not have to vote for the side for which they debated, but they should instead look at all the arguments presented and make their own balanced judgement. Activote devices or alternative voting methods could be used.

Whiteboard tools
Remove objects by double-clicking them and selecting Delete in the Object edit toolbox or by dragging them to the Flipchart bin.

🖊 Pen tool

🗑 Delete button

📖 Resource library

�֎ Backgrounds tool

◉ Activote (optional)

Temperature and thermometers

Learning objectives
QCA Unit 4C 'Keeping warm'
● That the sense of touch is not an accurate way of judging temperature.
● To use a thermometer to make careful measurements of temperature.
● That something hot will cool down and something cold will warm up until it is the same temperature as its surroundings.
● To explain temperature and temperature changes using scientific knowledge and understanding.

Resources 💿
'Temperature' flipchart file; non-mercury thermometers; three bowls containing the following: ice cubes; water at room temperature; warm water - one bowl for each group and one set of all three for the Starter. (Microsoft Excel is required to view the embedded spreadsheet in the flipchart.)

Links to other subjects
Mathematics
NNS: Record estimates and readings from scales to a suitable degree of accuracy.
● Use the ITP to work out different temperature word problems. For example: *In the morning, it is 18°C in the classroom. By the afternoon, the temperature drops by 5°C. What is the temperature in the afternoon?*

Whiteboard tools
Use the Handwriting tool to enter data into the spreadsheet in Desktop mode.

📱 Pen tool

🔦 Marquee select tool

📷 Camera tool

💬 Count down tool

🖥 Desktop mode

✏ Handwriting tool

📷 Return to main screen

Starter
Place three bowls containing ice cubes, water at room-temperature and warm water on a table. Invite a few children to judge how hot the contents in the bowls are using their fingers. Write their answers on page 2 of the flipchart 'Temperatures'.

Whole-class shared work
● Go to page 3. Ask: *What is a more accurate way of measuring temperature?* (A thermometer.) *What is a thermometer? How is it used?* Write their ideas on the board.
● Click on the thumbnail image on page 4, which opens the Interactive Teaching Program (ITP) *Thermometer*.
● Demonstrate how to read a thermometer. Point out where the pointer is placed. (It is at 0 when the ITP is initially opened.) What do the children think the negative numbers mean?
● Practise changing the temperature on the thermometer and working out the differences between readings.
● Encourage the children to place the pointer where they think the current temperature is.
● Show the children a real thermometer. Check the temperature of the room and set the actual temperature on the ITP. Take a snapshot of the thermometer using the Camera tool and add it to the flipchart page. Write the room temperature next to the snapshot.

Independent work
● Provide each group of four with a thermometer and a container of water (each group should have water of a different temperature).
● Ask each group to write the time and record the temperature of their water. Tell them they will be repeating this every ten minutes.
● On page 4 of the flipchart, select the Clock tool's Count down option 💬. Set the timer to ten minutes and choose a sound if speakers are available. Set the action to Turn to next page (to turn to page 5 automatically). Remember to return to page 4 to reset the timer while the children take their temperature readings.
● Each child should draw up a table to record their results.
● While the children are waiting they could work out the difference between the last two readings.

Plenary
● Click on the link on page 6 to open the spreadsheet. Collect the results from all the groups in the table on the first worksheet. Each group's chart will be automatically completed on the relevant worksheet.
● Discuss the results as a class. Ask: *Which bowls of water got warmer? Which bowls of water got colder? What is the difference between the coldest and warmest temperature at the beginning of the experiment? At the end of the experiment?* Return to Activprimary mode and write their responses on page 6.
● Lead the children to realise that all the bowls of water gradually returned to the temperature of the room. Remind them of this temperature by looking again at page 4 of the flipchart.

Keeping things cold

Learning objectives
QCA Unit 4C 'Keeping warm'
● To turn an idea about how to keep things cold into a form that can be investigated.
● To decide what evidence to collect.
● To make a table and record results in it.
● To draw conclusions from their results.

Resources
'Ice cube insulators' flipchart file; photocopiable page 129 and page 130 'Investigation report 1' and '2', one of each per child; one very cold ice cream; a selection of materials of differing textures (such as polythene, aluminium foil and bubble wrap), four pieces per group; four ice cubes and four jars for each group; backpack. (Microsoft Excel is required to view the embedded spreadsheet in the flipchart.)

Links to other subjects
Geography
QCA Unit 24 'Passport to the world'
● Investigate houses around the world, looking at how the construction materials insulate against heat or cold.
English
NLS Term 3 W7: Collect/classify words with common roots.
● Investigate the common root for thermal and thermometer. (From the Greek for *heat*.)

Whiteboard tools
Use the Count down tool as a reminder to record the thermometer readings. Enter data into the spreadsheet with the Handwriting tool.

🖊 Pen tool

🔝 Marquee select tool

⏲ Count down tool

🖥 Desktop mode

✍ Handwriting tool

🔲 Return to main screen

◉ Activote (optional)

Starter
Show the children an ice cream and a backpack. Ask them to imagine that you want to carry the ice cream in the backpack on a very hot day. What do they think will happen to the ice cream? Write their predictions on page 2 of the flipchart.

Whole-class shared work
● Discuss why the bag would not keep the ice cream cold, focussing on the properties of the material. Ask: *What would cause the ice cream to melt?* (The heat.) Add these ideas to their predictions on page 2.
● Go to page 3. Ask the children how you could stop the ice cream from melting. Add their ideas to the board.
● Show the children the materials you have brought and list them on page 4. Demonstrate wrapping the ice cream in one of the materials. Ask: *Which material do you think would keep the ice cream cold?* Use voting methods, such as Activote devices, to collect the children's predictions and make a note of the results.
● Ask them to investigate this using the ice cubes instead of ice cream. What will they keep the same and what will they change to ensure this investigation a fair test? Make notes on page 5.

Independent work
● Give each group of four children four ice cubes, four pieces of different material and four jars. Ask them to wrap each ice cube in a different material and place it into a jar.
● To find out how quickly the ice cubes melt, children should measure the amount of water in the jar after the following intervals: 5 minutes, 15 minutes, 30 minutes, 45 minutes and 60 minutes.
● Go to page 6. Select the Clock tool's Count down function ⏲. Set the timer for 30 minutes and set a sound alarm if speakers are available.
● Ask children to use the photocopiable pages to write a report. Support less able learners by reviewing the annotated flipchart pages to remind them of what was discussed during the lesson.

Plenary
● Open the spreadsheet on page 7 and collect the results from all the groups on the first page of the spreadsheet. Ask: *Which materials kept our ice cubes the coolest for the longest amount of time? Which materials let the most water out? Which let out the least?*
● Each group's results will be automatically transferred to the line graphs on the relevant pages of the spreadsheet. These can be printed out and kept as records.
● Explain to the children that a material which keeps warmth or cold in is called a *thermal insulator*. (The word *thermal* refers to heat.) Challenge them to suggest a material which is an excellent thermal insulator and another which is a really poor insulator.

Keeping warm

Learning objectives
QCA Unit 4C 'Keeping warm'
● To make careful measurements of temperature at regular time intervals.
● To record results in a table and to use these to draw conclusions.
● Some materials are good thermal insulators.

Resources
'Keeping warm' flipchart file; materials to test thermal insulation (bubble wrap, aluminium foil, thick and thin fabrics, paper); selection of summer and winter clothes; plastic containers (eg beakers); hot water (not so hot that it will soften plastic containers); box or tray for each group; photocopiable pages 129 and 130 'Investigation report 1' and '2', one of each per child; graph paper. (Microsoft Excel is required to view the embedded spreadsheet in the flipchart.)

Links to other subjects
Geography
QCA Unit 24 'Passport to the world'
● Investigate what people wear in different parts of the world. What kinds of fabric are worn in places near the north pole and the equator?

Whiteboard tools
Use the Clock tool's Count down function as a reminder to record the thermometer readings. Use the Handwriting tool to enter data in Desktop mode.

🅰 Pen tool

🅺 Marquee select tool

🅲 Fill tool

🅴 Count down tool

🅾 Desktop mode

🅶 Handwriting tool

🅼 Return to main screen

🅾 Activote (optional)

Starter
Display page 2 of the flipchart 'Keeping warm'. Ask the children to sort the clothes you have brought in into two piles: summer and winter clothes. What would they wear to keep warm? To stay cool? Why? Identify that different materials have been used to make the clothes and discuss the properties of these materials. Annotate the flipchart page with their suggestions.

Whole-class shared work
● Ask: *What else do you do to stay warm?* Make notes on page 3.
● Go to page 4. Read the problem together and encourage the children to suggest possible solutions. Discuss their ideas.
● Look at the materials named on page 5. Ask: *Would these materials help? Why? Why not?* Change the colour of the bad choices to red, using the Fill tool 🅲, and drag them out of the circle. Fill the good choices in blue and leave them in the circle.
● Tell the children that they will be conducting an investigation to see which materials keep a hot liquid the warmest for the longest amount of time.
● List the materials you have brought for the investigation on page 6. Can children predict which material will keep the hot chocolate hotter for longer, and give their reasons why? They could using voting methods, such as Activote devices, to vote on their prediction.
● On page 7, discuss how to make this a fair test. What will the children keep the same and what will they change? (Children should use one control container with no insulation, and two with different materials.)

Independent work
● Give each group of four children three containers, two pieces of material and a tray or box.
● The children should wrap each container in a different material, ensuring that the containers can stand upright in the box or tray.
● Fill the containers with hot water and tell the children to measure the temperature of the water every ten minutes. They should record the material, temperature and the time in a suitable table.
● Go to page 8 and select the Clock tool's Count down function 🅴. Set the timer for ten minutes, setting the sound alarm if speakers are available.
● Hand out the photocopiable sheets to help children write their reports. Provide more support to less able learners by looking at the pages annotated during this lesson to remind them of what was discussed.

Plenary
● Open the spreadsheet on page 9 and collect the children's results. Ask: *Which materials kept the water the hottest for the longest amount of time? Which materials kept the water warm? Which did not?*
● Each group's results will be transferred automatically to the relevant pages in the spreadsheet to create line graphs. These can be printed out and kept as records.
● Explain that the materials that kept the water hot for the longest time are good thermal insulators because they stop the heat from getting through. Remind them that the word *thermal* relates to heat.

Flowing materials

Learning objectives
QCA Unit 4D 'Solids, liquids and how they can be separated'
● To make careful observations and measurements of volume recording them in tables and using them to draw conclusions.
● That liquids do not change in volume when they are poured into a different container.
● That solids consisting of very small pieces behave like liquids in some ways.

Resources
'Flowing materials' flipchart file; photocopiable page 133 'Flowing materials'; different shaped measuring containers (six per group); a range of different materials for the children to *pour*, such as water, undiluted squash, sand, rice, salt, plastic blocks.

Links to other subjects
Mathematics
NNS: Measure and compare using standard units (l, ml).
● Support the children in making accurate measurements. Use measuring containers with different scales to show that 500ml is the same as 0.5l.

Starter
Display page 2 of the flipchart, which shows pictures of different kinds of materials. In pairs, children should discuss how to sort the materials. Invite children to use the Marquee select tool to sort the pictures on the whiteboard and explain their reasons. Encourage them to describe the properties of the materials.

Whole-class shared work
● Go to page 3 and watch the video clips. Ask: *What type of material is this? Does it move or stand still? What sound does it make? What do you think it feels like?* Make a note of the children's responses. Repeat for the video clips on page 4.
● Go to page 5 and invite the children to sort these pictures into two groups. Ask them to explain their reasons.
● Introduce and discuss the terms *solids* and *liquids*, exploring similarities and differences, and thinking about the properties that solids and liquids possess.
● Ask the children to complete the photocopiable sheet, supporting less able learners in the written work.
● Go to page 6 of the flipchart. Click on the thumbnail to open the ITP *Measuring Cylinder*. Revise how liquids are measured. Talk about the scale and measurements. Ask questions, such as: *Is 100 more likely to refer to 100 litres or 100 millilitres?*

Independent work
● Ask the children to copy the table on page 7 of the flipchart onto a piece of paper or into their books.
● Give each group of four a measuring jug and a set of measuring containers.
● The children should measure out 300ml of four different materials and record their observations in the table.
● They should then transfer one of the liquids from one measuring cylinder to another that is a different shape. Is the measurement the same? Ask them to test this again with another liquid.
● They should observe closely what the material looks like when it is poured. Are there any similarities or differences in the way the materials behave?
● Extra adult support will be helpful to monitor the groups as they measure out the materials. Support less able learners in reading the measurements.

Plenary
● Discuss children's results and make notes on page 8 of the flipchart. Ask: *Did the materials all behave in the same way? What happened when a liquid was poured from one container into another of a different shape?*
● Lead the children to understand that, although liquids change shape when they are poured into a different container, their volume will stay the same. Some solids consisting of particles (or very small pieces), such as salt and sand, will behave in a similar way to a liquid.

Whiteboard tools
 Pen tool

 Marquee select tool

Mixing solids and liquids

Learning objectives
QCA Unit 4D 'Solids, liquids and how they can be separated'
● That changes occur when some solids are added to water.
● To make careful observations, recording results in tables, and make comparisons.

Resources
'Mixing solids and liquids' flipchart file; water; a range of different soluble and insoluble solids, such as sand, coffee granules, and marbles; tea; sugar; full kettle; individual whiteboards and pens; exercise books and pens.

Links to other subjects
Art and design
PoS (2b) Pupils should be taught to apply their experience of materials and processes.
● Follow up this work by experimenting with mixing different quantities of powder paint with the same amounts of water. What kind of effects does this produce when the paint is applied to paper?

Starter
Divide the children into small groups and click on the image on page 2 of the flipchart to start the quiz. The children should decide on the correct answer as a group and write it on an individual whiteboard, to show after the count of five. (Alternatively, use Activote devices to gather their responses.) Click on the answer with the majority vote, to check whether it is correct.

Whole-class shared work
● Make a cup of tea in front of the class, adding a spoonful of sugar and stirring.
● Ask: *What has happened to the sugar? Can you still see it?* Note children's responses on page 3.
● Compare the state of the sugar before it goes in your tea and after. Ensure that the children understand that the sugar is solid.

Independent work
● Provide each group with a selection of transparent containers, water and a mixture of different solids. Go to page 4 and discuss what children think will happen to the solids when they are added to water. Change the names of the solids on the board or add more if necessary. Write the children's predictions on the board. Tell them they are going to carry out an investigation to find out if these predictions are correct.
● Tell the children to copy the table on page 5 to record their results and observations.
● Explain that they should measure out 500ml of water into each container. They should then add two teaspoons of one of the solids to the water in each container. Ask: *What happens when you mix the materials? What does the mixture look like after it has had time to settle?*
● Ask the children why they think the amount of water and solid have to be kept the same. Remind them of the importance of a fair test.
● Less able learners may need help in making sure the same measurements are used each time.
● Challenge more able learners to investigate what happens if they have the same amount of water but double the amount of solid.

Plenary
● Encourage the children to look carefully at their results. Ask: *What do you notice about your results? Were your predictions correct? What happened when you added one of the solids to the water? Did everyone get the same result? Did the same thing happen when you added marbles to the water?*
● Make a note of the children's conclusions on page 6 of the flipchart (changing the names of the materials or adding more if necessary). Pressing the button will bring up a list of key words.

Whiteboard tools
Double-click on existing text and select Edit text in the Object edit toolbox to amend or delete the text. Add text using the Floating keyboard in the Text editor tool tray.

📱 Pen tool

🖎 Marquee select tool

⊜ Floating keyboard

Ⓣ Edit text tool

◉ Activote (optional)

Learning objectives
QCA Unit 4D 'Solids, liquids and how they can be separated'
● That when solids do not dissolve or react with the water they can be separated by filtering.
● To choose apparatus to separate an undissolved solid from a liquid.

Resources
Two clear containers, one with sand and water and one with glass beads or marbles and water; sieve with large holes; loose tea leaves; fine sieve; tea strainer; filter teapot; tea bag; materials to filter tea leaves (net, muslin, tissue paper, foil with pinpricks); jug of water, bowl and clear measuring container for each group; exercise books and pens; a data-handling application such as Microsoft Excel.

Links to other subjects
ICT
QCA Unit 4D 'Collecting and presenting information'
● Ask children to use a data-handling package to create a bar chart and use this to interpret the children's results.

Whiteboard tools
Switch to Desktop mode to open and use a data-handling application. Use the Handwriting tool to enter data into the spreadsheet.

⬤ Pen tool

⬤ Desktop mode

⬤ Handwriting tool

⬤ Return to main screen

Sieving and filtering solids

Starter

Show the children the marbles and water and the sieve. Ask them to predict what will happen when you pour the marbles and water through. Carry out the experiment to confirm their prediction. Repeat for the sand and water. They should predict that the sand and water will fall through the holes in the sieve and the mixture will not separate easily. Ask: *What could you use to separate the sand?* Make a note of their responses.

Whole-class shared work

● Show the children some loose tea and tell them that, when you make a cup of tea with it, tiny parts float around on the top. Ask: *What could I use to prevent this?* They may suggest a sieve, tea strainer, or filter teapot. Show these items, if available.

● Show the children a tea bag. Gently pull it apart so they can see the loose tea inside. Allow them to handle the material of the tea bag. Establish that it has tiny holes that let the water through but that the bag keeps the tea leaves inside it. Explain that the bag is a filter and separates the tiny particles from the water.

Independent work

● Give each group of four a selection of different filtering materials, a container of loose tea leaves, a jug of water, a bowl and a measuring container.

● Explain that you want them to test the materials to find out which is the best filter to make a cup of tea.

● On a blank flipchart page, write down what they will change and what they will keep the same each time, to ensure a fair test. They could investigate which filter lasts the longest, which filter is the fastest or which filter lets the most water through without letting tea through.

● Open a data-handling application, such as Microsoft Excel, and together create a suitable table to record results. The children should copy this on to paper.

● Ask: *Which material do you predict will be the best filter? Why?* Note their responses on the whiteboard.

● Allow sufficient time for each group to complete their investigation.

● Support less able learners, by helping them to analyse the properties of the different materials.

● Challenge more able learners by adding a timed element to the task. Will the best filter also be the fastest filter?

Plenary

● Invite the children to report their findings to the rest of the class. Ask: *Which material was the best filter? Why? Which was the poorest? Why? What was it about the structure of that material that made it the worst?*

● Compare their findings with their prediction. Did they predict correctly?

Dissolving solids

Learning objectives
QCA Unit 4D 'Solids, liquids and how they can be separated'
● That some solids dissolve in water to form solutions and that although the solid cannot be seen it is still present.
● To predict whether sugar can be separated from a solution by filtering and to test the prediction.
● To decide what apparatus to use.
● When it is safe to taste things to test them.

Resources
Kettle; mug; instant hot chocolate; clean cold water; recently boiled water; sachets of sugar; clean teaspoons, bowls, sieves and jugs; clean materials for filtering (filter paper, different sieves, kitchen towel, foil with pinpricks); digital images of solids, liquids, and the processes of filtering, dissolving, melting and sieving (copyright permitting).

Links to other subjects
PSHE
PoS (3a) To consider what makes a healthy lifestyle.
● Explain that although we can't always see the salt and sugar in our foods, that does not mean that they are not present. Remind them of the disadvantages of too much salt and sugar in a diet and discuss how we can find out about, and reduce, the amount of sugar and salt that we consume.

Starter
Make a cup of hot chocolate and ask: *What has happened to the instant hot chocolate granules? What has happened to the water?* (The granules, a solid, have dissolved in the water, a liquid). Write *dissolve* on a new flipchart page.

Whole-class shared work
● Dissolve sugar in a mug of hot water. Add cold water to cool it. Ask: *Can you see the sugar?* (No.) *Does that mean it has disappeared? How could you test that the sugar is still in the water?* (By tasting the solution.)
● Ask the children to predict whether the sugar can be separated from the water by filtering, and the reasons for their prediction. Discuss how they could investigate this prediction.
● Remind the children that it is only safe to taste the solution because they are using clean water and clean teaspoons and cups, and because they know exactly what they are putting in it. The sugar is from sachets, so it has not been contaminated. Stress the importance of never tasting anything in experiments unless they know that clean equipment and non-toxic ingredients have been used.
● Impeccable hygiene must be observed for all activities that require tasting. Ensure that all equipment and surfaces are clean and washed with antibacterial spray. Ask children to wash their hands thoroughly before the activity.

Independent work
● Give each group a jug of warm water, a bowl, a teaspoon, a sugar sachet, a sieve and a filtering material.
● Ask each group to predict whether their material will filter the sugar from the water. They should then make up the sugar solution in the jug, line the sieve with the filtering material, place it over the bowl and carefully pour the solution through it. Warn them not to pour too fast. They can then taste the filtered solution to see whether or not the filter has worked.
● Compare results, and ask the children to explain why filtering cannot separate the dissolved sugar. (The holes in the filters are big enough for the sugar to get through because the sugar has dissolved into tiny particles.)
● Explain that some solids dissolve in water and that the mixture is called a solution. Although the solid cannot be seen it is still present.

Plenary
● On a blank flipchart page, place pictures of everyday examples of solids, liquids, filtering, dissolving, melting and sieving.
● On the same page place the words *filtering, dissolving, melting* and *sieving*. Ask the children to sort the pictures into the different processes.
● Encourage them to explain their decisions.

Whiteboard tools

⬚ Pen tool

✖ Marquee select tool

📖 Resource library

In a spin

Learning objectives
QCA Unit 4E 'Friction'
● That air resistance is a force that slows objects moving through air.
● To plan a fair test saying what to change, what to keep the same and what to measure.
● To make measurements of time.
● To identify a pattern in the results and to explain it in terms of air resistance.

Resources
Ten sheets of large sugar paper; two large tissues (one screwed up into a ball and one flat piece); photocopiable page 134 'Spinners' for each child; stopwatches, one per pair; data-handling program, such as Microsoft Excel; paper clips, pencils and scissors.

Links to other subjects
ICT
QCA Unit 4D 'Collecting and presenting information'
● Use a bar chart created in a data-handling package to interpret the children's results.

Starter
Take the children outside and ask them to run from one end of the playground to the other. What can they feel on their faces? (Air.) Provide each pair of children with a large sheet of sugar paper and ask them to run again with the paper held in front of them. What can they feel this time? Explain that what they are feeling is air *resistance*: air pushing against them.

Whole-class shared work
● Throw a flat piece of tissue up into the air. What do the children notice? (It falls slowly.)
● Now throw a screwed up piece of tissue up into the air. What do they notice? (It falls much faster.) Explain that the flat tissue has a bigger surface area than the screwed up tissue. The air cannot get round it so easily. Therefore, the air acts as a brake on the tissue, slowing it down.
● Demonstrate how to make a spinner, using the photocopiable sheet. Tell the children they are going to find out whether the size of the spinner affects how fast it falls.
● Open up a blank flipchart page and plan the investigation, using headings such as *Prediction, Method, Equipment* and so on.
● Ask: *How will you make the test fair?* (Dropping spinners from the same height; measuring the time in the same way for each spinner.)

Independent work
● Provide the children with a stopwatch, a photocopiable sheet, pencils, paper clips and scissors. Ask them to make the spinners and carry out the experiment, using the stopwatches to make their time measurements. The times can be recorded on the back of each spinner.
● Extend the experiment for more able learners by asking them to make another set of spinners and see what happens if the wings are made narrower or wider. Less able learners may need support in taking careful measurements of time.

Plenary
● Go into Desktop mode and use a data-handling program such as Microsoft Excel to collect the children's results. Use the Sort function to arrange the data in order, beginning with the spinners that took the longest time to reach the ground.
● Look at the spinners that have the longest times, and then at those that have the shortest times. Can the children see a pattern emerging? (The larger spinners take longer to fall.)
● Ask the children why they think the large spinners take longer to fall. Link their explanations to the idea of air resistance. Write their ideas on to a flipchart page.
● Children who extended the experiment could explain their findings, relating them to the concept of air resistance.

Whiteboard tools
Switch to Desktop mode to open and use a data-handling application. Enter data into the spreadsheet with the Floating keyboard.

▪ Pen tool

▪ Desktop mode

▪ Floating keyboard

▪ Return to main screen

Complete circuits

Learning objectives
QCA Unit 4F 'Circuits and conductors'
● To learn that a circuit needs a power source.
● To learn that a complete circuit is needed for a device to work.

Resources
'Circuits' flipchart file; sets of crocodile wires, bulbs and batteries – one for each group; photocopiable page 135 'Making circuits work'.

Links to other subjects
PE
PoS (4b) To warm up and prepare appropriately.
● As a warm-up exercise, get children to link hands in a circle. Then ask them to jump up and down, or run on the spot. If someone breaks the circuit by letting go, they all have to stand still.

Starter
Tell the children that in this lesson they will be looking at electricity. Invite them to look at the pictures on page 2 of the flipchart and sort them into two groups: those that need electricity to make them work, and those that do not. Ask: *How do you know that these objects need electricity? How does the torch light up even though it is not plugged into the mains?* Explain to the children that all objects that use electricity need a circuit to make them work.

Whole-class shared work
● Show the children the picture of a simple circuit on page 3. Use the Pen tool to label the wires and battery.
● Ask the children to point out the component that provides the power to the circuit. (The battery.)
● Can they explain what will happen if a bulb is added to the circuit? Invite a volunteer to add a bulb to the circuit.
● Challenge the children to explain in their own words what a circuit needs to make something work. For example, it needs a battery, and the wires need to connect to both ends of the battery.
● Show the children the pictures of different circuits on page 4. Ask them to predict if each circuit will light the bulb up or not, encouraging them to give reasons for their predictions. Ask: *Why do you think the bulb will not light up? What component is missing?* (Activote devices can be used to gather yes or no responses for each circuit.)
● Write *yes* or *no* to indicate whether they predict the circuit will or will not work.

Independent work
● Organise the children into groups of three or four. Provide each group with a set of wires, a bulb, a battery and a copy of photocopiable page 135 'Making circuits work'.
● Ask the children to make each circuit and then complete the table at the bottom of the sheet. They will need to explain why the circuit did or did not work.
● Mixed-ability groups should provide support to less able learners in making the circuits. Challenge more able learners to consider how they could change the incomplete circuits to make them work.

Plenary
● Ask the children to tell you which circuits did and did not work, and to explain their results. Review the predictions they made on page 4 of the flipchart. Address misconceptions, if any of the predictions were incorrect. Ensure that the children understand why a circuit is incomplete.
● Show the two pictures of circuits on page 5 and ask the children to explain if these circuits would work. Activote devices, or alternative voting methods, could be used to gather yes or no responses for each circuit. Challenge them to explain what could be done to make the circuits work.

Whiteboard tools

 Pen tool

 Marquee select tool

 Activote (optional)

Circuits and switches

Learning objectives
QCA Unit 4F 'Circuits and conductors'
● To understand that a circuit needs a power source.
● To know that a complete circuit is needed for a device to work.
● That a switch can be used to make or break a circuit to turn things on or off (using batteries or mains).

Resources
'Circuits' flipchart file; *Crocodile Clips Elementary* (available on the CD-ROM *Learning and teaching using ICT: Example materials* DfES 0315 2004G, or download from **www.crocodile-clips.com**); mains and battery operated devices with switches (mains appliances must have had an electrical supply check); crocodile wires, bulbs and batteries: one set for each group; materials to use as a switch (paper clip, tin foil, drawing pins, card).

Links to other subjects
Design and technology
QCA Unit 4E 'Lighting it up'
● The work in this lesson links well with this unit, as children need to understand how to make a bulb light up in a simple electric circuit and how switches work.

Whiteboard tools
Change to Desktop mode before starting the *Crocodile Clips* program. Use the Clock tool's Count down function to add a timed element to the lesson.

🖵 Desktop mode

📖 Return to main screen

🖊 Pen tool

⏱ Count down tool

Starter
Revise the children's previous knowledge about circuits. Open page 6 of the 'Circuits' flipchart. Tell the children that you are going to use the *Crocodile Clips* program to draw a simple circuit.

Switch to Desktop mode and start the *Crocodile Clips* program. Discuss what is needed to make a circuit work. Ask: *What would happen if I put a bulb into my circuit? What would happen if I put a bulb and a buzzer into my circuit?* Create a circuit that includes a bulb and a buzzer. Use the bigger 9V battery rather than the 1.5V battery, as these components will need more power.

Whole-class shared work
● Return to the flipchart and go to page 7.
● Show the children a selection of devices that use switches and demonstrate how each one works.
● In pairs, children should discuss what the devices have in common, and how each device works. Give three minutes for this. (You could use the Clock tool's Count down function ⏱ here.)
● Ask the children to name the devices and write the names as headings on page 7. Ask what the devices have in common, and write responses on the same page.
● Ask how each device works. Make notes on the board.
● Explain that in each circuit there is a component (or part) called a switch. Go to page 8 and look at the different ways to make switches.
● Invite the children to use the *Crocodile Clips* program to make a circuit with a switch and a bulb.
● Turn the switch on and off and ask what is happening in the circuit. Emphasise that a complete circuit is needed to make the item work. When the switch is off, it means that there is a break in the circuit.

Independent work
● Provide each group with a set of wires, a bulb, a battery and a selection of resources to make a switch. (Safety note: This activity must not be carried out using mains electricity!)
● The children should construct a circuit with a switch and make a diagram of it.
● Monitor the groups to ensure that they understand how to use a switch to break or complete a circuit. On page 9, compile an *Electricity* word bank to support the children in their drawing of their circuits.
● Give them 15 to 20 minutes to make and draw their circuits.
● Challenge more able learners to think of a different way of making a circuit.
● Encourage discussion in mixed-ability groups to provide support for less-able learners.

Plenary
● Go to page 9 of the flipchart. Ask groups in turn to demonstrate how their switch works. Ask: *What type of material did you use to make your switch work?*
● Write or draw diagrams on the board to illustrate the different ways in which the groups devised and used switches. Alternatively, take digital pictures and insert them into a flipchart to keep as a record of the children's work.

Using switches

Learning objectives
QCA Unit 4F 'Circuits and conductors'
● To know that a circuit needs a power source and needs to be complete for a device to work.
● To understand that a switch can be used to make or break a circuit to turn things on or off.
● To construct a circuit with a switch.

Resources
'Circuits' flipchart file; the Hasbro board game *Operation*, if available; photocopiable pages 136 and 137, 'Sounding it out' and 'What's the answer?', enlarged to A3 and photocopied on to card; crocodile clips, bulbs, buzzers, batteries, tin foil and large paper clips to make switches and dice – one set per group.

Links to other subjects
English
NLS Term 1 T25: To write clear instructions.
● Write instructions to explain how the board game works.
NLS Terms 1-3 T25: Identify phonemes.
● Use the sound cards to practise reading and spelling words through identifying phonemes.
Design and technology
PoS (5c) Design and make assignments using a range of materials.
● Create their own board game using a circuit with different components.

Starter
Display page 11 of the flipchart. Discuss how the game *Operation* works and how it uses the idea of circuits and switches. (The tweezers are attached by wire to the gameboard. When the tweezers touch the metal sides of the cavities, this completes a circuit and the buzzer and light are activated.) Make a note of children's ideas.

Whole-class shared work
● Show page 12 of the flipchart. Explain that the children will be making a game, using switches, called *Sounding it out*. Players from two teams will take turns to turn over a letter card and a word or picture card (which they are going to make). If the cards match, the players press a switch to sound the buzzer. The quickest player has to say the letter and word out loud. If correct, their team gets a point. If incorrect, the other team gets a point. The players then swap places with another team member.
● The children have to:
  ● write the alphabet around the edge of the gameboard
  ● cut out the holes for the switch and buzzer
  ● cut out the blank cards and draw pictures or write words on them to match the letters
  ● build a circuit to place underneath the gameboard, the switch and buzzer positioned in the cut-out holes.
● Provide groups with copies of the photocopiable pages as appropriate (see Independent work, below). Each group will need extra cards.
● Show page 13, *What's the answer?* One child has to be quizmaster. Two others compete to be the first to answer a question. One player presses a switch to light a bulb; the other presses a switch to sound a buzzer.
● The children have to:
  ● cut out the holes in the gameboard as indicated
  ● cut out the cards and devise questions and answers based on a subject of their choice (the children can swap quiz cards with another group so that the game is fairer)
  ● build one circuit with a switch and a bulb, and another with a switch and a buzzer, to place beneath the gameboard.

Independent work
● Provide groups with the resources and get them to make and then play their board games.
● *Sounding it out* is more suitable for less able learners, while more able learners should find *What's the answer?* more challenging.

Plenary
● Choose one group and ask the children to explain how they used circuits and switches in their board game.
● On the appropriate page, ask the children to draw where they placed the components for their circuit and explain what materials they used and why.
● Use page 14 to summarise what the children have learned.

Whiteboard tools
Use the Pen tool to annotate the gameboards on pages 12 and 13 to show how the children built their circuits.

🖉 Pen tool

How bright?

Learning objectives
QCA Unit 4F 'Circuits and conductors'
● To make predictions about the effect of including additional batteries in a circuit, and check whether results support the prediction made.
● That bulbs can burn out if components in a circuit are changed.
● How to change the brightness of bulbs in a circuit.
● To plan to change one factor and keep others constant.

Resources
Crocodile Clips Elementary (see Resources for Lesson 18); bulbs; crocodile clips; wires; batteries; motors - one set per pair; one sheet of A4 paper for each child.

Links to other subjects
Design and technology
QCA Unit 4E 'Lighting it up'
● Design circuits with lights for different purposes, for example, a night light for a small child, or a light to dazzle burglars.

Whiteboard tools
Change to Desktop mode before starting the *Crocodile Clips* program. Select the Return to main screen button in the Desktop toolbar to return to the flipchart.

▢ Desktop mode

▣ Return to main screen

▢ Pen tool

Ⓣ Text editor tool

◥ Marquee select tool

Starter
Review the children's knowledge on electricity. Ask: *Can anyone tell me what I need to make a complete simple circuit? Where does the bulb get its power from? What would happen if I replaced the bulb with a buzzer or motor?*
　Ask the children to draw a circuit on paper, showing how to make a bulb light up.

Whole-class shared work
● Using the *Crocodile Clips* program, draw these simple circuits and ask children to decide whether each device will work.

● Ask: *Why is one bulb brighter than the other? Why are some bulbs unlit? Is it because the circuit is not complete?*
● Challenge the children to predict what would happen if an extra battery were added to each circuit and to explain their reason. Write their responses on a blank flipchart page.
● Add an extra battery to each circuit to check the predictions.
● The children are not expected to know the term *voltage* but should understand that the battery is a source of power and that more batteries will produce more power. They also should understand that bulbs on the same circuit share the power.
● Explain that if too much power were supplied to the light bulb it would explode. Tell them that you cannot show them this because it is dangerous.

Independent work
● Provide each group of three or four with crocodile clips, wires, bulbs and batteries (9V and 1.5V).
● Set a context for the investigation, for example, a lighthouse's light has become too dim and it needs to be made brighter.
● Ask: *How could you change the brightness of the bulb?* (Change the number of bulbs in the circuit, the type of bulb, the number of batteries used to make the circuit, the voltage of the battery.)
● Ask the children to plan and draw the way in which they would make the bulb burn brightly. What type of circuit will they use? How will they set up their circuit?
● How can the children ensure a fair test? Help them to recognise the importance of changing only one thing at a time.
● Allow the children time to make and test circuits.

Plenary
● Encourage the children to explain their results, saying which circuits helped to make the bulb burn brightly?
● Place some incorrect and correct concluding statements on the right-hand side of the board and ask the children to drag the statements that are correct to form a sound scientific conclusion. For example:
　● The bulbs burned brightly when the number of batteries was the same as the number of bulbs.
　● The bulbs burned brightly when there were more batteries than bulbs.

 127

Similar skeletons?

■ Look carefully at the two pictures of skeletons that your teacher has given to you. What animals are they from?

Picture 1

This skeleton is from _____

I can tell because _____

_____

Picture 2

This skeleton is from _____

I can tell because _____

_____

■ Use the word bank below to label the parts of the skeleton.

☐ Are any parts the same?

☐ Are any parts different?

These parts of the skeletons are similar:

These parts of the skeletons are different:

Word bank

skull	rib cage	knee bone	arm bone
shoulder bone	teeth	spine (backbone)	pelvis
foot	toes	hand	fingers
hard	fragile	brittle	curved

Investigation report 1

◣ **Aim**

Our aim was to find out _____

_____

◣ **Method**

First we _____

_____

Then we _____

_____

Finally, we _____

_____

◣ **Equipment**

```
┌────────────────────────────────────────────────┐
│                                                │
│                                                │
│                                                │
│                                                │
│                                                │
└────────────────────────────────────────────────┘
```

◣ **Making the investigation fair**

We made the test fair by _____

_____

_____

◣ **Predictions**

We thought the end result would be _____

_____

We thought this because _____

_____

_____

Investigation report 2

◀ Results

These are the results from our investigation:

Our results show that _____

_____

_____

◀ Conclusion

Our investigation showed that

_____

_____

_____

◀ Evaluation

We could have improved our test by _____

_____

_____

▶ S C H O L A S T I C
www.scholastic.co.uk

Organisms cards

Wasp

Spider

Woodlouse

Hummingbird

Snail

Squirrel

Dog

Fly

Tiger

Sunflower

Jellyfish

Crab

Shark

Sparrow

Killer whale

Conifer

Duck

Frog

Daffodil

Seaweed

Ladybird

Zebra

Mouse

Starfish

Food chains

Grass

Ferns

Lettuce

Algae

Eagle

Seal

Carrots

Frog

Shark

Rat

Cat

Seeds

Sparrow

Worm

Slug

Fish

Fly

Zebra

Mouse

Lion

Producer	Consumer	Predator	Prey
Producer	Consumer	Predator	Prey

■ SCHOLASTIC
www.scholastic.co.uk

Flowing materials

◼ Draw a picture of a solid and a liquid in these boxes:

This is a picture of

_____

This is a picture of

_____

◼ Complete these explanations.

A solid is:

A liquid is:

Can you explain how solids and liquids are different?

_____

_____

_____

Spinners

■ Cut out these spinners. Clip the tail end together with a paperclip.

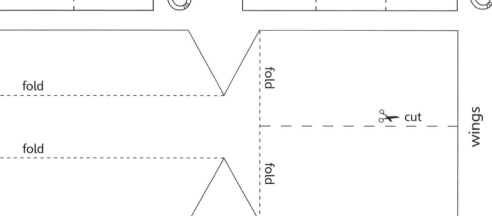

Making circuits work

- Make each of the circuits below with your group, and find out if they work.

- Record what you find out in the table.

- Can you explain why some of the circuits work and some do not?

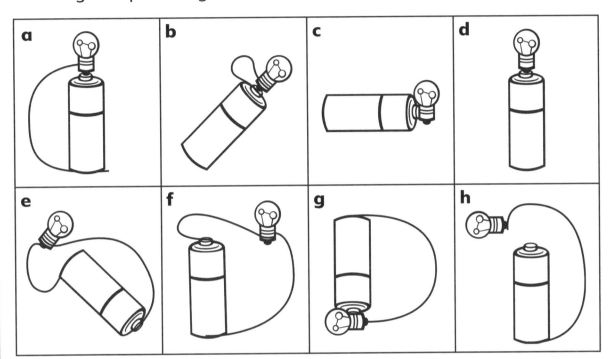

Circuit	Does the circuit work? (Yes/No)	Why?	Circuit	Does the circuit work? (Yes/No)	Why?
a			e		
b			f		
c			g		
d			h		

Sounding it out

✂ cut

Sounding it out

sounds

buzzer

switch

words
and
pictures

Bb   Zz

Illustrations © Jim Peacock / Beehive Illustration

▪SCHOLASTIC
www.scholastic.co.uk

What's the answer?

cut

What's the answer

new questions

buzzer

light

used questions

The Scores

Q _____	Q _____	Q _____	Q _____
A _____	A _____	A _____	A _____
Q _____	Q _____	Q _____	Q _____
A _____	A _____	A _____	A _____
Q _____	Q _____	Q _____	Q _____
A _____	A _____	A _____	A _____
Q _____	Q _____	Q _____	Q _____
A _____	A _____	A _____	A _____

Foundation subjects

The following lessons offer ways to use an interactive whiteboard to teach the foundation subjects, using different whiteboard tools to target different learning styles.

Using an interactive whiteboard gives teachers and children a unique opportunity to project, annotate and save large-scale images. The children will be able to study and focus on details of historical artefacts, maps and aerial photographs, as well as audio and video resources. This in turn facilitates group discussion. In practical lessons, such art and design, and design and technology, you can film techniques and processes with a digital camera or take pictures of children's work, and then display the results on an interactive whiteboard. This allows you to annotate the images and it provides a great opportunity for assessment, as well as a way to record the children's progress and achievements throughout the year.

Lesson title	Objectives	What children should know	Cross-curricular links
History			
Lesson 1: Rich or poor?	**QCA Unit 8** 'What were the differences between the lives of rich and poor people in Tudor times?' • To use inventories to identify characteristic features of different types of people in Tudor times. • To draw conclusions about life in Tudor times from different sources of information. • To learn that there are different ways of interpreting the same information.	• That there are a range of sources of evidence, including written and pictorial sources and artefacts. • About the lives of people in other societies and periods.	**Mathematics** NNS: To solve word problems involving money, using one or more steps, including converting pounds to pence.
Lesson 2: In short supply	**QCA Unit 9** 'What was it like for children in the Second World War?' • To learn why rationing was necessary. • To learn about the impact of rationing on the way of life of people living in England during the Second World War.	• What life was like when their parents/carers and grandparents were children. • When the Second World War occurred and some of the effects on people living in Britain.	**Mathematics** NNS: Use informal pencil and paper methods to record multiplications. **Science** PoS Sc2 (2b) To understand the importance of diet. **PSHE** PoS (3a) To understand what makes a healthy lifestyle.
Lesson 3: Preparing for the afterlife	**QCA Unit 10** 'What can we find out about ancient Egypt from what has survived?' • To learn about Egyptian tombs, pyramids and burial sites. • To learn that what we know about the past is dependent on what has survived.	• The way of life of people who lived a long time ago.	**English** NLS Term 1 T25: To write clear instructions using conventions learned in reading. **Geography** QCA Unit 24 'Passport to the world'
Lesson 4: Living here in the past	• To learn that the area has changed at different times in the past. • To learn to use maps to help describe some of the characteristic features of the past.	• They should have worked with sources, for example pictures and artefacts. • They should have studied, photographed and classified local buildings according to age.	**Geography** QCA Unit 9 'Village settlers' **Geography** PoS (2c) To use maps and plans at a range of scales. **Mathematics** NNS: To solve a problem by collecting, organising, representing and interpreting data in tables, charts, graphs and diagrams.
Geography			
Lesson 5: Too much rubbish	**QCA Unit 8** 'Improving the environment' • To explore how people improve the environment or damage it. • To ask and respond to geographical questions. • To collect and record evidence to answer questions.	• That data can be represented in a pictogram for easier analysis. • That materials can be recycled.	**Mathematics** NNS: To solve a problem by collecting, organising, representing and interpreting data in tables, charts, graphs and diagrams. **ICT** PoS (1b) To prepare information for development using ICT. **Science** QCA Unit 4B 'Habitats'

Lesson title	Objectives	What children should know	Cross-curricular links
Lesson 6: Virtual village **P**	• To recognise that settlements have specific features and are located in response to physical features and human choice. • To draw a map of the layout of a settlement.	• Maps have various features that are represented by symbols. • They should understand how to drag items from the Resource library.	**History** PoS (7) Local history study
Lesson 7: What did we do?	**QCA Unit 19** 'How and where do we spend our time?' • To be able to analyse and communicate findings. • To understand that collecting and storing information in an organised way helps to find answers to questions. • To interpret and analyse information in graphs.	• That data can be represented in tables and graphed by a computer.	**ICT** PoS (1c) To interpret information. **English** NLS Term 3 T25: Design a poster on paper or screen.
Lesson 8: Where on Earth is it? **P**	**QCA Unit 24** 'Passport to the world' • To investigate places. • To analyse evidence. • To use secondary sources of information.	• That there are features of places that can be memorised.	**English** NLS Term 2 T21: To make short notes. **ICT** QCA Unit 4a 'Writing for different audiences'

Design and technology

Lesson title	Objectives	What children should know	Cross-curricular links
Lesson 9: What makes a good bridge? **P**	• To understand and analyse how bridges are constructed. • To recognise the features of a strong bridge. • To develop ideas and explain them clearly.	• That bridges connect areas of land together and need to be strong to support the weight of vehicles.	**Mathematics** NNS: To describe 3D and 2D shapes. **Geography** QCA Unit 24 'Passport to the world' T **Speaking and listening** Objective 37: To use and reflect on some ground rules for dialogue.
Lesson 10: Designing a bridge **P**	• To generate suitable and realistic ideas to build a bridge. • To communicate personal ideas clearly when working in a group.	• How to analyse the features of good bridges. • How to work together to achieve a common goal.	**Speaking and listening** Objective 43: To use time, resources and group members efficiently by distributing tasks, checking progress, and making backup plans.
Lesson 11: Building bridges	• To display effective teamwork skills when constructing their group bridge. • To select appropriate tools, materials and techniques for making their bridge. • To assemble, join and combine components and materials accurately. • To reflect on the progress of their work and identify ways they could improve their work.	• How to work as a team. • How to appraise and evaluate their own work.	**Mathematics** NNS: To solve word problems involving money. **English** NLS Term 1 T27: To write a non-chronological report. **Science** PoS Sc1 (2d) To make a fair test or comparison.

Art and design

Lesson title	Objectives	What children should know	Cross-curricular links
Lesson 12: Viewpoints	**QCA Unit 4A** 'Viewpoints' • To collect information about viewpoints. • To explore ideas about dreams.	• How to empathise with another's situation. • How to work with plans.	**PSHE** PoS (2e) Reflect on spiritual, moral, social and cultural issues, using imagination to understand other people's experiences.

Lesson title	Objectives	What children should know	Cross-curricular links
Lesson 13: Take a seat	**QCA Unit 4B** 'Take a seat' • To identify different types of chairs, their parts, uses and materials from which they are made.	• How to look at photographs and pictures from past and present, identifying key features	**History** PoS (2) Knowledge and understanding of events, people and changes in the past **ICT** QCA Unit 4B 'Developing images using repeating patterns' **English** NLS Term 2 S1/T13: To use adjectives and to write own examples of descriptive, expressive language based on those read.
Lesson 14: Journeys	**QCA Unit 4C** 'Journeys' • To describe personal journeys that are made. • To design symbols/pictures that shows aspects of their journey.	• Map-reading skills and how to identify key features. • Road signs and their meanings. • Symbols that convey instructions, warnings and information.	**Religious education** Non-statutory national framework (3i) To think about symbols and religious expression are expressed. **Geography** PoS (2e) To draw plans and maps at a range of scales. **Mathematics** NNS: To recognise positions and direction.
Lesson 15: Making mosaics	• To understand how mosaics are made.	• That mosaic artwork was used to provide decoration during Roman times. • That mosaics were created using clay tiles and pieces of broken crockery.	**History** QCA Unit 6A 'Why have people invaded and settled in Britain in the past? A Roman case study' **Mathematics** NNS: To describe and visualize 2D shapes; to make shapes. **ICT** QCA Unit 4B 'Developing images using repeating patterns'

Music

Lesson title	Objectives	What children should know	Cross-curricular links
Lesson 16: Rhythmic patterns	**QCA Unit 10** 'Play it again - Exploring rhythmic patterns' • To recognise repeated rhythmic patterns. • To listen carefully and repeat a rhythmic pattern. • To combine two different rhythms with a steady pulse.	• That music has a pulse and often is made of layers of sound. • Children should have experience of playing one line of music against another.	**Art and design** PoS (4a) To learn about visual elements, including colour, pattern and texture, line and tone, shape, form and space.
Lesson 17: Painting with sound	**QCA Unit 13** 'Painting with sound - Exploring sound colours' • To identify descriptive features in art and music. • To analyse and comment on how sounds are used to create different moods.	• The music can make us feel different emotions, and that art can have a similar effect.	**Art and design** PoS (5d) Investigate art, craft and design in a variety of genres, styles and traditions.
Lesson 18: What's the weather like today?	• To understand how symbols can represent sounds. • To be able to follow a sequence of sounds and play as an ensemble.	• That weather can be represented using symbols.	**Geography** QCA Unit 16 'What's in the news?' **English** NLS Term 2 T13: To write own examples of descriptive, expressive language based on those read.

Religious education

Lesson title	Objectives	What children should know	Cross-curricular links
Lesson 19: What is God like?	• To think carefully about what God means to them. • To recognise and respect how different people seek comfort in God. • To develop a sense of awe and wonder in terms of God as an entity.	• That people have different ideas about God.	**English** NLS Term 2 T11: To write poetry based on the structure and/or style of poems read.
Lesson 20: Visions of light	• To think about light and dark as symbols.	• That light and dark are used in various religious festivals.	**PSHE** PoS (2e) Reflect on spiritual, moral, social and cultural issues, using imagination to understand other people's experiences.

Rich or poor?

Learning objectives
QCA Unit 8 'What were the differences between the lives of rich and poor people in Tudor times?'
● To use inventories to identify characteristic features of different types of people in Tudor times.
● To draw conclusions about life in Tudor times from different sources of information.
● To learn that there are different ways of interpreting the same information.

Resources 🅿
Prepared flipchart showing pictures of rich and poor Tudor people, and rich and poor Tudor homes (check copyright); photocopiable page 161 'Rich or poor?' for each child; computers with internet access; pencils; PDF of 'Rich or Poor?' (provided on the CD-ROM).

Links to other subjects
Mathematics
NNS: To solve word problems involving money, using one or more steps, including converting pounds to pence.
● Set up a spreadsheet to convert £.s.d. values to £.p and ask the children to work out modern-day values of the goods in the inventory. (£1 = 20s; 1s = 12d; £1 = 240d)

Whiteboard tools
View the website and PDF in Desktop mode and use the tools in the Desktop toolbox to annotate and highlight the screen. Select the Return to main screen button to return to the flipchart.

◔ Spotlight tool

◉ Recognition tool

🖊 Pen tool

🔦 Marquee select

▢ Desktop mode

📈 Return to main screen

Starter
Display the two Tudor people in your prepared flipchart. Ask: *Which do you think is richer? What is the evidence for this?* Annotate the pictures with the children's observations.

Whole-class shared work
● Ask the children if they think the people would have had the same kind of home.
● Focus on the images of rich and poor homes. Ask: *Who lives in this house? Why do you think that?* Invite a volunteer to the whiteboard to put each person in front of the correct house.
● Do the children think the contents of each house would have been the same?
● Ask: *How do we know what people owned?* Explain that when a person died a list was made of all their property and this was called an inventory.
● Open the site **www.windowsonwarwickshire.org.uk/spotlights/rich_or_poor/tedder_inventory.htm** and read through the inventory for David Tedder with the children.
● Challenge the children to decide whether David Tedder was rich or poor, and to give their reasons. Highlight any words that are indicative of wealth.

Independent work
● Give each pair of children a photocopiable sheet. It shows part of an inventory made in 1596.
● Ask the children to transcribe the inventory into their exercise books or a on separate piece of paper, using the glossary to help them. They need to decide whether the person was rich or poor and explain their reasons.
● The children should start by reading the inventory out loud in pairs or as a class. Remind them that Roman numerals have been used.
● More able learners could use all the material from the lesson to construct an inventory for a person in a different social class.
● Less confident pupils could be given a much-simplified inventory.

Plenary
● Display the PDF of the photocopiable sheet and read through it together. Ask if there were any sections the children did not understand and work through these together.
● Challenge the children to tell you whether they think the owner was rich or poor and to justify their answers. Highlight the text in the inventory that is evidence of wealth. Discuss any differences of opinion, helping the children to understand that evidence can be interpreted in different ways.

In short supply

Learning objectives
QCA Unit 9 'What was it like for children in the Second World War?'
● To learn why rationing was necessary.
● To learn about the impact of rationing on the way of life of people living in England during the Second World War.

Resources
'Rationing' flipchart file; pictures of ration books; pictures of people shopping in wartime Britain; examples of quantities of rationed food to help the children visualise the quantities; printed copies of page 9 of the flipchart file, *My family's food* ration for each child; pencils.

Links to other subjects
Mathematics
NNS: Use informal pencil and paper methods to record multiplications.
● Use mathematical strategies to work out the family ration.
Science
PoS Sc2 (2b) To understand the importance of diet.
PSHE
PoS (3a) To understand what makes a healthy lifestyle.
● Look at what foods make up a healthy diet.

Whiteboard tools
The Floating calculator can be used to check answers to the sums in the Independent work.

● Pen tool

● Recognition tool

● Marquee select tool

● Floating calculator

● Print button

● Activote (optional)

Starter
List what children already know about the Second World War on page 2 of the flipchart. Ask: *Why were British docks targeted for bombing raids? What would the effects have been?* (Destruction of shipping, destruction of goods stored.) Tell the children that German submarines attacked the Merchant Navy ships that brought supplies to Britain. Do they know why rationing became essential? Note their suggestions on page 3 of the flipchart.

Whole-class shared work
● Explain that before the war most of Britain's food was imported. Scarcity usually results in price rises and the government didn't want this to happen, so some foods were rationed.
● Write children's thoughts on rationing on page 4 of the flipchart. Ask why rationing was fair.
● Display the picture of the ration book on the fifth page of the flipchart and explain how they were used. Rations for a household were combined. Ask: *Would it be better to be part of a large or a small household? Why?*
● Display the leaflets on page 6. The Ministry of Food produced many leaflets to help people make the most of their rationed foods. With the children, look at and discuss how the leaflets would have been helpful.
● Go to page 7 of the flipchart. Explain that not all foods were rationed at the same time. Ask the children why they think that was, and what foods were not rationed. (Food was only rationed if the government could guarantee a regular supply; some foods were never available.) Move the shapes to reveal the foods that were rationed in each of the years shown.
● Go to page 8 and show the children how rations varied in different years of the war. Ask them to guess which items could you get less or more of in 1942, compared with 1940. Move the shape to reveal the answers.
● Show the children the examples of rationed food and compare these quantities to what they may eat in a day or a week.
● Explain that some people supplemented their ration by, for example, bartering goods grown or produced at home.

Independent work
● Give out copies of page 9 of the flipchart, *My family's food ration*, for children to complete in pairs.
● Less able learners could work with you on the whiteboard version.
● Challenge more able learners to work out a food ration for a different family.

Plenary
● Do the multiple-choice quiz on page 10 of the flipchart with the children. Use this as an opportunity to assess and clarify misconceptions. Activote devices, or alternative voting methods, can be used to choose the correct answer.
● Ask: *Would you have enjoyed wartime food? What would you have missed most?* Page 11 can be used to gather the children's opinions about rationed food.
● Ask: *Do you think the diet was healthy? Why/why not?*
● Page 12 offers an opportunity for the children to think more about the effects of rationing. The question asks them to consider the alternatives for sugar. (Answer: Potatoes were not used to sweeten cakes.) This could be used as a stimulus for a subsequent lesson to look at what people used instead of the rationed foods.

Preparing for the afterlife

Learning objectives
QCA Unit 10 'What can we find out about ancient Egypt from what has survived?'
● To learn about Egyptian tombs, pyramids and burial sites.
● To learn that what we know about the past is dependent on what has survived.

Resources
'Ancient Egypt' flipchart file; computer with internet access; plain paper; pencils; copies of completed page 5 of the flipchart file, one for each less able learner; scissors; glue; blank sheets of paper.

Links to other subjects
English
NLS Term 1 T25: To write clear instructions using conventions learned in reading.
● Write clear instructions for mummifying a body.
Geography
QCA Unit 24 'Passport to the world'
● Use the internet and reference books to find out what it was like to live in Ancient Egypt, and compare this to life in Egypt today.

Starter
Recap what the children already know about Ancient Egypt, making notes on page 2 of the flipchart. Explain that they are going to learn how the dead were prepared for the afterlife.

Record what the children know about funeral customs in Ancient Egypt on page 3.

Whole-class shared work
● Display page 4 and click on the link to open the British Museum's Ancient Egypt website (**www.ancientegypt.co.uk/mummies/home.html**).
● Click on *Story* on the left-hand side of the page. Begin with the embalming process and then go on to the wrapping and burial of the body (clicking on underlined text opens a glossary).
● Ask: *Why do you think it was important to the Ancient Egyptians that the body was preserved?*
● Discuss the differences between the rich and poor. Were they prepared for burial in exactly the same way? In what way were they different?
● Ask questions about the mummification process, for example: *Why was the heart left inside the body? Why was it important to fill the body with dry materials?*
● Discuss the ritual involved: *Why was the opening of the mouth an important ritual? What would happen if it wasn't performed?*
● Complete the activity on page 5 of the flipchart, putting the instructions for mummifying a body in the correct order.

Independent work
● Hand out sheets of plain paper. Tell the children to pretend to be master embalmers, and write a manual explaining how to prepare a body for burial.
● Encourage the use of annotated illustrations and diagrams (neither the embalmers nor their apprentices would have been able to read or write).
● Give less able learners copies of page 5 of the flipchart, as prompts for the instructions.

Plenary
● Write any interesting facts that the children have learned on page 6 of the flipchart.
● Address any misconceptions that have arisen. (For example, if the master embalmers could not write, how do we know about the embalming process?)
● Discuss the sources of evidence that tell us about the Egyptian belief in life after death. Remind the children of artefacts from the story, such as the canopic jars and amulets.
● Question the children about the reasons for each of the processes, for example, why were amulets wrapped with the bandages? Use page 6 to note down questions to research in a subsequent session.
● Page 7 offers an opportunity to assess the children's understanding of what they have learned. The children can use Activote devices or alternative voting methods to answer the question. (Answer: The heart.)

Whiteboard tools
Add annotations with the Pen or Recognition tools. Activote devices can be used to vote on the correct answer.

 Marquee select tool

 Pen tool

 Recognition tool

 Print button

 Activote (optional)

Living here in the past

Learning objectives
● To learn that the area has changed at different times in the past.
● To learn to use maps to help describe some of the characteristic features of the past.

Resources 🅿
Internet access; prepared flipchart showing plan of area, with digital pictures of old and modern buildings (copyright permitting) and hyperlink to **www.old-maps.co.uk** Modern, large-scale map of same area, showing individual buildings (include in flipchart, copyright permitting); one copy of both maps for each child (copyright permitting); paper and pencils; PDF of photocopiable page 162 'Streets past and present' (provided on the CD-ROM).

Links to other subjects
Geography
QCA Unit 9 'Village settlers'
● Consider why the area in the old and new maps has changed.
Geography
PoS (2c) To use maps and plans at a range of scales.
● Consolidate and apply map skills learned in geography.
Mathematics
NNS: To solve a problem by collecting, organising, representing and interpreting data in tables, charts, graphs and diagrams.
● Make a Venn diagram to sort the information into *Past, Present* and *Past and present*.

Whiteboard tools
Use the Spotlight tool to focus on your locality when you visit the website.

Ⅰ Lines tool

Ⓣ Text editor tool

▪ Pen tool

◔ Spotlight tool

⊜ Floating keyboard

Starter
Revise with the children any earlier work regarding study of the local area, reminding them of the locations of older and newer buildings in the region. Mark these on the simple plan of the local area in the flipchart. Remind the children of some of the features of older properties.

Whole-class shared work
● Ask the children to imagine what the area might have looked like in the past. Can they suggest familiar buildings or features that would not have existed?
● Explain that they are going to look at an old map of the area. Click on the hyperlink **(www.old-maps.co.uk)**. Locate your town, centre the map on your locality and focus on it using the Spotlight tool ◔.
● Point out the date of the map and ask the children to tell you how long ago that was. Encourage them to relate this date to other periods in history that they have studied.
● Ask the children if they can identify any features on the map.
● Look at the names of any old buildings. Ask: *Are the names familiar? Are these used in modern features, such as roads, or housing estates?*
● Draw attention to the modern map and ask the children to say briefly how the locality has changed: perhaps there was a railway in the past that isn't there now, for example. Annotate this map to show the changes.

Independent work
● Tell the children that they are going to pretend to be time travellers. Using the old and new maps of the area as a starting point, they will describe in detail walks between two familiar points in the past and the present.
● Discuss with the children the sorts of information they could include, for example, the styles and functions of the buildings.
● Encourage the children to describe other things that they might have seen or heard, such as transport or clothing.
● Less confident children could be given more supportive writing frames.
● More able learners should be encouraged to summarise the changes.

Plenary
● In this session children will sort the names of objects into those from the past and those from the present.
● Display the PDF of 'Streets past and present' on the CD-ROM.
● Read through the list of things and ask children to come up to the whiteboard and, using the Lines tool Ⅰ draw arrows from the words to the correct heading.
● Discuss the things that can go under both headings. How have these things changed over time.
● Discuss and clarify any misconceptions as they arise.
● Type other words suggested by the children onto the flipchart. Can the children classify these words, too?

Too much rubbish

Starter
Organise a survey of the rubbish thrown away in the classroom every day for a week. Put a tally sheet by the bin for people to fill in when they throw something away. Use the categories on the pictogram on page 3 of the flipchart. Decide on sensible units of measurement for each item (a certain number of sheets could constitute one *bundle* of paper). Put up a sign reminding people to use the tally chart. At the end of the week, total each day's rubbish.

At the start of this lesson, go to page 2 of the flipchart. Recap on what the survey was about, fill in the dates and discuss children's predictions about results.

Whole-class shared work
● Go to page 3 and click on the image to open the pictogram. Ask one child to read out the survey results for the first day and drag the relevant quantities of each symbol on to the pictogram.
● Use the Camera tool 📷 to take a snapshot of the day, reduce it to fit, and paste it into the relevant box on page 3 of the flipchart. Repeat the process for the other days of the week.
● Discuss the results. Ask what the items made of the different materials might have been. Use mathematical vocabulary to compare quantities of different materials.
● Go to page 4. Discuss what materials can be recycled and make notes. Drag and drop the items to the correct recycling box.
● Display page 5 and discuss which materials in the children's survey will have been recycled. Complete the spider diagram.
● Go to page 6. Ask whether there were any items that could have been recycled, and weren't? What items would have been hard to recycle?

Independent work
● Return to page 4, about recycling different materials. Ask the children to draw a series of pictures, using arrows, to show how a recyclable material can be continually reused (for example, aluminium). Talk about the vocabulary they will need and write the words up for them to copy.
● Provide children who need more guidance with an information sheet on a particular aspect of recycling.
● Ask more able learners to add a title and persuasive text to their diagram.

Plenary
● Look at page 7 of the flipchart. Click on the link to see a contract to try to recycle more, to help save resources and energy. Discuss the statements. Do the children all agree that this is a good thing to do? The class can sign the contract and print out copies to display, or to stick in their books.
● Ask the children to find out more about recycling and its good effects as part of their homework.

Virtual village

Learning objectives
● To recognise that settlements have specific features and are located in response to physical features and human choice.
● To draw a map of the layout of a settlement.

Resources 🅿
Map symbols both from the Resource library and, if necessary, created in a paint program; photocopiable page 163 'Virtual village'; computer with internet connection; URL for Ordnance Survey *Get-a-map* **www.ordnance survey.co.uk/oswebsite/ getamap**

Links to other subjects
History
PoS (7) Local history study
● Use this technique to study or develop a map of a particular period in time. Decide on the features to include or exclude.

Starter
Bring up the Ordnance Survey *Get-a-map* site. Start with the map of the British Isles. Choose a location, and gradually zoom in by clicking on the map. Ask the children what is changing as you do this They should be able to see details of roads, rivers, buildings and land use. Alternatively, start zoomed in on a known place, and zoom out.

Whole-class shared work
● Open a new flipchart page. Tell the children that they are going to create a map for an imaginary village in the countryside. Ask: *What colour should the background be? What is the main colour in the countryside?* Use the Fill tool 🖌 to set the background colour as requested by the children. Put a compass rose, from the Resource library 📖 on the screen and explain its purpose.
● Ask the children: *What features in the village would be very hard to move or remove, even with a bulldozer or crane?* (Lakes, hills, and so on.) Invite children to draw a river running across the screen, using a sensible colour and thickness of line. Ask: *Why do many settlements have rivers?*
● Ask: *What features of a settlement often cross a river?* Draw a couple of roads and/or a railway onto the flipchart.
● Add appropriate mapping symbols from the Resource library. Ask the children to justify the sites of the features.
● Finally, add buildings to the map using the Shapes tool 🔷.

Independent work
● Save the map and leave it on display for reference. Tell the children that they are going to design their own village. They will need to think about all the points discussed as a class.
● Hand out the photocopiable sheet. Point out the compass rose, key, the space for a village name and the space for the map. Ask the children to design their village to include a river and a hill. Tell them that colour will play an important part in their maps.
● Adapt the sheet for less able learners, providing a framework of river and roads to start them off.
● More able learners could look at an Ordnance Survey map to see how the background is shaded different colours, depending on what it is used for.

Plenary
● Ask the children to work in pairs to discuss their maps. Challenge each child to describe a route though the other's village, commenting on what is seen on the journey.
● Invite pairs of children to describe a walk through the village on the interactive whiteboard. Ask them to relate to the key when they describe what they see.
● Tell the children that they will now be able to look at maps of real places and know what it is like there.

Whiteboard tools
Use the map symbols from the geography folder in the Resource library to add features and compass points. Create buildings using the Shapes tool.

📖 Resource library

🖌 Fill tool

🔦 Marquee select tool

🔷 Shapes tool

🖊 Pen tool

What did we do?

Learning objectives
QCA Unit 19 'How and where do we spend our time?'
● To be able to analyse and communicate findings.
● To understand that collecting and storing information in an organised way helps to find answers to questions.
● To interpret and analyse information in graphs.

Resources
'What did we do?' flipchart file. Prior to the lesson, insert digital photographs of places in the local area (eg, shops, the park) on to page 2 of the flipchart. Complete the spreadsheet on page 3 showing how children spent their time during the week. Re-link the spreadsheet and save the flipchart for this lesson. (Microsoft Excel is required to view the embedded spreadsheet in the flipchart.)

Links to other subjects
ICT
PoS (1c) Interpret information.
● Change one item of data to illustrate how a typing error would affect the graph.
English
NLS Term 3 T25: Design a poster on paper or screen.
● Design a poster for a leisure activity.

Whiteboard tools
In Desktop mode, use the Handwriting tool to enter data, and the Pen, Highlighter and Eraser tools to annotate the charts. Use the Camera tool to paste the data and charts to a new flipchart page, for saving or printing.

◤ Marquee select tool

▣ Desktop mode

⚖ Highlighter tool

✂ Design mode

🖊 Pen tool

📷 Camera tool

✎ Handwriting tool

▦ Return to main screen

Starter
In the week preceding this lesson, ask the children to record how they spent their time every day for a week. Use the spreadsheet on page 3 of the flipchart for the criteria. Collate the data and enter it into the spreadsheet prior to this lesson. Re-link the file to the button on page 3 of the flipchart file and save the flipchart.

Look at the series of photographs of places in the local area that you have placed on page 2 of the flipchart. Ask the children to arrange them in the Carroll diagram, according to the criteria of *work, leisure, near,* and *far.* Use this to remind the children of the data they collected. Ask: *Do we visit places less if they are far away? Why?*

Whole-class shared work
● Click on the link on page 3 to display the completed spreadsheet. Make sure that the percentage row is not visible.
● Look at the data. Which activity has the largest amount of time? Use mathematics skills to try and work this out. Scroll down to reveal the percentage row. Point out that a computer can do the calculations for us, so that we can spend longer on thinking about what the results mean.
● Identify highest and lowest hours spent on any of the activities.
● Ask questions about the data, relating to largest/smallest number of hours, and make annotations.
● Scroll down to the chart. Ask: *How does the bar chart help us to understand the data? Which things are easy to see and which difficult? Does the bar chart help to spot any obvious errors in the data?* (The chart doesn't show the hours each child spent on each activity, but it is easier to see which activity takes up the most and least time.) Annotate with the children's observations.
● Save the annotated screen to the flipchart using the Camera tool 📷.

Independent work
● Ask the children to make a poster to advertise one of the leisure activities. The posters might include information about the locality of the activity, its benefits and when it can be used. The posters could be displayed around the school.
● Print out several copies of the annotated data that has been saved to the flipchart. Distribute the printouts to the children to provide data and vocabulary.
● Provide a few relevant phrases for those children who need them.
● Encourage more able learners to include a witty slogan, including alliteration or a pun, as part of their poster.

Plenary
● Go back to the chart of activities. Discuss possible explanations for the different amounts of time spent on the various activities. Draw out the idea that some activities can only be done once in a while. Perhaps they just did not occur in this particular week. Travelling distance might be a factor, as might the weather.
● Discuss how the data collected could be improved? Make a note of the children's responses on page 4 of the flipchart.
● Ask: *What would the effect be of taking a sample over four weeks?*
● Discuss whether the data would be different for adults.

Learning objectives
QCA Unit 24 'Passport to the world'
● To investigate places.
● To analyse evidence.
● To use secondary sources of information.

Resources
'Investigating Europe' flipchart file; photocopiable page 164, 'Where on Earth is it?'; internet access; facts about the places to be investigated; photographs of the places if available; computers with desktop publishing package (optional).

Links to other subjects
English
NLS Term 2 T21: To make short notes.
● The children can practise note-making skills when they research the different countries.
ICT
QCA Unit 4a 'Writing for different audiences'
● Encourage children to think about their audience if they are putting together a multimedia presentation.

Whiteboard tools
Set the Reveal tool before turning each page. This will stop the children from seeing the facts too soon.

● Reveal tool

● Marquee select tool

● Pen tool

● Delete button

● Activote (optional)

Where on Earth is it?

Starter
Do this activity over a few days, for about 15 minutes each day. The final session will include the Independent work.

Click on the URL on page 2 of the flipchart to go the European Union website. Enter the portal through the English link (*en*). Select *The EU at a glance* in the left-hand menu, then *Countries*, and *Maps of Europe*. Allow children to select countries and explore the maps, commenting on what they see.

Whole-class shared work
● Return to page 2 of the flipchart. Enable the Reveal tool ●, and turn to the page 3. Gradually reveal the page from the top, asking the children to guess the European Country of the Day. (The features are mixed up from their headings.)
● Ask the children to drag each fact under the correct heading at the bottom of the page, rotating them if necessary.
● Delete the label *Mystery country* to check whether the children guessed the country correctly. Place each fact next to its appropriate heading.
● Discuss the outline map of the country and emphasise which parts of it border other countries and which border the sea. Make associations to help children remember the shape of a country (for example, *Italy is shaped like a boot*).
● Repeat this each day using pages 4 to 10. The children should be able to predict the items on each page when they have seen them a few times. They can record information about each country on the photocopiable sheet.

Independent work
● On the final day, group the children into pairs and give each pair a country.
● Ask each pair to produce a booklet about the country. Encourage them to use their photocopiable sheets as a source of information.
● If necessary, provide a template document for the children to build on. This could include key headings that match the data in the flipchart.
● Pages 11 and 12 summarise all the information given on the preceding pages. Printouts of these two pages can be used to support less able learners.
● More able learners could produce a simple multimedia presentation instead of a booklet. They could use a desktop publishing package to insert text, clipart, maps, photographs and numerical data.
● Ask those children who are more competent in using the internet, to include a couple of words (vocabulary) from their country's language in their booklet or presentation.

Plenary
● Visit the EU online website again. Click on *The EU at a glance* and then *The symbols of the EU* to look at the flag and listen to the anthem.
● Use the list of member states (*The EU at a glance > Countries*) to investigate other countries that form part of the European Union. Ask the children to click on the ones that interest them.
● Page 13 offers a sorting exercise as an opportunity for the children to recall what they have learned about Europe.
● Allow children to share their booklets on the various countries. Write any interesting facts on to page 14 of the flipchart. If possible, display the booklets in the classroom, or show them at a special assembly.

Learning objectives
- To understand and analyse how bridges are constructed.
- To recognise the features of a strong bridge.
- To develop ideas and explain them clearly.

Resources
'The bridge competition' flipchart file; photocopiable page 165 'What makes a strong bridge?' for each child.

Links to other subjects
Mathematics
NNS: To describe 3D and 2D shapes.
- Children should use correct shape vocabulary when describing the bridges.

Geography
QCA Unit 24 'Passport to the world' To use secondary sources of information.
- Use the internet and reference books to find out about famous bridges.

Speaking and listening
Objective 37: To use and reflect on some ground rules for dialogue.
- Children should make structured contributions, speak audibly and listen to others when discussing the images.

Whiteboard tools
Use the Spotlight tool to focus on particular areas of the images. Reduce the Page scale to write in the area surrounding the main flipchart page.

 Pen tool

 Teacher tools menu

Menu (select Page scale in the pop-up menu)

Spotlight tool

What makes a good bridge?

Starter
Begin by posing the following problem to the class:
> You are standing beside a river and you want to cross to the other side. The river is too deep to walk through or drive through. How could you get across to the other side without getting wet?

Discuss the children's ideas, which will probably include building a bridge, and list them on page 2 of the flipchart. Explain to children that over the next few lessons, they will be looking at different types of bridges and how they are built. They will then design and build a bridge of their own. In this lesson, they will look carefully at what is needed to build a strong bridge.

Whole-class shared work
- Tell the children they are going to look at some pictures of bridges. Go to page 3 of the flipchart and draw their attention to the questions. Ask: *What makes each bridge different? What do you notice about the base of each bridge? What kind of material has been used? Why?* Use the Spotlight tool to focus on aspects of the bridges.
- Reduce the Page Scale (go to the Teacher tools menu, select Menu and then Page scale in the pop-up menu; click on Other and select 50% in the drop-down menu). Write up their suggestions in the area around the pictures.
- Reset the Page scale to 100% or *Best fit* (whichever is your preferred setting). Read the explanations of three different types of bridge on pages 4, 5 and 6. Ask the children to discuss, in pairs, real-life examples of these types of bridges.
- Look at pages 7 to 10. Discuss with the children the types of bridges that are being shown. Focus on particular features and annotate the children's ideas around the photographs (by reducing the Page scale).

Independent work
- Show the children page 11 and hand out the photocopiable sheets. Ask them to choose the bridge they like best, to draw it on the sheet and label the features that make it a really strong bridge.
- Halfway through the lesson, ask the children to complete their drawings.
- Go to page 12 of the flipchart and tell the children that, in the next two lessons, they will work in groups to design and build a bridge for the competition, using art straws.
- Ask the children to try designing a bridge for the competition on the second half of the photocopiable sheet.
- Encourage more able learners to use what they have learned about what makes a good bridge to inform their own designs.
- Less able learners may need further explanation of the task. Consider working with them as a group.

Plenary
- Ask the children to share their ideas for the bridge competition. Display good examples to share with the class.
- Tell the children that they will be using these designs in the next lesson.

Designing a bridge

Starter
Remind the children of the previous lesson. Display some of their bridge designs and discuss them. Encourage the children to describe the features they particularly like.

Tell the children that they will be working in groups to design a bridge for a competition. Their individual ideas will be important in the design process, but each group must come to an agreement about the final design.

Whole-class shared work
● Spend a few minutes discussing pages 12 and 13 of the flipchart. Explain the task to the children.
● Ask the children what they know about the word *force*? Give them a few minutes to think about their replies. Explain that it means pressure.
● At the bottom of page 12, draw a picture of a beam bridge across the river. Draw an arrow in the middle of the bridge. Ask: *What will happen if weights are placed in the middle of the bridge?*
● After discussion, ask: *How can we protect the bridge against that pressure?* Explain that for each force applied directly, there is an indirect force acting against it.
● Explain that the children will be competing to win a prize. The winner will be the group with the strongest bridge and the most money left.
● Go to page 14, which shows the materials they can use, and discuss. Show them page 15, and explain that they must use this to keep a tally of the materials that they use.

Independent work
● The children should work in mixed-ability groups of five, using their bridge designs from the previous lesson.
● Encourage the groups to think creatively of different ways of constructing the beam across the two bases. They should consider ways in which their materials could be strengthened.
● Allow the groups to spend five to ten minutes looking at the individual designs. They should look for a good idea from each sheet.
● Tell the groups that they have the remainder of the lesson to design their bridges.
● Each group should use plain paper to sketch and note down their ideas for a group design. The final design should be drawn on the photocopiable sheet.
● Provide each group with a few art straws for reference. As they work, encourage them to think about the different types of bridges that you have looked at.
● Ensure that the group's members work as a team, supporting those who are less able and allowing them the opportunity to contribute.

Plenary
● Encourage the different groups to share their ideas for their bridge.

Building bridges

Learning objectives
● To display effective teamwork skills when constructing their group bridge.
● To select appropriate tools, materials and techniques for making their bridge.
● To assemble, join and combine components and materials accurately.
● To reflect on the progress of their work and identify ways they could improve their work.

Resources
'The bridge competition' flipchart file; 40 art straws and a pair of scissors for each group; £1.50 in plastic money for each group (50 pence pieces and sufficient 5p and 10p coins for change); 10g weights to test the bridge (optional); two boxes to represent the villages; blue paper to represent the river that the bridges have to span.

Links to other subjects
Mathematics
NNS: To solve word problems involving money.
● Calculate change, keep to budget and compare how much each group spent.
English
NLS Term 1 T27: To write a non-chronological report.
● Use a report format when writing up the project.
Science
PoS Sc1 (2d) To make a fair test or comparison.
● Discuss how to keep the competition fair.

Whiteboard tools
Annotate and complete the charts with the Pen tool or the Recognition tool. Insert photos via the Resource library.

 Pen tool

 Recognition tool

 Resource library

Starter
This lesson will take more than the hour allocation. It can be extended at your discretion, depending on the detail required of the written work.

Ask the groups to show their bridge designs from the last lesson. Go through the previous pages of the flipchart to review the task and remind the children of the equipment they can use.

Whole-class shared work
● Go to page 16. Discuss the idea that teamwork is essential when designing and building any structure. Ask the children what skills they will need as they work in their groups, and note down their suggestions.
● Move on to page 17 and discuss how the class can make sure this will be a fair test. For example, the length that the bridge has to span must be established at the start. Note down children's ideas.

Independent work
● Within their groups, allow the children sufficient time to build their bridges.
● Set up the shop next to the whiteboard. Use the table on page 15 to keep a tally of the resources that each group purchases.
● Monitor the children as they work. Discuss their different techniques for joining the straws, and the ways in which they use the available resources.
● Take digital pictures as the children work. If possible, use a digital camcorder to film children as they demonstrate and explain their techniques and bridge designs. (Remember to obtain permission from parents before filming the children.)
● Ensure that the weights are available for the children to test their bridges as they build them.
● Again, ensure that more able learners support those who are less able, and allow them to contribute.

Plenary
● Display the chart on page 18 of the flipchart. Ask each group to record how much money it has left.
● Test each bridge to see how strong it is. Add 10g weights until the bridge collapses and record the final load in the chart on page 18.
● Use a digital camera to take a picture of each group's bridge before, during and after the test. Insert these photos on page 19 of the flipchart.
● Discuss which bridge is the winner. The bridge must be strong, but also must not have cost too much to make. Discuss what made the bridge strong.
● Encourage the children to evaluate their models in a positive light using the *two stars and a wish* approach: name two things about making your bridge or working in a group that you really liked; then name one thing you would change or improve.
● Use pages 20 to 23 to talk through the process of producing a written report and evaluation of the project. (This can be done in a subsequent lesson.)

Viewpoints

Learning objectives
QCA Unit 4A 'Viewpoints'
● To collect information about viewpoints.
● To explore ideas about dreams.

Resources
Prepared flipchart page showing digital photographs (copyright permitting) of the following:
● a *bird's eye view* (aerial) or oblique view (taken from the top window in building, for example)
● a *worm's eye view* (taken from the ground looking upwards)
● a view from a normal perspective.
Viewfinders, one for each child; paper; pencils; crayons.

Links to other subjects
PSHE
PoS (2e) Reflect on spiritual, moral, social and cultural issues, using imagination to understand other people's experiences.
● Encourage the children to empathise with the characters. Discuss with the children moments when they have felt small or big.

Starter
Display the flipchart page showing photographs taken from bird's eye/oblique, worm's eye and regular perspectives. Ask the children what they notice about these photographs. Ask: *How are they different?* Lead them to think about the notion of viewpoints: these could be scenes viewed by a bird or a giant, a worm or insect, and a person.

Whole-class shared work
● Open the Resource library and browse to English and then Stories. Select two contrasting characters, for example a boy and a witch, or a child and an animal, and paste them onto a new flipchart page. Make sure the characters are the same size.
● Ask the children to describe what the characters may be thinking. Ask: *What might be happening in this situation?* Write up their ideas.
● Increase the size of one character and ask the children if the character's viewpoints have changed. How have they changed? Why? Write their comments, using a different coloured pen.
● Think about the characters in isolation. Ask the children to look at the big character. What would the world look like from this viewpoint? Would you feel really powerful if you were this big?
● Think about the small character. What does everything look like from this viewpoint? How would it feel to be the size of an insect? Would the children feel scared, or would they feel safe because they could hide in lots of small places?

Independent work
● Tell the children to think about their classroom. Ask: *What would everything look like to a person as tall as the ceiling/no taller than a ruler?* Encourage the children to pick up objects and to look at them from different perspectives.
● Give out sheets of paper, pencils and crayons. Ask the children to draw a particular object from a bird's eye, or worm's eye, point of view.
● Next, ask them to draw their own pictures, imagining that they are looking at a scene from a bird's eye or worm's eye viewpoint. This can be a real-life scene, such as the classroom or playground, or it can be a fantasy scene, from the viewpoint of a giant, for example.
● Remind the children that they need to think about their viewpoints. How do things look if you are really big or small? Does everything look frightening? Do you feel safe? Do things get in the way?

Plenary
● Invite some of the children to share their work.
● Ask the class to guess from which viewpoint the picture has been drawn.
● Encourage the children to describe what they have drawn. How did the different viewpoint make them feel about the things in the picture?

Whiteboard tools
Select images from the Resource library.

 Marquee select tool

 Resource library

 Pen tool

Take a seat

Learning objective
QCA Unit 4B 'Take a seat'
● To identify different types of chairs, their parts, uses and materials from which they are made.

Resources ◉ 🄿
'Take a seat' flipchart file; photocopiable page 167 'Take a seat', one for each pair.

Links to other subjects
History
PoS (2) Knowledge and understanding of events, people and changes in the past.
● Study furniture and how it has been used in different periods of time.
ICT
QCA Unit 4B 'Developing images using repeating patterns'
● Design a repetitive pattern for the back and seat panel.
English
NLS Term 2 S1/T13: To use adjectives and to write own examples of descriptive, expressive language based on those read.
● Use new vocabulary to write a short story based on the drawings.

Whiteboard tools
Use the Spotlight tool to focus on particular chairs. Annotate the children's suggestions with the Pen or Recognition tools.

🄺 Marquee select tool

◔ Spotlight tool

▱ Recognition tool

◉ Activote (optional)

Starter
Start by telling the children that in this lesson they will be looking at different types of chair, and designing a chair of their own. Go to the second page of the flipchart. Ask the children where they use chairs in their daily life, and what they use them for. Write up their suggestions.

Whole-class shared work
● Show them the photographs of the different chairs on page 3 and ask: *What do we use chairs for? What are they made from?* Ask the children to compare the chairs and to tell you what is similar about each chair and how they differ. Group the chairs according to their similarities.
● Use the Spotlight tool to focus on particular chairs or to focus on special details. For example, the high chair is very different to the wicker chair, although they are both made for sitting.
● Focussing on individual chairs, ask: *How is this chair used? What is it used for? What material has the chair been constructed from? Why do you think that material has been chosen? Is the chair meant to be portable?*
● Look at page 4 together. Ask the children to vote on their favourite chair. Discuss the results and the reasons why a particular chair is preferred. *Which chair is the most popular? Which is the least popular? Why?*
● Go to page 5 of the flipchart. Discuss why we use chairs. Add the children's suggestions to the list.
● Display page 6. Ask children to drag the labels to the correct features of the chair. Once they have done this, they can answer the questions on the tabs. Discuss the different ways in which chairs are made.

Independent work
● Group the children into pairs. Provide each pair with a copy of photocopiable page 167 'Take a seat'.
● Talk through the task, explaining the terms *front view, back view, side view* and *plan view*.
● Encourage the children to spend some time thinking before they begin designing. They should consider the purpose of the chair. Is it for a special occasion, or a particular person?
● Go to page 7 and draw attention to the Character box. The children can pick a character for whom to design a chair. You can also use this page to note down ideas for different purposes of chairs, to stimulate thinking.
● If groups finish early, encourage them to think of patterns that could be used for the seat and back panels of their chairs. They could draw and colour these in their sketchbooks.

Plenary
● After completing their drawings, ask the children to show their chair designs to the rest of the class. Invite each child to point out the features they particularly like. Ask questions such as: *What type of occasion could* (for example) *Eve's chair be used for? How do you know this chair is fit for a King?* Write any interesting findings on to page 8 of the flipchart.

Journeys

Learning objectives
QCA Unit 4C 'Journeys'
● To describe personal journeys that are made.
● To design symbols/pictures that shows aspects of their journey.

Resources
Internet map site, such as *Multimap* (**www.multimap.com**) or the AA (**www.theaa.org.uk**); Digital photographs of different landmarks from the local area (copyright permitting); selection of road traffic signs from the Resource library; sketchbooks, one per child; selection of collage materials.

Links to other subjects
Religious education
Non-statutory national framework (3i) To think about symbols and religious expression.
● Look at how symbols are used by different religions.
Geography
PoS (2e) To draw plans and maps at a range of scales.
Mathematics
NNS: To recognise positions and direction.
● Lay a grid over a digital area photograph and number the axes. Use for work on coordinates, for example, *Who can show me where the shopping centre is?*

Whiteboard tools
Select images of road traffic signs from the Resource library. Use the Shapes tool to help in building symbols. Use the Spotlight tool to focus on aspects of the photographs.

🔳 Camera tool
🔳 Shapes tool
🔳 Pen tool
🔳 Spotlight tool
🔳 Resource library

Starter
Ask the children to explain what a journey is (the way you get from one place to another). Ask them to spend a few minutes thinking about a journey that they often make, for example, from home to school, from home to town, or from home to a grandparent's house.

Display a map of the local area (copyright permitting) and ask volunteers to describe their journeys. Encourage them to describe in detail the places of interest they notice on the way. Ask: *Why do you notice that house more than the others? Describe what the entrance to the church looks like. Do you like that sculpture that is in the park? Can you explain why?*

Whole-class shared work
● Write the phrase *Every picture tells a story*. Discuss what it means.
● Display a selection of road symbols and ask the children to tell you what each symbol means. Record the suggestions the children give.
● Return to the map and focus on a small section by the school. Ask the children to point out the road signs they pass each day and to explain what the signs show.
● Display a few photographs of landmarks on the map, such as the church, shopping centre, theatre or playground. Ask the children how these things could be shown using a symbol.
● Focus on particular aspects of the photographs using the Spotlight tool 🔳. Encourage the children to think carefully about the shapes that they see and recognise in the landmarks.
● To support less able learners, insert actual shapes by the landmarks. Which shape would the children choose for a background?

Independent work
● Tell the children to look carefully at the photographs on the board and to choose two aspects of their particular journey that always catch their eye.
● Using their sketchbooks, ask the children to think of as many different ways of showing that landmark in pictures. For example, if they pass a church, they could draw a dove or a stained glass window.
● Encourage them not to draw the obvious representations but to think creatively about different ways to represent the landmark. They should consider how this landmark makes them feel when they see it?
● Once they are happy with their designs, the children should create a collage of the symbols using different materials.

Plenary
● Take digital pictures of some of the children's work and display them on the whiteboard.
● Challenge the rest of the class to guess what the symbols depict.
● Ask children to explain why they chose to represent the landmark in this way, and to explain their choice of materials.

Making mosaics

Starter
Display page 2 of the flipchart. Ask the children to explain what they know already about mosaics and write up suggestions on the board. Show the examples of mosaics on page 3 to 7. Share other examples, using your printed resources (for example, postcards, photos or books), or examples from the internet, copyright permitting (for example, the Roman Mosaics page from the BBC website **www.bbc.co.uk/history/ancient/romans/mosaics_gallery.shtml**). Explain to the children that in this lesson they will be making their own alphabet mosaic.

Whole-class shared work
● Look in detail at the mosaic examples. Encourage the children to identify the features they notice. Ask: *How have these mosaics been created? How have the colours been used? What shapes can you see?*
● Display page 8, which shows letters made out of mosaic tiles. Discuss the image and let children build up their own letter using the grid on page 9, and the Fill tool .
● Use the Page reset button to start again.

Independent work
● Give each child a photocopiable sheet and some sheets of scrap paper. Ask them to design their initials using the mosaic grid.
● Explain that they need to think about the colours that they want to use and whether they would like to include other elements, such as a patterned border.
● Encourage the children to mix different types of media to add interest to their mosaics. They can cut up coloured paper or pages from colour magazines to use as mosaic tiles.
● Suggest that they plan out the shape of their mosaic pattern before sticking everything down.
● Less able learners may find it easier to concentrate on the initial letter of their first name only. Extend more able learners by encouraging them to fill the entire grid with colour, ensuring that their letters are clearly visible.

Plenary
● Encourage the children to show their work, and to draw attention to any elements of their mosaics which they particularly like. Ask the children to explain why they chose different types of materials.
● Write any points of interest up on to page 10 of the flipchart.

Rhythmic patterns

Learning objectives
QCA Unit 10 'Play it again - Exploring rhythmic patterns'
● To recognise repeated rhythmic patterns.
● To listen carefully and repeat a rhythmic pattern.
● To combine two different rhythms with a steady pulse.

Resources
Prepared flipchart, each page showing a different four-beat rhythm, for example:

Prepared flipchart: the first page with the words to *Polly put the kettle on*, the second page showing the same rhyme with musical notes showing the rhythm under each line; selection of percussion instruments.

Links to other subjects
Art and design
PoS (4a) To learn about visual elements, including colour, pattern and texture, line and tone, shape, form and space.
● Identify how artists evoke different moods through their paintings.
English
NLS Term 2 T10: To develop use of settings in own writing.
● Use the children's work as a stimulus to create a setting for a story. Encourage them to think about the moods and scenes that music can evoke.

Whiteboard tools
Use the music symbols from the Resource library to create rhythm patterns. Use the Lines tool to divide the screen into three parts to separate the rhythms that groups play.

 Resource library

 Marquee select tool

❘ Lines tool

❋ Background

▨ Highlighter tool

Starter
Play *Switch* with the children. Ask them to tap out a four-beat pulse on their knees. Encourage them to keep the pulse steady and not to rush. Then call out *Switch* and show the first page of the prepared flipchart. The children have to change to this rhythm. After repeating this rhythm a couple of times, tell the children to return back to the four-beat pulse. Repeat for the other rhythms.

Whole-class shared work
● Show the flipchart page with *Polly Put the Kettle On*. Ask How many lines/phrases are there in each verse? (Four.) Say the rhyme out loud with them.
● Go to the second page and show the musical notes under each line.
● Practise clapping the rhythm with the children. Point out that the same rhythmic phrase repeats itself several times. Tell them this is called an *ostinato*.
● Go to a blank flipchart page and divide it into two parts using the Lines tool ❘. In the top part, draw four crotchets. Explain that this is the pulse of the rhythm. Ask the children to clap out the pulse.
● When the pulse is steady, clap the rhythm of the song *Polly Put the Kettle On* over it. Ask: *What is the difference between your rhythm and mine?* (Theirs is quicker.)
● Duplicate the pulse rhythm five times across the board.
● In the next line, duplicate the rhythm of the whole song under the last four pulse patterns, leaving the first part blank.

Pol-ly put the ket-tle on

● Divide the class into two. Explain that one half will clap the first line and the other half the second line. Ask the class to perform both parts together a few times.

Independent work
● Ask the children to select an instrument and get into small groups of about six. Label each child in the group *A* or *B*. Ask the *A* children to play the steady pulse on their instruments and the *B* children to play the rhythm of *Polly Put the Kettle On*.
● Stop the children halfway through and listen to some of the groups.
● Then, ask them to devise their own repeated rhythmic pattern. When they practise the pattern, half the group should maintain the steady pulse whilst the other half performs the rhythmic pattern. They should then swap roles.

Plenary
● Listen carefully to each group as it performs its rhythmic pattern.
● Add the children's patterns to a new flipchart page. Build up a set of rhythmic patterns and ask groups to try and play each other's.

Painting with sound

Learning objectives
QCA Unit 13 'Painting with sound - Exploring sound colours'
● To identify descriptive features in art and music.
● To analyse and comment on how sounds are used to create different moods.

Resources
Digital pictures of an elephant, a tortoise, a swan and a lion (copyright permitting); recording of Saint-Saens *Carnival of the Animals;* print of Van Gogh's *Starry Night* and an example of music to accompany it (for example, Beethoven's *Moonlight Sonata*); digital and printed versions of paintings that evoke a sense of mood and allow scope for aural interpretation (copyright permitting); large pieces of sugar paper, one for each group; selection of tuned and untuned instruments

Links to other subjects
Art and design
PoS (5d) Investigate art, craft and design in a variety of genres, styles and traditions.
● Identify how artists have created impression/effects in their paintings.

Whiteboard tools
Use the Lines tool to point to specific points of interest and relevance with the pictures.

 Pen tool

Lines tool

Sound recorder (optional)

Starter
Paste pictures of an elephant, a tortoise, a swan and a lion on to a blank flipchart page. Play the appropriate pieces from the *Carnival of the Animals*, and ask the children which animal is being described. What is it about the music that makes them think of that animal? Encourage words that describe the music, such as *loud, soft, fast, slow, high, low* and so on. Tell them about the music, and that Saint-Saens wanted to *paint* a picture of each animal in sound.

Whole-class shared work
● Display the picture of Van Gogh's *Starry Night*. Ask the children what it shows, what effect it creates and how it makes them feel.
● Invite the children to describe what sounds they would hear if they were in the picture, or what sounds the picture make them think of. Write up their suggestions.
● Play a recording of Beethoven's *Moonlight Sonata*. Ask: *Does this music go with the picture? What kind of sounds would you choose to use?* Add their ideas to the board.
● Look at other paintings. Discuss how each picture makes the children feel and what kind of music they think could accompany it.

Independent work
● Divide the class into small groups and provide each group with a large piece of sugar paper.
● Explain that each group will create a piece of music to accompany one of the pictures.
● Ask each group to select a picture. Give the group the printed version of its chosen picture to place in the middle of the piece of sugar paper.
● Tell the groups to annotate the features they would particularly like to illustrate in their composition, for example, the stars, or the hustle and bustle of the town.
● After completing this, encourage each group to think about the instruments they will use.
● Ask each child to select an instrument to help them with their composition (children could use their own instruments if appropriate).
● Ask: *What instruments, or combinations of instruments, will you use at different points to give different effects?*
● Give the children sufficient time to complete their group compositions.

Plenary
● Invite each group to perform their composition for the rest of the class. If a microphone is available, use the Sound recorder to record the children's compositions.
● Display the pictures on the whiteboard. Ask: *Can you guess which painting this group's composition is for? What helped you to guess? How did they create the feeling of stars high up in the sky?* Encourage the children to use musical terminology when they give their answers.
● If possible, add the children's music to the flipchart containing the images. The music can then be played as the pictures are viewed.

What's the weather like today?

Learning objectives
● To understand how symbols can represent sounds.
● To be able to follow a sequence of sounds and play as an ensemble.

Resources
'What's the weather like today?' flipchart file; extracts from Debussy's *La Mer*, or another orchestral piece about the sea; printouts of page 4, one for each group; selection of classroom instruments; writing materials.

Links to other subjects
Geography
QCA Unit 16 'What's in the news?'
● Study weather conditions in different parts of the world and compose a range of weather scores to reflect the varying conditions.
English
NLS Term 2 T13: To write own examples of descriptive, expressive language based on those read.
● Write short descriptive pieces that reflect the weather scores.

Starter

Begin the lesson by playing Debussy's *La Mer*. Ask the children what the music makes them think of. Tell them the title of the piece and what it means (*The Sea*). Explain that Debussy's piece is written for an orchestra, which is a large group of different instruments. Debussy used different combinations of instruments to get different effects.

Tell the children that in this lesson they will be using symbols to create a piece of music about the weather.

Whole-class shared work

● Go to page 2 of the flipchart and ask the children to look at the symbols. Suggest that these symbols could be used to represent different kinds of sounds.
● Ask the children to think of different sounds they could make for each of the symbols. Make a note of the instruments that they suggest, and any sound-related vocabulary, such as *loud* and *soft*.
● Go to page 3 and explain that this is a graphic score: it gives instructions for playing a piece of music.
● Discuss the symbols and the timeline. Explain that the symbols stand for different kinds of sounds, and that the timeline keeps everyone in step and shows them when they have to make their sound.
● Discuss the wavy line. Explain that this tells the players how loud or soft to play. Ask the children how they would do this. For example, for a loud sound, ask: *Do you need a big sound from one instrument, or do you need to add more instruments at this point?*
● Seat the children in a circle and place the instruments in the middle. Ask them to name the instruments and describe how they are played.
● Discuss and agree upon a sound for each of the weather symbols in the graphic score. Divide the children into groups and assign each group a weather symbol and sound.
● Give the groups a few minutes to practise their sounds.
● Keep page 3 of the flipchart on display and perform the score as a class. Use the Clock tool's Count up function 🕐 to keep time and move the vertical line across the board to show when each group must perform their sound.

Independent work

● Distribute the printouts of page 4 of the flipchart and ask the groups to compose their own weather score. They can use the symbols on the sheet or create new ones of their own.
● Allow less able learners to use a limited range of symbols and sounds.
● Encourage more able learners to consider different combinations of sounds to achieve particular effects.
● Invite one of the groups to recreate its graphic score on the whiteboard, using page 4 of the flipchart. Duplicate the symbols as required.

Plenary

● Invite the class to perform the score on page 4.
● If there is time, allow all the groups to perform their score for the rest of the class.
● Discuss which scores the class liked the best and what they enjoyed the most about this lesson. Write the children's responses on page 5.

Whiteboard tools
If a microphone is available, use the Sound recorder to record the children's scores. Use the Clock tool's Count up option to keep time.

🕐 Count up tool

🔍 Marquee select tool

📇 Duplicate function

🖨 Print button

🔊 Sound recorder (optional)

What is God like?

Learning objectives
- To think carefully about what God means to them.
- To recognise and respect how different people seek comfort in God.
- To develop a sense of awe and wonder in terms of God as an entity.

Resources
Photocopiable page 169 'What is God?'; prepared flipchart page showing variety of contrasting scenes, from different cultures and countries (for example, a peaceful rural landscape, a busy market scene in a different country, a majestic mountain range, a busy city street); some meditative music; calming music and a calm landscape picture.

Links to other subjects
English
NLS Term 2 T11: To write poetry based on the structure and/or style of poems read.
- Link this to the work in this lesson by providing existing poems as models for children to base their own poems upon.

Starter
Display the prepared flipchart page of contrasting scenes. Above the images, write the questions *Where is God?* and *What is God like?* Tell the children you would like them to think about these questions quietly for a short time. Play the meditative music to them while they look at the flipchart page.

Whole-class shared work
- Ask the children to share their thoughts about the questions on the board. Ask: *How do you imagine God? Where do you think He is?* Make notes of their suggestions.
- Display the photocopiable sheet, which shows some of the names given to God by three different religions.
- Discuss the names, and what they tell you about God. Annotate a blank flipchart page with the children's ideas.
- Point out that in Islam, Muslims learn the 99 names of God (Allah), of which only three are given on the sheet. The many names relate to different attributes of God.
- Talk about other names that could be given to God, relating these to different aspects of Him. These could include forgiveness, protection, justice and so on.

Independent work
- Give each child a copy of photocopiable page 169 'What is God?' Ask them to answer the questions. The last question requires them to make notes about what God means to them, what they think he is like and where they think he can be found. They should then use these notes to write a poem entitled *What is God?*
- Work with less able learners in a group, to help them organise their ideas and to write a collaborative poem.
- Challenge more able learners to use interesting similes and imagery in their poems.

Plenary
- Gather the children on the floor with their poems. Darken the room and light a candle.
- Ask the children to look quietly at the stillness of the candle.
- Explain that you will ask them to read their poems to the class. Tell them that you will tap their shoulders to show when they should read out their poem.
- Invite one children to begin. When that child has finished, tap a different child on the shoulder to signal that they should read their poem to the class.
- Continue until all the children have read their poem aloud.

Whiteboard tools
 Highlighter tool

 Pen tool

 Marquee select tool

Resource library

Learning objective
● To think about light and dark as symbols.

Resources
'Visions of light' flipchart file; calm music; candles.

Links to other subjects
PSHE
PoS (2e) Reflect on spiritual, moral, social and cultural issues, using imagination to understand other people's experiences.
● Encourage the children to listen to and respect each other's ideas.

Visions of light

Starter
Before the lesson begins, open the flipchart, enable the Reveal tool and go to page 3. Turn off the lights and play the children some calm music. Gradually reveal the two questions on the screen.
   Give the children a few minutes to think carefully about each question.

Whole-class shared work
● Discuss children's responses to the questions. Write their ideas on the board. Encourage them to think about the actual use of light as well as the feelings that light brings.
● Go to page 4. There is a picture on the page, hidden in darkness. Slowly reveal the picture by repeatedly clicking on the button in the bottom right-hand corner.
● Explain to the children that when we are in the dark, we use lights to find our way around. Relate this to experiences of power cuts or camping at night.
● The words *light* and *dark* do not always refer to the presence or absence of a light source. Go to page 11 and discuss the phrase *to be kept in the dark*. Ask: *Does it mean to put someone in a dark room?*
● Delete the objects covering the next three words and phrases. Talk about what they mean. Lead the children to think about *light* and *dark* in terms of knowledge or truth.
● Drag proverbs out of the box at the bottom of the page and discuss their meanings. Are they literal sayings?
● Use the Fill tool to fill the occurrences of the word *light* in a different colour to highlight it.
● Bring the children to the understanding that light can mean knowledge, truth and joy. Light is also used in many celebrations, such as Divali, Advent and Hanukkah, to represent happiness.
● Display page 12 and read the words out loud. How do they make the children feel? What are light and dark feelings? Work together to place the words on the scale. Discuss any different opinions regarding the words as the children may rate words according to different degrees of light and darkness.

Independent work
● Ask the children to think carefully about the meanings of *light* and *dark*.
● Challenge them to write new proverbs and/or sentences that relate to light and dark. For example, *I feel full of light when I'm happy*.
● Focus less able children on the feelings that lightness and darkness bring. More able children may be able to think more about *light* and *dark* in terms of religion.

Plenary
● Invite volunteers to add their proverbs or sentences to the page 13. End the lesson by lighting a few candles and turning off the lights. Play some calm music and allow children to read out their sentences in turn.

Whiteboard tools
Use the Reveal tool to show the flipchart pages bit by bit. Use the Fill tool to emphasise words on the page.

🖳 Reveal tool

🖌 Fill tool

🖊 Pen tool

🗑 Delete button

🏹 Marquee select tool

Recognition tool

Activote (optional)

Rich or poor?

🔲 This is part of an inventory taken in 1596.

In the Hall there.-In primis, three tables, foure fourmes, sixtene holbeardes, and one paire of tables, praised at iij^{li}. xii^{js}. iii^{jd}.

In the Parlor.-Itm , iij greene carpetts, ij greene clothe cheyres, one blacke wrought velvet cheyre laide wth silver and golde lace, iij long cussins of redde sattyn laide wth golde lace, preised at xj^{li}.

In the Warthrope.-Itm, one litle table wth a frame, one playne presse of elme, j iron-bound cheast, two playne cheasts, j cofer, ij paire of olde virginalls, preised at [torn]

In Sr Henrie Unton's Studie.-Itm, vij hanginges of gilded lether, one table there, shelves, wth many bookes of diverse sortes, to the number of ccxx, and one cheast, praised at xx^{li}.

In the Drawing Chamber.-Itm, one fielde bedstede wth a cover of yelowe sattyn layde wth silver lace, and five riche taffitie curtyns layde wth silver lace, one fetherbedde, j bolster, j paire of pillowes, j paire of blankettes, i yelowe rugge, j matterys of flockes preised at xl^{li}.

Inventory extracts from *The Unton inventories printed for the Berkshire Ashmolean Society in 1841.*

Glossary

bolster .... *long pillow*	gilded.................. *decorated with gold or silver*
cheast .... *chest*	holbearde ....*long shafted axe used as a weapon*
cheyres...*chairs*	
cofer...*coffer, chest*	In primis..*firstly*
curtyns ....*curtains*	Itm .... *item*
cussins ....*cushions*	matterys of flockes............ *a mattress stuffed with wool*
diverse... *different*	
fetherbedde............................*mattress stuffed with feathers*	playne ....*plain*
	praised/preised at............................... *priced at*
fielde bedstede..................... *bed with curtains hanging from a central point*	presse of elme ....*elm cupboard*
	sattyn......... *satin, an expensive shiny material*
forme or fourme..................*bench decorated with gold or silver*	taffitie ....*taffeta, a glossy silk fabric*
	virginals.......*keyboard instruments like pianos*

Streets past and present

◾ Which things would you only have seen a long time ago, and which things would you only see today? Draw an arrow to link each thing to the right column.

◾ Underline with a coloured pencil the things that you could have seen long ago and today? Would they have looked the same? How would they have been different?

A long time ago	Today
Cars	
Bicycles	
Horse and cart	
Railway station	
Burglar alarms	
Telephone boxes	
uPVC windows	
skateboards	
Traffic lights	
Blocks of flats	
Mobile phone masts	
Terraced houses	
Gas mantles	

◖SCHOLASTIC
www.scholastic.co.uk

Virtual village

- ◀ Design your own village!
  - ☐ Create a map and give it a name and a key.
  - ☐ Remember to include a hill and a river.
  - ☐ Give your village a name.
  - ☐ Make a key, showing the symbols you have used and what they stand for.
- ◀ Find a partner. Ask them to describe a route through your village. What do they see on the way?

Name of village:

Key

_____

Where on Earth is it?

◀ Find out about these European countries. Record your information in the table below. If you have time, add more countries of your own choice.

Country	Capital	Language	Famous sight	Area in square km	Physical feature
Ireland					
United Kingdom					
France					
Spain					
Germany					
Italy					
Netherlands					
Switzerland					

◀ S C H O L A S T I C
w w w . s c h o l a s t i c . c o . u k

What makes a strong bridge?

◢ Look at the bridges on the whiteboard.

◢ Draw the bridge you like best on the whiteboard screen. Use a ruler to draw the straight lines.

◢ Give your picture a heading saying what kind of bridge it is.

◢ Label the features that make the bridge strong.

My favourite bridge. It is a _____ bridge.

◢ Read about the bridge competition on the whiteboard. Imagine you are going to enter it.

◢ Draw what your bridge would look like. Remember, you will only have art straws to build your bridge.

My bridge design. It is a _____ bridge.

Designing a bridge

◀ What type of bridge will your group make?

A beam bridge   An arch bridge   A suspension bridge

◀ Or something new?

Remember! You can use:
● 40 art straws   ● A pair of scissors

You have £1.50 to spend in the shop on:
● Paperclips – 20p each   ● Sticky tape – 20p for 2cm
● Sticky tack – 25p for 1cm square   ● String – 25p for 30cm

◀ Draw your group's design here:

◀ The people in my group are: _____

_____

▲ S C H O L A S T I C
www.scholastic.co.uk

Take a seat

- ◾ Use this sheet to help you design a chair.

- ◾ What purpose (or use) is your chair going to have?

My chair is designed for: _____

- ◾ What special features does your chair have?

The special features of my chair are: _____

_____

_____

- ◾ Draw a picture of your chair:

Side view	Front view
Back view	Plan view

Making mosaics

■ Use the grid to help you make your own mosaic.

■ Think about the colours you want to use.
Cut the tiles from coloured paper or pages
from magazines.

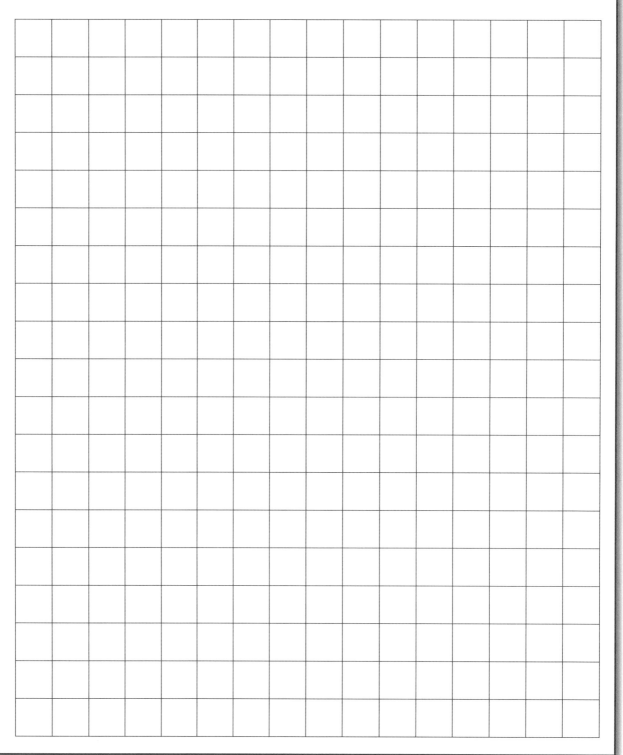

SCHOLASTIC

w w w . s c h o l a s t i c . c o . u k

What is God?

- Many religions have different names for God. The different names reflect the many aspects of God. Here are some examples:

Judaism
Jehovah-Jireh (The Lord our Provider)
Jehovah-Ropheka (The Lord our Healer)
Jehovah-Shalom (The Lord our Peace)

Christianity
The rock
The shepherd
The creator

Islam
Al-Ghafur (The All-Forgiving)
Al-Wadud (The Loving)
Al-Hakeem (The Wise)

- What do these names tell you about God? _____

_____

- What names would you give God? _____

_____

- On the back of this sheet, draw or write down a few notes about what you think God is like, what God means to you, and where you think God can be found. Use the notes to write a poem entitled 'What is God?'

Whiteboard diary

Teacher's name: _____

Date	Subject/ Objective	How was the whiteboard used?	Evaluation

◖ S C H O L A S T I C

w w w . s c h o l a s t i c . c o . u k

Whiteboard resources library

Teacher's name: _____

Name of resource and file location	Description of resource	How resource was used	Date resource was used

Using Activprimary

This brief guide to Activprimary offers a few tips on using the application. It is based on the training manual *An introduction to Activprimary (Version 2 for Windows)*. The PDF of the manual is distributed as part of the Activprimary software package, but it is also available online and on the CD-ROM that accompanies this book (under the Help section). To learn more about how to use Activprimary, try the online tutorials at **www.prometheanworld.com/uk/html/training/tutorials.shtml** (the hyperlink is provided on the CD-ROM in the Web Links section).

Flipchart mode and Desktop mode

Desktop mode 🖵

Return to main screen 📖

When Activprimary is launched, it automatically takes you away from your desktop screen to Flipchart mode. A flipchart will be open and ready for use. Click on the **Desktop mode** button to access your desktop and any other applications, without closing Activprimary. The Desktop toolbox means that you can still use a selection of Activprimary tools with other applications. To get back to Flipchart mode, click on the **Return to main screen** button in the Desktop toolbox.

Design mode and Presentation mode

Design mode
Toggle between
red Design mode and
yellow Presentation mode

Teacher tools menu 🖌

Switch between Design mode and Presentation mode by clicking on **Teacher tools menu** and then **Design mode**. When you are in Design mode, the Teacher tools icon border is red; it is yellow in Presentation mode.
Use Presentation mode when giving classes. Design mode allows access to all the design features of Activprimary to create or change a flipchart. Some features are only available in Design mode, including:

- The Properties button is available in the Object edit toolbox. The options available will depend on the object selected.
- Right-clicking (or barrel-clicking) shows a menu for any selected object or background.
- New folders can be created in the Resource library.
- Page organiser button is available via the Page number button.

Navigating your flipchart

Next and Previous page buttons ▶ ◀

Page organiser

Use the **Next page** and **Previous page** buttons to move through the pages in the flipchart. If you are on the last page of the flipchart, clicking the Next page button will add a new page. You can view the pages in the flipchart by clicking the Page number button. The Tool tray will display thumbnails of the pages; access a desired page by clicking on its thumbnail. In Design mode, you can move or copy objects from one page to another by dragging it to the thumbnail in the Tool tray. The **Page organiser** button will appear in the Tool tray; this allows you to move, copy and delete pages.

Selecting and manipulating objects

Marquee select tool ▶

Use the **Marquee select tool** to move objects on the screen and to drag resources from the Tool tray (such as shapes, lines, backgrounds, grids or images). Click on an object to select it. Select multiple objects by clicking on

3. Rotation

the background and dragging a selection box around the objects. The selected object(s) will be surrounded by a number of squares called Pick-up boxes (see the numbered diagam on the left).
Click and drag these boxes:
1. to move the object around the page
2. to resize the object
3. to rotate the object
4. to change the size of a shape without changing its proportions.

Adding text to a flipchart page

Text editor tool

Floating keyboard

Pen tool

Recognition tool

Handwriting tool

Text editor tool: Use this to enter a block of editable text. Click on the page, where you would like to insert the text. You can then input text using your computer's keyboard or use the **Floating keyboard** in the Text tool tray.
Pen tool: This allows you to add free-hand writing to the screen, in the same way that you would use a conventional whiteboard.
Recognition tool (in Special tools): This tool recognises free-hand writing and converts it to editable text. A **Floating keyboard** is also available in the Recognition tool tray. The **Handwriting tool** in the Desktop toolbox also allows you to convert free-hand writing to text in a word-processing document or in a spreadsheet.

Use the Dice tool as a random number generator

Dice tool

would be written as *643*.

The **Dice tool** (in the Special tools menu) is a useful and fun way to generate random numbers. You can select and roll up to five dice; click on the equal-sign button to add the sum of the dice roll to the flipchart page. However, you can also use the dice to test the children's understanding of place value, for example, by using three dice to create a three-digit number. So *643* would be written as shown left.

Using the Camera tool

Camera tool

The **Camera tool** is useful for taking snapshots of annotated screens. Use it, for example, to take a snapshot of a completed sequence from one of the activities on the CD-ROM, which can then be saved to a flipchart page and annotated. You can also take screenshots of annotated documents to show, for instance, highlighted headings and subheadings. It is advisable to exercise caution if taking screenshots of published material or anything on the internet and to check for copyright permission first.

Using the Eraser tool

Eraser tool

Activprimary's **Eraser tool** does not technically remove images from the page; it creates a colourless object over the top, which displays anything on the middle or bottom layer of the flipchart. This eraser object can be moved around to cover other elements on the flipchart page. It can be moved and manipulated like any other object. The spyglass, which is provided in some of the flipcharts on the CD-ROM, incorporates an eraser object that allows the user to see through objects to *hidden* answers.

The Activprimary toolboxes

The information is taken from the training manual *An introduction to Activprimary (Version 2 for Windows)*. The PDF of the manual is distributed as part of the Activprimary software package, but it is also available online and on the CD-ROM that accompanies this book (under the Help section). Try the online tutorials at **www.prometheanworld.com/uk/html/training/tutorials.shtml** (the hyperlink is provided on the CD-ROM in the Web Links section).

The Main screen and toolbox

Across the bottom of the screen is the Tool tray. When certain tools are selected, additional options for them will appear in here. You can reposition the Tool tray and the Main toolbox through settings (Teacher tools menu button>Menu>Settings>Toolboxes).

In the corner of the flipchart page, you will see the Flipchart Bin. Use the Marquee select tool to drag objects into the Bin to delete them.

At the side of the screen is the Main toolbox. It is divided into two main areas: the Teacher Area (the upper section) and the Pupil Area (the lower section). The Teacher Area contains administrative tools aimed solely at the teacher.

Teacher tools menu

New flipchart

Open a flipchart

Save a flipchart

Print

Page reset

Page notes

Web browser (AP2.5 only)

Notes and pointer (AP2.5 only)

Tickertape (AP2.5 only)

Design mode Switch between Design mode and Presentation mode.

Menu Customise preferences for Activprimary.

Exit

Activities explorer Access pre-made activities, including the Interactive Teaching Programs.

Sound controller/recorder

Special tools (See page 175 for details.)

Clear tool With this tool you have three options: Clear Screen, Clear Objects and Clear Annotations.

Desktop mode Access your desktop without closing the program.

Activote Take an interactive vote (with voting devices only).

Page number button Click on the Page number button to open the Page Organiser in the Tool tray.

Next/Previous page buttons If you are on the last page, clicking the Next page button will add a new page to the end of the flipchart.

Marquee select tool

Pen tool Select this to access the Highlighter and Eraser tools.

Lines tool

Shapes tool

Text editor tool

Fill/Colour picker tool Select a colour using the Colour picker tool and add it to the Colour palette.

Grids

Backgrounds

Resource library

Undo/Redo buttons

The Resource library

The Resource library is a series of folders whose contents can include images, word banks and sounds. You can also create your own folders and store your own flipchart items in the Resource library.

Rubber stamp tool Place multiple copies of an image.

Previous / More images

Categories Access the Resource library directory and browse the categories.

Shared collections

Personal collections

Other location Access other resources on your computer using the Browse to Another Location button.

Create new folder Create a new directory to store your own resources in. (This option is only available in Design mode.)

ACTIVPRIMARY

The Special tools toolbox

These options will appear in the Tool tray when the Special tools button is clicked.

Spotlight tool Cover the screen apart from a re-scalable area that follows the cursor, revealing parts of the flipchart beneath. There are options for rectangular or circular spotlights.

Reveal tool Cover up the desktop and then reveal the flipchart from the top, bottom, left or right.

Dice tool Roll up to five dice and add the totalled number to the flipchart.

Protractor tool

Ruler tool

Compass tool (AP2.5 only)

Fraction creator tool Handwrite a fraction and add it to the page as text.

Recognition tool Convert handwriting to editable text.

Floating calculator Add the entire calculations to the flipchart as editable text. The Floating calculator remains on screen in Desktop mode

Camera tool Capture part of the screen as a picture.

Screen recorder (AP2.5 only) Record actions performed on screen as a video file.

XY Origin tool Place a rotation point on the page and rotate objects around this point.

Clock tool You can also set a timer to perform an action after a specified amount of time.

The Object edit toolbox

When you double-click on any object the Object edit toolbox will open. This toolbox contains appropriate tools for editing the selected object.

Increase object size Increase the size of a selected object in 10% increments.

Decrease object size Decrease the size of a selected object.

Delete button Click this button to remove the selected object.

Duplicate function Make an identical copy of the selected object.

Edit text tool Enables you to change the text on your flipchart. Available options appear in the Tool tray.

Properties This is only available in Design mode and lets you change an object's attributes.

- **Identification** Set the name of the object or group a collection of objects.
- **Position** Manually alter the object's position on the screen, or lock it in position.
- **Appearance** Change aspects of an object appearance, such as its layer, translucency, outline and fill colour.
- **Container** Allows an object to carry with it a smaller object placed on top.
- **Actions** Set an action that an object will perform when clicked in Presentation mode.

The Desktop toolbox

The Desktop toolbox appears when you click on the Desktop mode button. The tools work in the same way as they do with an Activprimary flipchart.

Return to main screen Return to the main flipchart.

Marquee select tool Operate your desktop as you would if Activprimary wasn't running.

Pen tool

Highlighter tool

Clear Screen

Spotlight tool

Reveal tool

Undo button

Redo button

Activote

Colour palette   **Line thickness**

Handwriting tool Convert free-hand writing to text.

Camera selector

Camera tool

Floating keyboard (AP2.5 only)